THE REALITY OF
THE SUPERNATURAL
WORLD

Exploring Heavenly Realms and Prophetic Experiences

TODD BENTLEY

D0326080

DESTINY IMAGE® PUBLISHERS, INC.

P.O. Box 310, Shippensburg, PA 17257-0310

"Speaking to the Purposes of God for this Generation and for the Generations to Come."

This book and all other Destiny Image, Revival Press, Mercy Place, Fresh Bread, Destiny Image Fiction, and Treasure House books are available at Christian bookstores and distributors worldwide.

For a U.S. bookstore nearest you, call 1-800-722-6774.

For more information on foreign distributors, call 717-532-3040.

Reach us on the Internet: www.destinyimage.com.

ISBN 10: 0-7684-2670-7

ISBN 13: 978-0-7684-2670-0

For Worldwide Distribution, Printed in the U.S.A.

2 3 4 5 6 7 8 9 10 11 / 12 11 10 09 08

This book is dedicated to God the Father, the Ancient of Days who sits upon the throne; Jesus Christ, our Chief Apostle and Prophet; and the Holy Spirit of God who is my ministry partner, the source of all true revelation, and the one who reveals Himself as the seven Spirits of God (see Isa. 11:2).

Acknowledgments

A special thanks to Bob Jones, who is like a grandfather of the faith. His example of living in the Spirit daily has helped me develop the understanding that I don't just do ministry but that I am a spiritual being. Bob encouraged me not to shrink back or back off from sharing my examples because initially I wondered if I was the only one having these somewhat strange experiences. Bob, however, helped me settle things in my heart and to know that it was OK to experience the spiritual realm as often as I was.

Thanks to Patricia King for her years of advice and mentoring, her love of the simplicity of the Gospel, and her desire just to go for it all! She is a great inspiration for me. Patricia also told me to be sure to build a biblical framework around each supernatural experience I had, not only to validate my encounter, but also to make it available to others.

Bill Johnson is a tremendous prophetic teacher whom God has raised up—I'm thankful for his wisdom and inspiration. He's so loving and grounded in the Word, but at the same time, because of his love for Jesus, he's open to some "sensational" realities of the spiritual realm.

I'm thankful to the many prophets who were forerunners before me and who continue to pay the price for the cross and the prophetic ministry. Also, thanks to the ones, like Sundar Singh, who have already gone home, but whose lives continue to be an example of how to live in the realm of the Spirit.

Thanks to Kenneth Hagin for having been so into the Word and accepting visions, revelations, and Holy Ghost visitations. Many people don't realize that in the early days of his ministry he had many visitations and third Heaven encounters. His belief in visions compelled me to move forward.

I'm very grateful for my editors of the first edition of this book: Kevin Paterson, Shae Cooke, and Jackie Macgirvin, who edited and reworked my many words, then polished and put them in logical, readable order—no small task! For this second edition, thanks again to Shae Cooke for her editing work.

Thanks goes to Janelle Mierau for her work collecting, researching, and editing the supernatural testimonies, as well as her proofreading help on the book. Thanks also to Katherine Martin for her proofreading as well.

Endorsements

For many, "being seated in heavenly places" (see Eph. 2:6) has been reduced to a doctrinal statement. It stirs up pleasant feelings in times of difficulty, but could never be considered a lifestyle or an ongoing experience. In the following pages, Todd bravely bares his soul in sharing his personal encounters with God, restoring heavenly places to their rightful status in our life's experience. While jealousy will no doubt provoke some to reject this message, it is a risk worth taking. Today a whole generation of reality seekers is hoping there is more to the Christian life than what they've seen so far. They were born to shape the course of history, but must be anchored into the highest purpose of all. In *The Reality of the Supernatural World,* Todd provides a priceless road map to the fulfillment of life's ultimate quest, seeing the face of God. I highly recommend this book, as I highly recommend this quest.

BILL JOHNSON
Senior Pastor, Bethel Church
Author, *When Heaven Invades Earth* and
The Supernatural Power of a Transformed Mind
Redding, California, USA

Todd Bentley has gone into the treasury room of Heaven and brought down jewels of the Kingdom to be released into earthen vessels in his marvelous book, *The Reality of the Supernatural World.* Experience,

Scripture, and insight all kiss one another in his life, ministry, and now his writings. An amazing read, indeed!

James W. Goll

Co-founder of Encounters Network

Author, *The Lost Art of Intercession, The Seer,* and

Praying for Israel's Destiny

Franklin, Tennessee, USA

Todd's book, *The Reality of the Supernatural World,* establishes that the supernatural realm, sanctified by the Holy Spirit, is available to all Christians in every nation. It is your inheritance through the work of Calvary. This is an essential manual as you learn about angels, dreams, the prophetic, hearing God's voice, open heavens, decrees, and more. It is God's heart that His children go deeper to possess their full inheritance. This book is your road map.

Dr. Mahesh Chavda

Senior Pastor, All Nations Church

Fort Mill, South Carolina, USA

Do you want more of God? I sure do, and here is how you get it. Jesus said He only did what He saw the Father doing and only said what He heard the Father saying. Todd's book will catapult you into hearing and seeing with much more clarity, resulting in an increase of effective ministry. We are *all* called to be "Seers" and "Hearers."

Carol Arnott

Senior Pastor (with husband, John Arnott)

Toronto Airport Christian Fellowship

Toronto, Ontario, Canada

I love Todd Bentley's ministry—his faith is contagious, and his heart is for other people to step into God's fullness for themselves. *The Reality of the Supernatural World* encourages the reader to expect that the God who moves through Todd can use all of us in the same way, whether we are old or young, male or female. Today I encourage you to read this book, do what it says, and win your part of the world for Jesus!

(WESLEY AND) STACEY CAMPBELL
Founders of New Life Church, Revival NOW!
Ministries, and Be A Hero
Kelowna, British Columbia, Canada

This book leaves me longing for more of the supernatural world now! My already desperate hunger for more of God grew as I read. If you desire to experience the invisible Kingdom realm, you want to read Todd's book. Thank you, Todd, for showing us the way up and in....

DR. HEIDI BAKER
Director, Iris Ministries
Co-author, *There Is Always Enough*
Pemba, Mozambique, Africa

So often folks complicate the supernatural by believing it is too far out there to attain. In *The Reality of the Supernatural World,* Todd deflates the mystical mind-sets that tend to block believers from embracing valid Kingdom encounters. Read and be launched into an adventure with JESUS. I love this book!

PATRICIA KING
President, Extreme Prophetic
Author, *Light Belongs in the Darkness* and
Third Heaven, Angels, and *Other Stuff*
Kelowna, British Columbia, Canada

Brilliant! Anointed! Cutting-edge! *The Reality of the Supernatural World* will captivate your heart and engage your spirit. Todd gives revelatory keys to unlock supernatural mysteries. Everyone can understand the profound yet simple language used to explain the vast expanse of the supernatural dimensions of Heaven touching earth. This wonderful book is replete with extensive scriptural references, biblical examples, and personal experiences to support the revelation, teaching, and understanding Todd imparts. This revelation sparks passion, and you will go deeper into the heart of Jesus and higher into the dimensions of the Spirit as you embrace the gold nuggets of truth that are freely being offered to *you*! You will revisit this book many times in order to grasp everything Todd shares.

JILL AUSTIN

President and Founder, Master Potter Ministries

Los Angeles, California, USA

Table of Contents

Foreword

Authentic apostolic Christianity brings demonstrations of Heaven to earth. Jesus not only taught us to pray, "Thy Kingdom come on earth as it is in heaven," but He also demonstrated the "how to's" by His life, actions, and ministry. Can we do the same? That's the challenge that this book delivers.

By the grace of God, not only does Todd Bentley believe in the reality of the supernatural world, he brings it to bear in everything he says, does, and envisions. Todd believes and acts as if the prayer of Jesus is and will be answered through his life! He wants to infect you with that very same kind of faith.

Some years ago, the Holy Spirit whispered to me, "There is a new young champion I am raising up on the scene. His name will be Todd. You will need his raw faith, and he will need your wisdom." What was even more interesting was the way the Holy Spirit pronounced the name to me—it had a distinctive tone to it that did not sound like the "English" that I was used to hearing! So, I kept my eyes and ears open for this new young champion.

For the next three years, I kept wondering who and where this "Todd" was and when I would meet him. Then one day at a School of the Supernatural, I met a young zealous Canadian believer moving in impacting power and revelatory accuracy. *Who is this robust young man?* I thought. Then the Holy Spirit reminded me, "Remember—this is 'Todd!'" I looked again and for sure—he met the description—one who would walk in raw faith.

It has been a joy over these past few years to join in gatherings and minister alongside this brave heart in Christ. I have been challenged, amazed, and impacted by the life of Jesus through Todd Bentley and Fresh Fire Ministries. Believe in the supernatural? Todd lives in the supernatural. It is as common to him as breathing air!

The pages that follow are filled with demonstrative experiences and biblical accounts of the reality of the supernatural world. Want Heaven to come on earth? Then devour this book! It will rock your world so much that you will never recover to live a boring Christian life ever again.

Warning—if you believe and act on the contents that follow, you too will be a demonstrator of authentic apostolic Christianity in the earth. Go on a journey with the God of the supernatural and watch the impossible become possible.

JAMES W. GOLL

Co-founder of Encounters Network

Author, *The Seer, The Lost Art of Intercession*

and *Praying for Israel's Destiny*

Set your mind [affections] *on things above, not on things on the earth* (Colossians 3:2).

In December 2001, I had a prophetic experience in Fairfield, Iowa. I found myself in an ocean that went on farther than my eyes could see. I felt the pull of the tide, like an invitation, drawing me deeper into this huge sea. I resisted for a moment because of fear of the unknown. As I ventured out a little deeper, the water flowed over my head. It was overwhelming.

"God," I asked, "what's this?" The Lord said, "Todd, this is the sea of glass." He continued, "The knowledge and the glory of the Lord shall cover the earth as the waters cover the sea. You're in the waters of knowledge. You're in the waters of revelation. You're in the waters of the knowledge of the glory of the Lord that comes by the revelation of the Holy Spirit."

"And before the throne there was a sea of glass like unto crystal…" (Rev. 4:6 KJV). This sea before God's throne is like crystal; it's transparent. This is a prophetic picture of God's ability to see and know all things at once. Everything is before God's eyes. Nothing is hidden from His knowledge.

After the experience, I thought to myself, *Great! That was a blast*. It wasn't until a few weeks later that I began to understand what this vision meant. During a church service in Salt Lake City, I saw angels descending into the service and ascending toward Heaven again. I immediately thought about Jacob's ladder (see Gen. 28:12). These angels were descending with revelation knowledge.

Then the Lord said, "Look and see what they have in their hands." I saw eyes and wings. The Lord said, "Eyes and wings represent the seer anointing and the signs prophet. The wings are a picture of an increase of the prophetic; they are wings to fly higher than you ever have before. I will release the seer and the signs anointing this year." (We'll discuss the seer and signs prophets later in the book.)

After these visions in Salt Lake City and Fairfield, the Lord said there was an invitation to experience a new dimension of revelation, knowledge, and the prophetic, not just to a few specific prophets, but to the corporate Church.

It is time to lift our standard and expectations of how much of God we can have and see now. In the same way that we can teach people to move in the prophetic and discern God's voice in the realm of impressions and thoughts, I believe that we can teach the Body to exercise their spiritual senses (see Heb. 5:14) and position themselves to receive visions, trances, sight into the Spirit, and even third Heaven experiences.

I am tired of the world, satan, mediums, wizards, TMers, and the New Age movement stealing and counterfeiting our genuine inheritance to walk in the Spirit of wisdom and revelation. It's time to understand the reality of the supernatural. We should actively seek and expect it in our lives. God's ability to keep you is far greater than the devil's ability to deceive you if you're walking right with the Lord. I believe that the word of the Lord for this generation is, "Come up here."

The Reality of
The Supernatural
World

BOOKS BY TODD BENTLEY

Journey Into the Miraculous
The Reality of the Supernatural World

AVAILABLE FROM DESTINY IMAGE PUBLISHERS

Chapter One

THE REALITY OF THE SUPERNATURAL

Do you want to have greater intimacy with the Lord? Do you long to know Him better and hear His voice more frequently? Even though this book is about the supernatural realm, the underlying theme is *deeper intimacy with God*. The more you know Him the more you will love Him— it's inevitable. The good news is that you aren't the only one who is longing for greater intimacy. God is longing for deeper intimacy with you! He wants to draw His people closer by giving them revelation of the reality of the spiritual realm and supernatural encounters.

Shortly after I started in ministry, the Lord spoke to me and said, "Todd, I want you to start speaking on the reality of the supernatural. I want you to make it available to everyone. Take the spookiness out of it. Build a platform of faith and expectation so that everyone can have a greater experience of Me."

Maybe you're opening this book with fear and trembling, feeling like a heretic for even considering these things. Maybe you think signs and wonders have passed away or that the whole thing is somewhat weird. Perhaps you're wondering whether the supernatural experiences you read about in Scripture are for today and you're hungry to learn more about these things. To start off, I want to lay a biblical foundation so you can see that the supernatural realm is more real than the physical realm and that it's for all believers to experience today as part of a normal Christian life. I want you to receive revelation and impartation for supernatural living, and I want you to grow in faith that the Lord would open the eyes of your heart.

Sometimes when I talk about dreams, visions, and translation in the spirit, people start thinking, *Oh, that's it…astral travel, witchcraft, New Age!* They automatically think it's the occult realm and inspired by the devil; however, if there is a counterfeit, you can be sure there is a genuine article. Satan counterfeited these spiritual experiences, and now Christians are afraid of them. We're being deprived of our spiritual inheritance because of fear; we're allowing the devil to steal our blessing right out from under us.

A great host of men and women in the Bible, from Genesis through to Revelation, experienced trances, visions, dreams, angelic visitations, prophecy, visitations of God, and even the audible voice of the Lord. As God's children today, we should all be having genuine encounters in the Spirit of Truth. The Holy Spirit is the One who inspires all truth and all true supernatural encounters, no matter what form they take. In this chapter, we will define and carefully lay some biblical guidelines for these supernatural experiences, which will bring us into deeper intimacy with the Lord and greater fruitfulness.

SUPERNATURAL EXPERIENCES: PATHWAY TO INTIMACY

Every spiritual encounter is about intimacy with Jesus. Your motivation shouldn't ever be just to have a cool experience. It's not about "I want a spiritual thrill! So, God, let angels come to my house, OK?" Our desire for spiritual experiences must be motivated by a passion to know, experience, and see Him. It's all about the "the spirit of wisdom and revelation in the knowledge of Him" (Eph. 1:17). God wants to take the spookiness out of our idea of the spirit realm and spiritual visitations and He wants to help us see just how "natural" it is to communicate with the One whom we love. I believe this is the direction He has for the Church.

Someone once said to me, "Todd, I saw Jesus come over, bend down on one knee, and kiss me on my forehead." The person sobbed as he shared his moving vision. Now that experience may not shake the nation. It's not necessarily going to do a whole lot as far as taking cities for God, but it sure did something for that believer. This encounter with Jesus deeply touched his life.

If the only reason God wanted to open our eyes was just so that we could see and know Him, to taste, touch, and smell things in Heaven as they are now, just to feel closer to Him, then that is what I want. Paul talks about this dimension and prays for us in Ephesians 1:17 that we would receive "the spirit of wisdom and revelation in the knowledge of Him." It's one thing for me to say, "God loves me," and it's another thing for me to feel His liquid love course through my body for an hour. I mean, that does it for me.

I believe that I see and experience things during intimate fellowship with God just because God and I love each other. I can tell you that these experiences cause my faith in God and His Word to grow; they make me love and trust Him more. The more that I see and experience Him and His Kingdom, the more I want to give all of myself to Him. In every loving relationship, it is important to understand the world of the one we love. How much more important is it for us to know the supernatural world of our God, the same world He has called us to know and experience? We just need to cultivate a lifestyle of seeking for, and living in, the presence of the One we love. Often, God may have a secondary purpose in giving us supernatural experiences that we may be unaware of. But until I find that out, intimacy with the Lord is good enough for me!

HEAVEN IS OUR INHERITANCE NOW

I know that when I teach about the supernatural, people think things like, *Buddy, I've been a Christian for 20 years, and I've only seen one vision,* or *God only gives us visions in a moment of need.* I agree that there is purpose in what God gives; however, God also wants us, in faith, hunger, and expectation, to simply come to Him and ask, "God, I want all the things of Heaven and I don't want to wait until I die. So, if I really do have spiritual eyes, would You show me a few glimpses of Heaven now? Is it OK if I have a few visions?"

Scripture speaks of believers having "access by faith into this grace in which we stand" (Rom. 5:2). I believe the verse applies not only to salvation, but also to access into the spiritual realm, the Kingdom we all become citizens of at conversion. We just need to make ourselves available to this realm by faith.

I really don't think that there is a problem with that! Heaven is my inheritance! Why can't I enjoy some of it now? People say, "We walk by faith and not by sight." That is true. So, I believe by faith that there is an unseen, invisible realm. I also believe by faith that this realm is available to me and that I can access it by activating some biblical principles. Therefore, I am walking by faith and not by sight when I venture into a spiritual realm that the Lord has invited me to experience. I want to make myself available if God wants to give me spiritual sight and I really can't find a reason why He wouldn't. No one has ever been able to show me in the Bible why this realm is not available to all Christians all the time.

I want to learn how to touch, access, and experience that invisible realm daily. You may be thinking, *Wait a minute, Todd… What if God doesn't want you to see?* First, if God doesn't want me to see, I won't see. Make no mistake about that. Yet I know that I have a heavenly Father called Daddy—Abba, Father—who really loves me. If my daughter asks me a question, I answer her. God also wants to answer us when we call on Him. However, when we call on God, because He is a spiritual being, He answers, not in a natural way, but in a supernatural way: "Call to Me, and I will answer you, and show you great and mighty things, which you do not know" (Jer. 33:3). God is very creative in how He answers us. The Bible tells us that in the past God has spoken "at various times and in various ways" (Heb. 1:1).

I don't ask God for specific experiences. I just make myself available and say, "God, whatever You want to give me or show me, or wherever You want to take me is fine." Then God usually does something, and I cooperate. You can't determine what you're going to see, where you're going to go, or what level of revelation you're going to receive, but you can ask and you can ask daily to receive heavenly revelation:

If then you were raised with Christ, seek those things which are above, where Christ is, sitting at the right hand of God. Set your mind on things above, not on things on the earth. For you died, and your life is hidden with Christ in God. When Christ who is our life appears, then you also will appear with Him in glory (Colossians 3:1-4).

God commands you to "seek those things which are above, where Christ is." Where is Christ? In heavenly places. Therefore, God is telling us to seek heavenly places. This is a biblical invitation—really, a command—to seek spiritual experiences. This verse also commands us to focus on the things above, not on things of the earth. If you focus on the earth, you can't enter into the things of the Spirit.

BIBLICAL EXAMPLES

Now you will notice that from the beginning to the end of the Bible, it was natural and common for believers to have supernatural visitations of God. I encourage you to study these passages:

- The Lord appeared to Abraham to make a covenant (see Gen. 17:1).
- Two angels visited Lot and spent the night at his house (see Gen. 19:1).
- Jacob had a vision of a ladder and the angels of God ascending and descending (see Gen. 28:12).
- An angel appeared to Gideon in the winepress (see Judg. 6:11).
- God appeared to Moses in the burning bush (see Exod. 3:2).
- Gehazi had his spiritual eyes opened to see angels and chariots (see 2 Kings 6:16-17).
- Daniel had visions (see Dan. 7:1-12; 8:1-14); Gabriel appeared to him (see Dan. 9:21).

- Ezekiel was transported (see Ezek. 3:12).

- Peter fell into a trance (see Acts 10:9-23).

- Paul was given a thorn in his flesh because of the abundance of visions and revelations he received (see 2 Cor. 12:7).

- John had many visions recorded in the Book of Revelation when he was taken in the Spirit on the Lord's Day (see Rev. 1:12-18).

- Mary and Joseph were directed by angels who appeared in dreams (see Matt. 1:20-21; Matt. 2:13).

- Philip and Elijah were transported in the spirit, and Elijah was caught up in a whirlwind (see Acts 8:39; 1 Kings 18:11-15; 2 Kings 2:11).

The Bible records many different methods that God uses to speak to His people. They weren't just for the prophets either. Later we'll look at these methods and biblical stories in detail. For now, let's examine a well-known story. As you read it, ask the question, "Why not me? Are God's experiences only for the people who lived when the Bible was written? Isn't it biblical to want to know Him more?"

GEHAZI'S SPIRITUAL EYES OPENED

The king of Syria had sent a great army that surrounded the city of Dothan. The army's sole purpose was to kill the prophet Elisha. Gehazi, Elisha's servant, was fearful because he saw only with his natural eyes. Elisha saw into the spiritual realm with his spiritual eyes. He saw the real situation:

So he answered, "Do not fear, for those who are with us are more than those who are with them." And Elisha prayed, and said, "Lord, I pray, open his eyes that he may see." Then the Lord opened the eyes of the young man, and he saw. And behold, the mountain was full of horses and chariots of fire all around Elisha (2 Kings 6:16-17).

The Lord's will is that your spiritual eyes open as Gehazi's did. It wasn't just for the prophet; it was for his servant too! Just because you have never seen into the unseen realm doesn't mean that it isn't right there under your nose. It was there right in front of Gehazi the whole time. As he peered out the window, all he could see was the temporal realm—Syria's chariots and army—and it caused him fear.

Elisha, however, remained calm, more moved by what was going on in that spiritual realm than what was going on in the natural. Perhaps he understood that the spiritual realm affects everything in the natural, since everything came out of the spiritual realm in the first place. Remember when God said, "Let there be light"? Light came out of the invisible. The prophet prayed that Gehazi's eyes would open, and guess what? Suddenly Gehazi could see into the spiritual realm. Guess what again? That same realm still exists today. You might not see it, but it's here right now. Angels are here right now. Demons are all over the city. Heavenly glory is all around. "The kingdom of heaven is at hand" (Matt. 4:17).

Sometimes we can see glimpses of the Kingdom with our natural eyes through miracles, salvation, healing, and deliverance, but I want to see into the spirit realm more often. Wouldn't it be a whole lot better in the area of intercession or deliverance if you could see into the spirit? It would be much more effective to see into that supernatural realm and pray specifically, rather than grope blindly and say, "Whoever you are and whatever your name is, if you are out there (and I think you are even though I can't see you), I am going to resist you in intercession anyway."

We are only taking shots in the dark if we are not able to discern or see what spirit(s) we are warring against (see Eph. 6:12). We need to say more than ever as a church, "God, enlighten the eyes of my understanding; open my spiritual eyes; give me ears to hear; give me discernment!" I want it to be just as easy for me to communicate supernaturally as it is for me to breathe.

Two Worlds

I want to talk about these two worlds—the natural and the spiritual—which we saw so clearly in the story of Elisha and Gehazi. Genesis 1:1 says, "In the beginning God created the heavens and the earth." God made man of two different substances. He took the dust of the earth, a natural element, and then He breathed into him the breath of life, a spiritual element, thus creating a spiritual/natural being. Although we are members of both worlds, our spirit-man doesn't come alive until we are born again. The Bible clearly describes these two worlds:

> *Therefore we do not lose heart. Even though our **outward man** is perishing, yet the **inward man** is being renewed day by day. For our light affliction, which is but for a moment, is working for us a far more exceeding and eternal weight of glory, while we do not look at the things which are seen, but at the things which are not seen. For the things which are seen are temporary, but the things which are not seen are eternal* (2 Corinthians 4:16-18).

Paul tells us to look at things that are not seen. God looks at these things—He lives in that realm. Desiring to see into the spiritual realm is biblical. Jesus prepared the way for us to enter the heavenly realms: "Not with the blood of goats and calves, but with His own blood He entered the Most Holy Place once for all, having obtained eternal redemption" (Heb. 9:12). Jesus obtained eternal redemption by the blood when He entered into the Holy of Holies once and for all; so now we have a way to come boldly before the throne of grace. Do you believe that?

It even gets more exciting! The Bible also says that we are citizens of Heaven *now*: "[He] raised us up together, and made us sit together in the heavenly places in Christ Jesus" (Eph. 2:6).

NATURALLY SUPERNATURAL

We are just as much a spiritual creation with spiritual senses as we are a natural being with natural senses. If you think about it, we will probably only average 80 or so years in this physical body, but our spiritual self is eternal. As for me, I want to use those spiritual senses to touch, taste, smell, hear, and feel. I want to experience the realm called Heaven, which is available now. That is why "the kingdom of heaven is at hand" (Matt. 4:17). That is why "the kingdom of God is within you" (Luke 17:21). That's why Jesus gives us an invitation to come boldly before the throne of grace. Come boldly! There is an invitation NOW to come: "Let us therefore come boldly to the throne of grace, that we may obtain mercy and find grace to help in time of need" (Heb. 4:16).

Start by saying, "I come by faith, and I believe that I am at the throne, because You said that I could come. I just believe that I am there right now." That kind of faith is a great start. Continue, and soon you'll know with certainty you are in the heavenly realm, because you'll truly be there. Your senses will come alive. You'll feel the rumble of thunder; you'll blink when the lightning flashes, feel your jaw drop when you first see the living creatures, stand awestruck when you first glimpse the glorious rainbow arched over the throne, and feel humbled as you watch the 24 elders bow before it.

I call it "the throne zone." I've had encounters where I've been before God's throne. I've seen it, touched it, and listened there. I don't have to wait 40 years, 50 years, or 60 years until I shed my natural flesh and die. The Bible encourages us to reach out in expectation that we can encounter and have what is in Heaven now. In fact, God expects you to take advantage of the free access He's offered you to His courts.

If my kids come in from playing to visit me, is Dad available? Of course I am. So is our heavenly Father when you come, saying, "I just want to know You more, Lord... I want to have an experience with You based on the Bible." So if the Bible talks about angels (as in Luke 4:10, "He shall give His angels charge over you..."), and God even gave Elisha's servant eyes to see angels, then I think I have pretty good support for asking God to also open my eyes to see angels.

I don't go seeking after angels or pray to them. I don't look for a trance, or predetermine where I am going to go in a heavenly experience. I just make myself available by faith, with the understanding of how real the spiritual realm is.

NATURAL AND SPIRITUAL SENSES

We were created with five natural senses: touch, taste, smell, hearing, and sight. In the following passage, John refers to hearing, seeing, and touching Jesus using his natural senses:

That which was from the beginning, which we have heard,
which we have seen with our eyes, which we have looked upon,
and our hands have handled, concerning the Word of life—
the life was manifested, and we have seen, and bear witness,
and declare to you that eternal life which was with the Father
and was manifested to us (1 John 1:1-2).

In the same way that we have physical senses, God created us with five spiritual senses to touch, taste, see, smell, and hear the spiritual realm. When you get up in the morning, do you have to tell yourself to breathe? Do you have to tell yourself to sniff or remind your eyes to work? No, you don't have to remind your taste buds to taste your coffee. You rarely concentrate on your natural senses, but it's not like that with your spiritual senses—we need to practice using them. The apostle Paul writes about mature Christians who "by reason of use have their senses exercised to discern both good and evil" (Heb. 5:14b). Paul implies spiritual eyes as he refers to the "eyes of your understanding being enlightened" that we might know what is "the hope of His calling, what are the riches of the glory of His inheritance in the saints, and what is the exceeding greatness of His power toward us who believe…" (Eph. 1:18-19).

When we die, we will be carried immediately into God's presence and we will see the throne in Heaven. According to Revelation chapter 4, we will see four living creatures around the throne, a rainbow, and a sea of glass like crystal. We are going to see the glory as Ezekiel described it. We will see God as the glorified Son of Man as described by Daniel, and that's just the beginning. What about the Ancient of Days, the golden streets, the mansions? Have you ever wondered how many angels there will be?

It's going to be heavenly and glorious up there, filled with unbelievable things!

Right now, you have five spiritual senses, including spiritual eyes. God's Word tells us that the Kingdom of Heaven is at hand—that it is within you and that right now, on this earth, you are a citizen of Heaven invited to come boldly before the throne of grace. How could it *not* be possible then for you to touch, taste, smell, hear, and experience what Heaven has to offer *now?* God makes it possible to enjoy the world now by the Spirit. We as Christians have to get used to the idea of Kingdom living.

Use wisdom. Let the basis for every experience be the Word of God. Believe that God's ability to keep you is greater than the devil's ability to deceive you, if you live right. If you ask for the Holy Spirit, those little demons of deceit won't pester you, unless you've left open doors for them. Yes, we need to examine our lives, but if we're washed by the blood of Christ, if we love God, if we're in the Word, if we're plugged into a church, and if we want to make ourselves more available to God, then, if we continue asking for the Holy Ghost, we're going to get the Holy Ghost. "If you then, being evil, know how to give good gifts to your children, how much more will your Father who is in heaven give good things to those who ask Him!" (Matt. 7:11). Trust in a loving, good, heavenly Father who gives good things to His children who ask Him. God doesn't deceive us. We're His children and heirs.

IF NOT YOU, WHO?

Supernatural experiences abound throughout the Scriptures; however, many Christians still say, "Well, those were for Daniel, for Paul, and for John...only for the saints." I tell you what. Forget about those stumbling-block arguments; those people were just like us!

> *These all died in faith, not having received the promises, but having seen them afar off were assured of them, embraced them and confessed that they were strangers and pilgrims on the earth. For those who say such things declare plainly that they seek a homeland. And truly if they had called to mind that country from which they had come out, they would have had opportunity to return. But now they desire a better, that is, a heavenly country. Therefore God is not ashamed to be called their God, for He has prepared a city for them* (Hebrews 11:13-16).

The great cloud of witnesses in Heaven is looking at our generation because they're not here anymore. They're gone already; they've run their race. Think about it—if supernatural revelation is not for me and it's not for you and the cloud of witnesses has gone on—who is going to have it now? If they all had it then, we should have it today. They didn't have revelation once in a while; they had it in abundance. When I realized this truth, I said, "God, then I want it too!" Thus, I positioned myself in faith, then contended and hungered for supernatural experiences.

If a biblical person of old had an experience that the Bible recorded, then I've come to believe that I can access the same experience by faith. If it's in the Scripture then there's an invitation to start there and go higher. So if Moses could communicate face-to-face, then I'm going to press in for that too. As you read further into these studies, you may think, *Oh, I don't know about that. I know the angels visited Abraham's house, but Todd, did they really come to your house...can they come to mine?* Well, why not? Why does rational thinking overtake our minds to rule out that supernatural experiences are for today?

One of the reasons I began to teach on the different levels of revelation and the open heavens is because of a unique prophetic experience I had in Iowa. The Holy Spirit spoke to me about the anointing that was on Maria Woodworth-Etter (one of the great Christian history-makers) and how her meetings weren't only filled with miracles, signs, wonders, healings, and evangelism. Rather, the Holy Spirit reminded me that many who attended Maria's meetings testified of a dimension of revelatory visitation, dreams, angels, being taken into Heaven, and trances that would sometimes last as long as three days. It was very common for children to see angels. The Lord said, "Todd, I want you to believe for that."

In the middle of one of our Iowa services, we hit such a place of the intensity of the Presence that it was as if everyone fell into the rest of God. Nobody moved, and I couldn't move anything on my body except for my lips. I didn't preach, but just stood on the platform in one place calling out words of knowledge while people received healing! Later, many attendees were taken into prophetic experiences—some saw the same thing at the same time. Shortly after 11:00 P.M., a flash of a bolt of lightning streaked across the auditorium, and then hit the altar, "Did anybody else see that?" I yelled, still frozen in place, and almost everyone there had.

The Lord reminded me then of a time at one of Maria's healing meetings when no one showed up. She decided right then to go and fetch them. She found a soapbox, stood atop it outside with the intention of preaching, and suddenly froze there as a statue. Eventually, people gathered around her, curious, wondering why she just stood there like that. When the crowd grew, she regained her mobility, and said, "Follow me!" and man, they followed her into that tent, and they had a healing revival! We need more of those experiences now.

Examine Second Corinthians 12:1: "It is doubtless not profitable for me to boast. I will come to visions and revelations of the Lord." Paul knows he's going to come into visions and revelations of the Lord because if you read verse 7, you understand that he had an abundance of revelations—frequently! "And lest I should be exalted above measure by the abundance of the revelations, a thorn in the flesh was given to me, a messenger of Satan to buffet me, lest I be exalted above measure" (2 Cor. 12:7).

I run into people all of the time who believe that God is quiet and only talks when He is angry. "He only talks when He wants to reveal your sin," they say. "God only talks to you when you need some deep revelation," or "God just doesn't want to speak to you in intimacy," and even, "Forget about it—don't even expect to hear from God." Well, I believe that God is far more personal than that. Every day when I wake up, I expect that I'm going to hear a word from the Lord. Those words won't always be about direction or the future. And, of course, I don't expect to be taken to the third Heaven every day, but I do expect to hear from God, in some manner, every day. I hope by the time you finish reading this book that this will also be your expectation and experience.

Chapter Two

LEVELS OF PROPHETIC REVELATION

I once heard my prophet friend, Bobby Connors, tell a story about a time he was asking the Lord to help him as he prepared a seminar about *How God Speaks Today*. "God, will You let me know the different ways You communicate with us?" he asked.

"You tell the Church, I speak any way I want to!" the Lord yelled back.

As this surprised prophet discovered (once again), God often answers in unexpected ways—we just can't box Him in. However, the Bible does give us numerous examples of how God speaks, so we can begin to understand His multifaceted ways. In this chapter, I've outlined some of the ways the Lord speaks. However, my list is definitely not exhaustive; it describes the most common ways that God speaks throughout the Bible.

Scripture records many ways that God spoke to His people—and not just the prophets either. God really does speak "at various times and in various ways" (Heb. 1:1). I believe, as we see throughout the Bible, that we are all to use our spiritual senses, and to have prophetic visionary experiences and revelations of Jesus because these experiences weren't just for the saints of old. They were also for the saints of the New Testament, and for us. James says that "Elijah was a man with *a nature like ours*" (James 5:17).

A very thin veil separates the natural realm and the spiritual world. Do you know how close you are to the supernatural realm now? Just because you've never seen it, doesn't mean it's not there. You're very close. William Branham, a healing prophet during the Voice of Healing revival (1946–1967), would pray, "God, just pull back the curtain." God would give him very detailed words of knowledge (see 1 Cor. 12:8) about people's lives and conditions. At times, I struggle to see beyond the veil, and other times I see through immediately.

Sometimes God will let you peek behind the veil quickly, get one picture or one glimpse of what you think is an angel, and then it's gone. People come to me and say, "Todd, I was slipping in…the veil was being pulled back. I could see light and then it was gone." Others say, "I felt like I was going to go, but my head bumped up against something." The devil will do everything he can to keep you out of the supernatural realm.

God will speak to you where you are. He'll speak in various ways, different for every person. Let's spend the rest of the chapter examining some of the ways that the Lord reveals Himself. I am going to cover the simple ones first and then I am going to examine some of the deeper ways He speaks.

IMPRESSIONS

God often uses impressions to give prophetic revelation to His people. Some people would call that ESP or déjà vu, but that's not really what it is. It's actually knowledge from the Holy Ghost. You just know something; you perceive it. How do you know? You just know. You know that you know. You have the knowledge as Jesus often did in Scripture: "But immediately, when Jesus perceived in His spirit that they reasoned thus within themselves…" (Mark 2:8).

Sometimes we get impressions in the form of a "gut feeling": *This doesn't feel good; I'm getting nauseous. I don't know why; it just doesn't feel right.* This sense is usually just the witness of the Spirit. We need to pay attention to these impressions. Most of us have had these kinds of experiences. Perhaps you sensed danger or felt like you should pray for someone. You may not have known why at the time, but it was an alert from the Holy Spirit.

People also get impressions in their bodies. When I'm ministering, I may feel a pain on the left side of my body, right below my ribs. I know it is not mine, so somebody in the room must have the problem. "Does anyone have a cracked right rib?" I may ask. Then somebody will say, "Hey, that's me," and be healed. As you can see, not every revelation is a third Heaven experience; some are just gentle impressions that are still powerful in releasing God's will in and through us.

THE VOICES OF GOD

Although we all long to hear God's audible voice, the *still, small voice* is much more common. God speaks most frequently through our thoughts:

> *…behold, the Lord passed by, and a great and strong wind tore into the mountains and broke the rocks in pieces before*

the Lord, but the Lord was not in the wind; and after the wind an earthquake, but the Lord was not in the earthquake; and after the earthquake a fire, but the Lord was not in the fire; and after the fire a still small voice. So it was, when Elijah heard it... (1 Kings 19:11-13).

In Elijah's case, God did not speak in a loud dramatic way in the wind, fire, or earthquake—He spoke in a still, small voice. When we learn to quiet our hearts and thoughts and listen for that quiet voice, we begin to hear from God far more than ever before. He wants to teach us to tune in to the still voice of His Spirit.

When the Lord does speak to us this way, many people struggle with the question, "Was that my thought, or was that from the Lord?" Here is a key to discerning between God's thoughts and yours. If you are thinking about something and then suddenly your mind takes a detour, it is probably a God thought. God sometimes invades our thoughts and changes the topic on us. It can be confusing, especially if you wonder: *Hey, I was thinking about what I was going to do after the meeting, and all of a sudden, I am thinking about cancer. Why would I be thinking about cancer?* It's probably because God just dropped one of His thoughts on you and is prompting you to pray for someone's healing. His thoughts often come out of nowhere or don't flow with what you were just thinking.

To determine the difference between your thoughts and God's, ask yourself these questions:

- Did I feel the presence of the Lord?
- Were there strong emotions connected to the words?
- Was I impacted during the encounter?

- Am I still impacted today as I look back on this encounter?

Often, God's voice and messages leave a strong spiritual memory, an impression, or a residue. When you think back on the experience, you remember laughter, tears, or other strong emotions. Pay attention to all of your senses.

When the Lord speaks through an *inner, audible voice,* it sounds like a clear voice, which seems to come from inside you, not actually registering on your physical ears. Every part of your being vibrates with it, and it seems as loud as if it's coming from the outside, though the words come from your belly. It's as if your whole being kind of explodes or vibrates. Your body becomes alert and you think, *What…what…what was that?* That's the inner, audible voice of God. You may not be able to shake it for hours, and it usually affects you for eternity.

The first time I heard the inner, audible voice of God was the day of my salvation. I was visiting my drug dealer in his trailer, and a friend who had recently come to Christ was witnessing to me. When the voice of God spoke on the inside, it sounded like He was yelling—it seemed to come from my belly area and then thundered through my whole body. I had the kind of feeling you get when you're sleeping and someone opens the door, yells your name, and wakes you from a deep sleep. Although God only spoke a few words, His words resounded with enough power to wake up my sleeping spirit as He said, "Listen now…listen now!"

God also speaks audibly to your physical ear. The *outer, audible voice* of God is like, "Hey, Peter, what are you doing down there?" You hear God as you hear any other person's voice. It's outside of you and comes in through your ears. As the Old Testament prophet says, "Whether you turn to the right or to the left, your ears will hear a voice behind you, saying, 'This is the way; walk in it'" (Isa. 30:21 NIV).

At times, God spoke to His people with an audible voice. Samuel heard the voice of God as a child so clearly that he thought Eli was calling him. Moses heard God's voice from the burning bush and at other times. Jesus and the disciples heard God's audible voice on the Mount of Transfiguration. Apostle John heard God's voice repeatedly when he received his revelations of things to come.

Sometimes I've heard the audible voice of the Lord, as described in Psalm 29:3, as a voice that thunders or comes over the waters. I've had many experiences in the third Heaven realm when God's voice thundered or even called out loudly like a trumpet (see Rev. 1:10). This powerful voice can actually shake the room. It sometimes sounds like someone is trying to speak to me under water; it's a muffled, booming sound, but I understand it through flowing thoughts that come to me.

However, outside of third Heaven experiences, when I hear God's audible voice, I normally hear Him speak to me conversationally, in plain speech, as a friend speaks to a friend. When I hear God this way, it's usually in intimate times of prayer. When the Lord visited me on Mother's Day in 1998, He spoke to me for four hours with the inner and the outer, audible voice. Sometimes I heard thoughts flowing from a voice inside my head. Other times the Lord stood behind me and spoke into my ear. His voice came in from outside.

SMELLS

God doesn't always speak verbally. He also communicates through smells. Does that sound funny? One of the first times that God showed me something in the heavenly realm, He did it through a smell. My drug dealer, Aaron, and I had just got saved. Then we got the town drunk saved, brought him to Aaron's trailer, and helped him clean up. He'd been an alcoholic for 25 years, and after three days of sobriety, he was ready to drink again.

All of a sudden, it smelled as if I was sitting in the sewer—nasty! I thought the toilet had overflowed or the sewer pipe had blown because it was a raunchy, swampy smell. I sensed the Lord saying to me, "It's the spirit of death." At that point, my spiritual eyes opened, and I saw the fellow's face melt off, then return to normal. His face looked like some kind of bad horror movie. I saw skeleton then skin, skeleton then skin. I would see with spiritual eyes then natural eyes. That revelation first came by smell, and then was confirmed by a vision. Soon after that revelation, this man died and went to be with the Lord.

Over the years, I've paid attention to my sense of smell. I know the smell of cancer now. It's a stinky, swampy smell. The other day, I walked up to a woman and I recognized the smell. I turned to her and said, "Cancer?" She began to cry.

I once prayed for a woman in my meeting who had been involved in temple worship in India. She is a Christian now. When I laid hands on her, instantly the whole place smelled like rotten eggs and the sewer. Many people smelled it, not just me. She had a demon in her stomach, and when it left, we could still smell it.

I can promise you, though, that smells from the Lord can be a whole lot better than that! How would you like to smell the fragrance of the Lord or the aroma of His perfume? Those are some good smells: "Your robes are all fragrant with myrrh and aloes and cassia" (Ps. 45:8a NRSV). I have been in meetings where God will manifest with the smell of vanilla, roses, cinnamon, and burning incense. He'll sometimes even give me a revelation of the direction of the meeting by allowing me one whiff of His fragrance. That's how God will get my attention, and I'll just know we're changing gears. Once while praying for someone, I started smelling roses! I knew God was leading me to speak prophetically about the Rose of Sharon as He gave me more revelation. Have your nose open for what God wants to say because He wants to speak to all your spiritual senses.

Visions

> *And a vision appeared to Paul in the night. A man of Macedonia stood and pleaded with him, saying, "Come over to Macedonia and help us." Now after he had seen the vision, immediately we sought to go to Macedonia, concluding that the Lord had called us to preach the gospel to them* (Acts 16:9-10).

The Lord will also speak through another level of divine revelation called "visions." At times in meetings as I preach, I start to "see" visions of miracles. As soon as they come, I stop, switch gears, and let the healing anointing fall.

Some visions are like movies in which the pictures come alive and move like a "moving picture," otherwise known as *panoramic* visions as John had on Patmos. More common are pictorial visions that are like still pictures or snapshots. You might hear someone say, "I saw a picture of…."

A vision can be either external/open (appreciated by the open physical eyes) or internal/closed (appreciated with the "mind's eye" of understanding as when one sees in a trance, a dream, a mental image). In an open vision, you would "see" something outside of your mind with your physical eyes while at the same time aware of your surroundings or things happening around you. You may also experience an *inner* open vision where you see something that appears to be on the outside but you're viewing it with your "mind's eye"—so you may not be aware of your surroundings.

In a closed vision you see something in your mind though your eyes are open. In an *inner* closed vision, your natural eyes are closed and you're seeing the vision with your mind's eye.

When the Lord gives me an *open* vision, my natural eyes are indeed open. I may be looking at someone or something, but I am seeing a panoramic or pictorial vision also unfold in my mind with my "spiritual eyes" at the same time. It's as if the vision is opaque and superimposed over everything around me, so I can still see my natural surroundings. When I saw the spirit of death on that town drunk, I was seeing an open panoramic vision, meaning I "saw" him transform into a skeleton and back again as I looked at him, while aware still of my surroundings.

In another open panoramic vision one day (while I was still single), I was telling my future wife's best friend that I felt sure I was going to marry Shonnah. The presence of God flooded the room and the air above my fireplace opened up like a large television screen where I saw an open, moving vision of Shonnah, beautiful in a white dress, running through a field toward me, as I (wearing a tuxedo) ran toward her. We met and embraced, and then I saw us get married.

Often, in open pictorial (still) visions, I'll see a stranger in a crowd who all of a sudden, and only for an instant, will look like someone I know. That's when I know that I'm supposed to release a spiritual gift (see Rom. 1:11), anointing, or mantle similar to that on the life of the person I know to that individual. For example, once I saw a person whom I thought for a moment was the prophetic teacher Bill Johnson. I immediately knew that the Lord wanted me to pray for a mantle of teaching and revelatory ministry over the person.

One day I looked out over the sanctuary and "saw" a large, golden shield at the back of the room. My eyes were open but I was actually viewing it with my mind's eye. If I were to say to a gathering, "I see a golden shield," most would turn around to see if they could see it too. "I see" or "I saw" doesn't always mean that the person is seeing it through their spiritual eyes *out there*. They may be seeing the vision through spiritual eyes *in their mind,* as I did with the golden shield. Many don't see more in this realm because they are looking for outer divine sight, for the open vision. It's similar if someone says, "I saw an angel last night." Did the person really see the angel as he or she would see a person in the natural, or did the person see the angel in the spirit? Many people search hard with the "wrong" eyes when what really needs to happen is for their spirit to engage so that they can "see it" in their mind. This is where most prophetic experiences happen.

DIVINE REVELATIONS

Divine revelation is an instant download, almost like a flash of light, through which you get instant knowledge of Scriptures and what they mean. It's like illumination—instantly you are flooded, verses come to mind, and you suddenly know what they mean and how they connect to each other. This is every preacher's dream. Divine revelations can replace years of pouring over a commentary trying to glean insight for sermons.

DREAMS

Do you know that the word *dream* means "to firmly bind"? That's because a dream from the Lord will have a lasting impact on you. Dreams are visions that you have when you are asleep. Sometimes, if God can't get you to quiet your mind or believe that He is trying to speak to you when you are awake, then He may speak to you through dreams. Sleep is a strategic time when God can talk to you without interruptions. Sometimes when God visits me, His presence is so thick that I fall into a deep sleep. Then I think, *Why is it that every time I soak in His presence I fall asleep?*

Sometimes we will see visions involving colors, signs, symbols, or numbers—these require interpretation. This symbolic revelation usually happens more in the dream realm. Christian authors have written entire books on dream interpretation. (I highly recommend material on dreams by a prophet friend of mine, John Paul Jackson.)[1] Here are just a few samples of verses that mention dreams:

Now Joseph had a dream, and he told it to his brothers... (Genesis 37:5).

While he was sitting on the judgment seat, his [Pilate's] *wife sent to him, saying, "Have nothing to do with that just Man, for I have suffered many things today in a dream because of Him"* (Matthew 27:19).

...behold, an angel of the Lord appeared to Joseph in a dream, saying, "Arise, take the young Child and His mother,

flee to Egypt, and stay there until I bring you word; for Herod will seek the young Child to destroy Him" (Matthew 2:13).

Charlie Robinson is a prophet and member of our Fresh Fire Ministries (FFM) apostolic team. Before joining the ministry, he had two dreams about eagles. He dreamed he came to my house and saw a bald eagle fly over and land in a tree. The next night he dreamed he was in my house, and he looked out the window and saw a family of golden eagles and bald eagles in a tree.

He understood the first dream to mean that God was calling him to be involved in prophetic ministry (symbolized by an eagle) with FFM. The second dream involved Charlie joining a family of eagles, which the Lord showed him included our apostolic team as well as those prophetic people and associates that connect through Fresh Fire Ministries.

The next morning when Charlie arrived at my home, he "saw" a large picture of an eagle on the wall. That day I felt that I should ask him to come on board as an FFM itinerant minister. Then about a year and a half later, I asked him to join the apostolic team. Charlie allowed God to lead him through prophetic dreams and today he's very much a part of our ministry as a seer prophet.

TRANCES

A trance is not an experience! Rather, a trance is a state that one enters to have an experience. Here is an illustration to help you relate to what a trance is. When a dentist or a doctor sedates you for a procedure or an operation, you enter a dreamlike state, but you're awake through it. It's almost as though you are experiencing the procedure in your subconscious. You see images similar to the ones that you see in your sleep, yet you know you are awake! Thus it is with a biblical trance-like state that you fall into for an "experience." It's God's supernatural anesthetic.

In Acts 10, Peter fell into a trance while praying on a rooftop, and had a vision where Heaven opened and a sheet containing unclean creatures came down (see Acts 10:9-16). Paul too fell into a trance quite suddenly while praying in the temple in Jerusalem (see Acts 22:17).

Occasionally I have trances in which people will come to me and say something like this: "Hi. My name is Judy and I have cancer. I'm going to be in your meeting tonight sitting in the fourth row on the left side. Will you call me out and pray for me?" Later, at the meeting, I will see that same woman and know exactly how to pray for her.

The Lord performed a miracle in Grants Pass, Oregon, years ago because of a powerful trance He gave me. While praying one night, I went into a trance in which a woman visited me. She shook me violently and said three times, "The headlines report, 'BOY COMES OUT OF A COMA.'" When I asked the Lord what He wanted me to do, He said, "There will be a man instructed to come tonight to take an anointing back to a boy who is in a coma in another city."

When I described my trance at the meeting that night, a man ran down the aisle and said, "You're not going to believe this, but I was just at the hospital with a woman whose son is in a coma, and she asked me to come tonight to stand in the gap to get an anointing for that boy's healing." Later I heard a report that the boy received healing and got up from his hospital bed! Then the local newspaper ran a headline just as I had seen it in my vision.

Once, while preaching in Australia, I felt the atmosphere change in the room and I knew something was going to happen. I even said, "I'm about to have an experience," then *boom!* I was in a trance that lasted for about 25 minutes after I fell out under the power on stage. (My pastor, Ken Greter, later told me that he'd seen the same thing happen once while Kenneth Hagin preached.) Then I called people out of the crowd for the next hour and gave detailed prophetic words. As I prophesied, I called out specific years of transitions in the church, and included details about plans, blueprints, and buildings from 20 years earlier. The Lord also revealed the secrets of people's hearts. Later, I didn't remember what I'd said. Pastor Ken said that during my experience and prophetic flow, he had seen a huge angel, about three stories in height, hover over the building. He also saw angels ascending from and descending to the church, in answer to prayers from saints in the congregation.

Later, the church pastor took us into his office and showed us dated plans inscribed with the exact years I had mentioned in the prophecy. Through revelation in my trance, the Lord had spoken to many people's hearts and given powerful confirmation and encouragement to this pastor to resurrect the dreams and plans for his church from 20 years before.

Another time in Iowa, I froze on the platform during a meeting. I was awake, but my whole body froze except for my lips. I called out words of knowledge and people received healing. I'd call out physical conditions about people, some as they walked in the room, even though I couldn't see them. I was stuck like that for 45 minutes; the Holy Spirit worked powerfully and many were saved and healed!

ANGELIC VISITATIONS

It's biblical for angels to visit people with messages: "Do not forget to entertain strangers, for by so doing some have unwittingly entertained angels" (Heb. 13:2). Why would God bring revelation through an angel? God sent angels to bring messages to Abraham, Gideon, Elijah, Mary, John, and many others. They are ministering spirits sent to do His word (see Heb. 1:14). When Jesus came out of the wilderness after being tempted by the devil for 40 days and nights, "Angels came and ministered to Him" (Matt. 4:11). Also, when Jesus was in the Garden of Gethsemane, an angel ministered to Him (see Luke 22:43).

I have had several different angelic visitations. I've seen an angel of financial blessing, warrior angels, and an angel called "Revival." I've seen the healing angel like the one from the Book of John chapter 5 in the New Testament. This angel's job was to release healing in geographic areas. I've also seen the angels that participate in gathering the harvest. In a later chapter, we will examine the subject of angels in more depth.

HOLY GHOST FLASHBACKS

Sometimes the Lord reminds us of revelation He's given before, and then reveals how it applies in our present situation. Scripture speaks of these divine reminders: "I will remember the works of the Lord; surely I will remember Your wonders of old" (Ps. 77:11). These flashbacks are one of my favorite types of revelation—through them God can bring back something that He previously said to give us new direction. Those who lived in the hippie days or who lived in the world for a season will probably remember having flashbacks. I know what flashbacks are because I used drugs before my salvation. Now I have something better: *Holy Ghost* flashbacks!

I'll be in a meeting, surveying the crowd, and God will give me a flashback to a time when somebody gave a testimony of how his right ear opened up. Then I'll ask, "Who has a deaf ear?" and tell the person who responds that their ear is going to open! Sometimes I'll have a flashback and see someone, for instance, worrying about a bunch of bills, and then I know that there is a financial issue or concern in the life of the person I'm praying for. Often the Holy Spirit will cause me to remember an event from my own past, and I'll know what an individual is involved in—drugs or addiction, for example.

While ministering, don't discount flashbacks or memories that come to mind because they may be God's way of alerting you to something going on in the individual's life, or giving you a method for dealing with it. He is renewing His past works, though in a different setting.

Visitations of the Lord

Sometimes, when God wants to send revelation, He will deliver it personally, as He did with the apostle John:

Then I turned to see the voice that spoke with me. And having turned I saw seven golden lampstands, and in the midst of the seven lampstands One like the Son of Man, clothed with a garment down to the feet and girded about the chest with a golden band. His head and hair were white like wool, as white as snow, and His eyes like a flame of fire; His feet were like fine brass, as if refined in a furnace, and His voice as the sound of many waters; He had in His right hand seven stars, out of His mouth went a sharp two-edged sword, and His countenance was like the sun shining in its strength. And when I saw Him, I fell at His feet as dead. But He laid His right hand on me, saying to me, "Do not be afraid; I am the First and the Last. I am He who lives, and was dead, and behold, I am alive forevermore. Amen. And I have the keys of Hades and of Death" (Revelation 1:12-18).

This passage provides an awesome description of the glorified Christ. (No wonder John became afraid and needed consolation.)

That's what we want—visitations of the Lord like John had. Sometimes they'll overwhelm us; the Lord's presence has touched me so deeply that I've wept, and sometimes I don't see Him, but I can feel His presence and just know that He's there.

As the Lord called me into ministry, I had a visitation of the Lord. I sensed His form and presence with me. He spoke audibly to me for a long time about the ministry He was about to thrust me into, and then He described how Patricia King would call me out at a meeting and prophetically release me into full-time ministry. I've had many other visitations of the Lord since, and it appears in these last days similar experiences are on the increase in the Body of Christ.

In the early days of my ministry, my first visitation of the Lord occurred in Fort St. John, British Columbia. It was 3 o'clock in the morning, and I had just finished prophesying over everyone at a meeting. Back in my room, exhausted, I decided to lie on my bed for a while, and just wait on God for His presence. Just as I sensed He was about to draw near, however, my bedroom door opened, and I sensed someone enter, and then the door slammed shut. I couldn't see anyone and fear swept over me, yet I could still feel the Lord's presence with me. Then, Jesus stepped out of the darkness and toward me, and it was as if a kaleidoscope of color followed Him—blues, reds, yellows, and colors I have no words for. Jesus was like a living rainbow!

My Lord sat on the edge of the bed—the mattress even squished down and the sheets moved. He fed me—at least that's what it felt like—and then He placed His hand in front of my nose, and I inhaled the awesome aromas of vanilla, cinnamon, rose, and sweet incense. It was a vivid and wonderful visitation of the Lord.

This particular visitation of the Lord in human form is biblical. In Genesis 18, the Lord appeared to Abraham as a man. Note that most scholars interpret the *Angel of the Lord* as Jesus Christ, and not an angel. The "A" capitalized in a Scripture reference to an angel usually signifies that it's the Lord (see Exod. 3:2-4).

TRANSLATED IN THE SPIRIT

Out-of-body experiences, or *translation,* is another biblical spiritual adventure. Translation is different from being transported. Being translated in the spirit means that one's spirit leaves and one's physical body stays put.

Elisha received supernatural knowledge of his servant Gehazi's actions when he was translated in the spirit. He actually exposed Gehazi's lies by asking him: "Wasn't my spirit there when the man got down from his chariot to meet you? Is it a time to accept money and clothes, olive orchards and vineyards, sheep and oxen, and male and female slaves?" (2 Kings 5:26 HCSB).

People involved in the New Age movement sometimes speak of similar translation experiences called "astral travel." They have illegal access to the spiritual realm, but Christians have legal access. Remember, everything that satan does is a counterfeit of the real thing.

Once I was ministering in Mexico but I was staying in a hotel across the border in Texas. I'd heard that there was a lot of witchcraft in that

Mexican border town. Many witches and a head warlock started coming to my meetings. One of the nights, at my hotel, a witch appeared at the end of my bed—not her body, but her spirit. The first thing I thought was to rebuke her in Jesus' name, but she wasn't a demon, so the next thing that came to my mind to say was, "Leave or I'll cut the silver cord." She screamed and vanished. I asked the Lord, and He explained that even though demons allowed her to have that experience, she wasn't a demon, and so she could not be cast out.

This silver cord concept intrigued me. I'd vaguely remembered a Scripture verse tied into that, and it speaks of a silver cord that connects the body to the spirit, which may allow the spirit to return to the body after translation:

> *Remember your Creator before the silver cord is loosed, or the golden bowl is broken, or the pitcher shattered at the fountain, or the wheel broken at the well. Then the dust will return to the earth as it was, and the spirit will return to God who gave it* (Ecclesiastes 12:6-7).

In the case of the witch, perhaps this is why the Lord had me say this to her; for if the spiritual umbilical-like cord had been severed, she may not have been able to return to her body.

In scriptural translation, this verse seems to suggest that when people go out into the spirit, the silver cord acts like a spiritual umbilical cord. So it's possible that when the cord is broken the spirit returns to God and not the physical body.

There are several scriptural examples of God's people experiencing divine (legal) translation. In the following passage, most scholars believe that Paul is describing his trips into the third Heaven. He said that he didn't know if he was in his body or not. This may have also been an out-of-body experience:

> *I know a man in Christ who fourteen years ago—whether in the body I do not know, or whether out of the body I do not know, God knows—such a one was caught up to the third heaven. And I know such a man—whether in the body or out of the body I do not know, God knows—how he was caught up into Paradise and heard inexpressible words, which it is not lawful for a man to utter* (2 Corinthians 12:2-4).

Man, he really tripped! Today, God is giving these experiences to more and more believers. People ask me whether my body, soul, and/or spirit go when I'm taken to the third Heaven. I have to be honest with you; I don't know. All I can tell you is that I was caught up into the third Heaven. Whether I was in my body or not, I don't know. Now that sounds biblical, doesn't it?

I had a dramatic translation experience years ago, the first time I ever preached in Uganda, Africa. A witch doctor came to the healing festival one evening dressed in his full regalia. Some of the pastors, as well as the people, were very afraid that he would curse them and the festival—he was reputed to be the most powerful witch doctor in the region. As the man stood on the festival grounds shaking his stick and yelling at me in demonic tongues, black storm clouds gathered and rain began to fall. Wet and afraid, the people started to leave the grounds.

I then addressed the situation. In Jesus' name, I bound the demonic powers operating through the man and forbid witchcraft from operating through him. Soon the witch doctor left, the skies cleared, and we resumed the festival.

The next evening when I arrived at the crusade, the witch doctor was on stage talking to the pastors. A pastor came running up to me shouting, "He's saved!" When they asked this former witch doctor what had happened, he said, "the short, fat, white guy with a beard" showed up in his home. Although I don't remember visiting him in the spirit that previous night during my soaking time, he testified that I had come to tell him about how powerful and real Jesus is, and he accepted Jesus as his Savior.

When he returned to the festival the next night, he fell to his knees on stage. I prayed for him, and he fell out under the power of the Spirit. When he got up, this former witch doctor made a public statement to the crowd: "The power of Jesus is more powerful than the power of satan!"

Another time, while I was in Toronto to minister, I was taken in the spirit to Finland through England. I saw a great revival shaking the nation of Finland like the explosion of an atom bomb. Right afterward, in the natural realm, a woman called from England to speak to her husband at the Toronto meeting. Although I don't recall stopping in England in the spirit, she claimed I had visited her on my way to Finland.

In Grants Pass, Oregon, in December 2000, I was on the front row before a revival tent meeting when a man came to me and said, "Todd, I brought an angel with me from John G. Lake's ministry in Portland. He is standing at the back of the tent." I thought, *Right, you brought an angel, and he is standing at the back of the tent.* I turned around, and there was a huge angel standing there! I asked God, "What should I do?" I felt like running, so I ran to the back of the tent; and, as I did, it was as though somebody hit me in the head with a baseball bat. Wham! I didn't feel any pain, but I fell out of my body as it fell to the floor.

The next thing I knew, I was watching my body on the floor getting prayer from John Paul Jackson. My first thought was, *How am I going to get back into my body? What do I do?* I was about to panic. The Holy Spirit told me to calm down. Then I had this idea from God that I should walk around and see what was wrong with people. As I did, I had instant knowledge about who was sick and what they had. When I was done, I lay down, and my spirit returned to my body. Later I was able to call people out and name their sickness before praying for them.

I have also been part of a corporate translation experience. I was with a group of seven or eight prophetic people in Mission, British Columbia. We were praying at Patricia King's house when a few of us were translated to the streets of China. We actually spoke in Chinese tongues, and we saw everything as though we were there, even though physically we'd never left Patricia's house.

Another time, in the middle of my message in Wes and Stacey Campbell's church in Kelowna, British Columbia, I was translated to a hospital in Kenya where I laid hands on a crippled man. There I was, one moment preaching on a platform in Canada, and the next, frozen like a statue and translated to a different continent, where for only a moment, I left my body. Everyone in the meeting saw me freeze. As soon as I returned, I called to one of my team members, "Remind me when we get to Kenya to go the hospital and pray for a guy there who is crippled."

After the Kenyan crusade, I went into the hospital and prayed for terminally ill patients. The same man I visited in my experience was there. He looked like a toothpick because he had wasted away from AIDS. He wasn't expected to live for more than a few days, and he hadn't walked or even gotten out of bed in six months. When I laid hands on him, he jumped up and wanted to grab his mattress and run up and down the hallway with it. Talk about, "Arise, take up your bed and *walk*" (Mark 2:9)! Several other patients were instantly healed and sent home by the doctor—so that translation produced pretty good spiritual fruit, don't you think?

Note, I didn't just decide to have these translation experiences. You can't will yourself into an experience. But you can make yourself available for one by faith so that if God chooses to sovereignly come and initiate any of these experiences, He can.

TRANSPORTED IN THE SPIRIT

Enoch was transported in the spirit. This is where the body, soul, and spirit go along for the ride. Every part of you is sucked up and disappears. Enoch walked with God and was gone—he just stepped from this realm right into the next realm and that was it. "By faith Enoch was taken away so that he did not see death, 'and was not found, because God had taken him'" (Heb. 11:5a). Did you know that Ezekiel was transported in the spirit too? The Lord would pick him up and take him to different places in Israel. Look at this:

> *He stretched out the form of a hand, and took me by a lock of my hair; and the Spirit lifted me up between earth and heaven, and brought me in visions of God to Jerusalem, to the door of the north gate of the inner court, where the seat of the image of jealousy was, which provokes to jealousy (Ezekiel 8:3).*

Study the conversation between Elijah and the king's servant. Apparently, his spiritual travels were common knowledge.

And now you say, "Go, tell your master, 'Elijah is here'"! And it shall come to pass, as soon as I am gone from you, that the Spirit of the Lord will carry you to a place I do not know; so when I go and tell Ahab, and he cannot find you, he will kill me... (1 Kings 18:11-12).

Of course, the experience that we're most familiar with is described in the story of Philip and the Ethiopian eunuch: "Now when they came up out of the water, the Spirit of the Lord caught Philip away, so that the eunuch saw him no more..." (Acts 8:39).

I have never been transported in the Spirit, but I'm ready to go any time the Lord wants to send me. I know prophetic people who have experienced this. Here's an experience that happened to the well-known prophet John Paul Jackson, as told in his own words:

In 1990, I was on a twenty-one-day ministry trip through Europe, but after speaking in Geneva, Switzerland, I doubled over in pain from what doctors later told me was pancreatitis. Lying on my bed in excruciating pain that night, I told God that if He didn't heal me, I would cancel the rest of my trip and check into a hospital. Around 2:30 A.M., I sensed someone standing beside my bed. To my right was an elderly man with weathered skin and thick, knotted fingers. First, I thought I was hallucinating; then I thought it was an angel. As the old man reached out his hand towards me, he said, "I have come to pray for you." Placing his hand on top of mine, which rested on my stomach, he began to pray. I felt heat leave his hands and enter into mine. It felt thick like honey and glowing hot. Heat unrolled like a scroll—down my legs and out my feet and up my abdomen and out my head. As it steadily unrolled, the searing pain left my body. Then, we looked at each other and he disappeared before my eyes.

I jumped out of bed and began dancing around the room, thanking God for healing me and sending His angel. That's when He said it wasn't an angel. Nor was it the devil. A vision appeared to me of a man with outstretched hands and tears running down his face telling God, "I just want to be used by You, but I'm an old man in a small village. People think I'm crazy. Can You use me?" And God said to me, "I took him from an obscure village in Mexico, used him, and sent him back."

God does supernatural things like that. It's not a big deal to God. We make it a big deal because it violates physical laws. It seems out of the ordinary to us, but not to God. What is abnormal to us is normal to God.[2]

As you can see from the different examples in this chapter, God speaks to His people in a variety of ways. He is a very creative God. The examples I've covered are just some of the ways that God speaks. Each way He speaks impacts us differently. Even simple pictorial visions have pressed permanently into my soul, and now, years later, they still move me.

I hope I have stretched your faith and that you press in for these experiences. Remember, God gives good gifts to His children; He wants to speak to you as much as He did to His people in Bible days, and as He does for the spiritual generals of today. The Lord wants to communicate with you even more than you want to communicate with Him. He wants to open your spiritual eyes and ears to hear His voice and know His ways. Confess any ways you've placed God in a box by holding to wrong beliefs that limit how He can speak to you, or by doubting that He would speak. Then set aside time every day to be with Him, and get ready for supernatural encounters—sweet, great adventures in the spirit that will boost your faith and draw you into deeper intimacy with your awesome God.

Chapter Three

TOUCHING THE SUPERNATURAL REALM

I stood on a sea of glass—it was clear as crystal (see Rev. 4:6). *This is the third Heaven,* I thought. The sea changed color. "Why is the sea of glass taking on the color of amber?" I asked the Lord. As I watched it change, I remembered Ezekiel describing the glory of the Lord as amber, and like a rainbow (see Ezek. 1:27-28; 8:2), and I understood. Suddenly, I was before a pillar of fire and I recalled that Ezekiel, too, experienced God's presence as a pillar of fire. The warmth of His glory surrounded me, and I felt His glory on my face—like a warm summer sun shining on me. There's nothing in this world that compares with the glory of God! Then the Lord spoke these words to me (later confirmed by several prophetic people), "The Body of Christ is ready, on a corporate level, for the kind of anointing that you have touched and seen hidden away in back rooms."

This and other experiences have been so life changing for me. A few believers here and there are being taken into the third Heaven, having angelic visitations, and experiencing dreams, trances, and all those supernatural experiences we read about in the Bible, but now it's time for *all* His children to enter in. As you read this book, I want you to raise your expectations of how much of God you can receive now. Let's grow in faith to encounter and experience God in ways that we never have before.

SET YOUR MIND ON THINGS ABOVE

I'm going to say this repeatedly, but it's important to settle this issue in your spirit. The Bible encourages us to set our minds on things above where Christ is seated. Think about the reality of Heaven. Listen. It's more real than the world you live in. It's easy to set our mind on what we see in the natural—what the doctor said, what we feel, and what the situation looks like. It's so easy to be caught up in the temporal world, but the Bible says we need to set our minds on the eternal: "If then you were raised with Christ, seek those things which are above, where Christ is, sitting at the right hand of God" (Col. 3:1).

Remember, though, we don't wrestle against flesh and blood but against demonic powers and principalities (see Eph. 6:12). The devil is real, and he really does want to steal from you and destroy and kill you. No, you don't need to look for a devil behind every bush, but you do need to walk in a supernatural awareness of both demons and angels.

When I wake up in the morning, I make a conscious effort to thank God for the reality of angels. Because I make room for this reality as a part of my everyday life, angels are free to manifest themselves actively in my ministry. I may pray something like this: "Thank You, God, for the angels that are with me. Thank You for the angels—those ministering spirits that come to do Your work. Thank You for the healing angels. Thank You for the harvest angels. Thank You for the angels that encamp around those who fear You. They lift me up; they lift me above the warfare."

As I am in the shower I'll pray, "I thank You, Jesus, that the blind see and the deaf hear. I thank You that cripples walk. I just thank You for miracles and healing." I am constantly pulling that supernatural realm into my life and growing my faith levels by expecting miracles and reminding myself that they are easy for Jesus to perform. I thank God in prayers like this: "I thank You, God, for Heaven. Thanks, Lord, that I can see in the spirit. I want to travel in the spirit, Lord. I can go to Hawaii with my wife, God, why can't I go somewhere in Heaven too? Holy Spirit, take me there! Thank You for trances, visions, and dreams. Thank You that I hear Your voice, God. You said, 'My sheep hear My voice.' Yes, I can hear Your voice."

I may not see an angel, or anyone healed right then; I may not be in a place where I even need a miracle, but I stay aware of the supernatural realm by continuously setting my mind on things above and thanking God for them.

I always look for demonic powers and spiritual strategies: "God, what is happening in the service right now in the invisible realm? What is the enemy doing? What is the hindrance in the region?" The Kingdom of God is not in word only, but it is in demonstrations of the Holy Spirit's power (see 1 Cor. 2:4). I regularly pull on that divine realm, and then the heavens open up for me.

ONLY BELIEVE

I want you to live and to walk in God's power. I want you to encounter and to experience the reality of the supernatural and the spiritual realm. I've learned that these encounters, like everything in the Christian life, we receive by faith. "Jesus said to him, 'If you can believe, all things are possible to him who believes'" (Mark 9:23). One

New Testament story powerfully illustrates a Gentile's faith in the supernatural realm.

> *And Jesus said to him, "I will come and heal him." The centurion answered and said, "Lord, I am not worthy that You should come under my roof. But only speak a word, and my servant will be healed. For I also am a man under authority, having soldiers under me. And I say to this one, 'Go,' and he goes; and to another, 'Come,' and he comes; and to my servant, 'Do this,' and he does it." When Jesus heard it, He marveled, and said to those who followed, "Assuredly, I say to you, I have not found such great faith, not even in Israel!"* (Matthew 8:7-10)

The Lord once told me He is calling us to the same kind of faith the centurion demonstrated. "Todd," He said, "if you can get people to believe in the realities of the spiritual realm (the manifestation of Heaven touching earth—the prophetic word, angels, dreams, and people being healed and set free), then I will release more of My power."

"God, what do You mean 'get them to believe in an angel'—what about believing in You?" I asked.

"My people don't have trouble believing in Me, but when you mention that an angel showed up they quickly get into unbelief," He answered.

That made sense, and here's why: If I tell you that Paul, Elijah, and Daniel saw an angel you'll say, "Amen. I believe it." We expect the prophets to have those experiences. But if I say *I* saw an angel, then everyone becomes skeptical. We are the Daniels, Elijahs, and Pauls of today. If we aren't seeing into the supernatural realm, who else will?

We need the simple faith of a child. Today, we often hear reports of children who see angels. Angels will sometimes show a playful side of themselves to people. At a meeting in Edmonton, Alberta, I heard a report of Gabriel visiting a seven-year-old boy. The angel actually pulled up his gown to show the boy he was wearing running shoes!

"Only believe" (Luke 8:50) is the door that opens up the spiritual realm that brings Heaven; that brings all the miracles and all the signs and all the wonders. God wants to challenge your belief system. He wants to challenge your level of faith. God wants to challenge your mind-set and to make the supernatural natural and commonplace. He wants us to believe like the saints of old, and He wants to release miracles as He did, and as we see, from the beginning to the end of the Bible. This is the inheritance of His sons and daughters.

END-TIME RELEASE OF SIGNS AND WONDERS

But this is what was spoken by the prophet Joel: "And it shall come to pass in the last days, says God, That I will pour out of My Spirit on all flesh; your sons and your daughters shall prophesy, your young men shall see visions, your old men shall dream dreams. And on My menservants and on My maidservants I will pour out My Spirit in those days; and they shall prophesy. I will show wonders in heaven above and signs in the earth beneath: blood and fire and vapor of smoke. The sun shall be turned into darkness, and the moon into blood, before the coming of the great and awesome day of the Lord. And it shall come to pass that whoever calls on the name of the Lord shall be saved" (Acts 2:16-21).

Do the words "whoever calls upon the name of the Lord shall be saved" refer to a day yet to come or a day that is here? I believe we are living in the outpouring of God's Spirit right now. He is releasing prophecy, visions, and dreams to His people today: "I will pour out of My Spirit on *all flesh*"—sons and daughters are prophesying, young men are having visions, and old men are dreaming dreams in our generation.

God's purpose here is that we all will prophesy and have dreams and visions. What we are seeing now is progressive; it's a process. I believe that this divine promise is available today for anyone who is ready to receive it. A day is coming in the Church when all flesh will come into the dimension of visions, dreams, healings, and miracles. This calling goes way beyond the dimension of commonplace prophetic words, the still, small voice, impressions, words of knowledge, prophetic exhortation, or even "thus says the Lord" type of prophecies spoken to us in the first person (as though God is speaking the words). Every believer should be having profound, detailed, accurate words of knowledge for every person they encounter. Every believer should be having visions and dreams. Every Christian should be participating in healings and miracles. These experiences are available to all of us now.

I don't know if the last days are 500 years or 1,000 years away, but I do know we are certainly in the last days far more than the disciples were when the Spirit was poured out in Acts. I also know that these are the last days for anyone reading this book. Maybe your life is a third or even two-thirds of the way spent. It's the last days—the only days remaining that each of us has to serve the Lord.

Every saint has the opportunity to participate in the release of this prophetic dimension, which will come with signs and wonders. We are destined to carry that supernatural anointing, to walk in the reality of the Spirit of wisdom and revelation, and to have the eyes of our heart opened to see into the heavens. This is our inheritance. According to Scripture, God endorses ministry through signs and wonders: "Men of Israel, hear these words: Jesus of Nazareth, a Man attested by God to you by miracles, wonders, and signs which God did through Him in your midst, as you yourselves also know" (Acts 2:22).

This passage speaks of the days that God confirmed and endorsed Jesus' ministry with miracles, signs, and wonders. According to John 17 we are just as loved by the Father as Jesus is; we are just as much a child and just as much a joint-heir. Jesus asked this of the Father: "... that the world may know that You have sent Me, and have loved them as You have loved Me" (John 17:23). Jesus is seated at the Father's right hand in the heavenly places and, as part of His Body, we are made to sit in heavenly places with Him (see Eph. 1:20-23).

The Father wants to endorse ministry in North America with miracles, signs, and wonders. He wants us to reach for this inheritance. We need to say, "Thank You, Lord, that it's mine." The supernatural needs to become a part of our consciousness, part of our everyday thinking. We need to think about open heavens, angels, visions, and dreams. We need to talk about miracles, power, and healings. We need to thank God for angels and for the prophetic.

We are living in an exciting time! God wants to anoint you for prophetic vision and to give you spiritual eyes. As the Lord opens the eyes of your heart, you will come into the reality of the spiritual realm. God wants to make you naturally supernatural. It's time for your launch into new realms of the Spirit.

MADE FOR SIGNS AND WONDERS

God hasn't called us just to preach the Gospel. The Gospel "package" includes performing signs and wonders. Your destiny is to *be* a sign and a wonder! God created us to see signs and wonders, as well as to be signs and wonders. Delve deeply into this passage of Scripture: "Here am I and the children whom the Lord has given me! We are for signs and wonders in Israel…" (Isa. 8:18).

We're talking about a prophetic life, a prophetic message. People are crying out for revelation: "Give me illumination. I want an experience of the supernatural. I'm not seeing the signs and wonders in the church today, so I'll call the psychic hot line." When we don't have signs and wonders, the world looks for them somewhere else. They seek them in the New Age, the occult, and in the false expressions of genuine revelation. God wants us to have the genuine article, so the world can know there's revelation and understanding in the Church.

The world should be saying, "I've never met these people, but somehow they knew something about my past and about the sickness in my body. They also knew something about my younger brother and he got healed; that tells me there's a God." When these supernatural events begin to happen, you won't even need to preach the Gospel (but do!) because it will be evident to the unbelievers that there's a living God in Heaven.

Now look what happens if we are not for signs and wonders: "And when they say to you, 'Seek those who are mediums and wizards, who whisper and mutter,' should not a people seek their God? Should they seek the dead on behalf of the living?" (Isa. 8:19).

When we are not for signs and wonders, people seek out wizards, mediums, and dead gods. They consult the dead on behalf of the living, rather than the living God. Doesn't that verse just break your heart? So many people are turning to the counterfeit because we are not where we need to be spiritually. We need to live out our spiritual inheritance and be signs and wonders; then the world will turn to the Church for revelation.

We must understand the reality of the supernatural, the open heavens, and the heavenly glory and reach for that place in the spirit where supernatural signs and wonders happen. God wants to release this anointing upon His people. Are you ready for it?

SIGNS AND WONDERS TESTIFY TO GOD'S KINGDOM

What is the first thing that comes to mind when you think about Acts 2, or the Day of Pentecost? According to Acts 1:8, Pentecost was about receiving *dunamis* (miraculous) power. Likely, you picture a group of people gathered in a Jerusalem upper room who feel a rushing wind, see tongues of fire, and then who speak in other languages. In reality, the experience at Pentecost was not so much about speaking in tongues as it was about signs, wonders, prophetic experiences, power, and about God opening up Heaven as He poured out His Spirit. Think about it. Speaking in tongues was only one of the evidences or results of the Holy Spirit's outpouring that day.

Historically, many things happen when God pours out His Spirit. People have prophesied for days afterward, having visions and dreams. We don't see these things often, or on the same level, because we have a hard time believing that God allows people encounters with the supernatural world.

I'm going to make a statement that you might not believe; you might even find it offensive. Fortunately, it's not just my opinion; I got it from the apostle Paul who picked it up from Jesus—so don't get upset with me! Here it is: You haven't fully preached the Gospel of Christ if you haven't done it with miracles, signs, and wonders:

Therefore I have reason to glory in Christ Jesus in the things which pertain to God. For I will not dare to speak of any of those things which Christ has not accomplished through me, in word and deed, to make the Gentiles obedient—in mighty signs and wonders, by the power of the Spirit of God, so that from Jerusalem and round about to Illyricum I have fully preached the gospel of Christ (Romans 15:17-19).

Paul says that he had fully preached the Gospel because signs and wonders by the power of God accompanied his preaching. Chew on that one for a while.

In the context of the Gospel presentation, we should always see the manifestation of God's power. "Then Jesus went about all the cities and villages, teaching in their synagogues, preaching the gospel of the kingdom, and healing every sickness and every disease among the people" (Matt. 9:35). Notice that Jesus preached the Gospel *and* healed every sickness and disease. In every reference where Jesus proclaimed the Gospel, we see the demonstration of the Kingdom in power. Jesus never brought the message of the Kingdom without a demonstration of the Kingdom. "And Jesus went about all Galilee, teaching in their synagogues, preaching the gospel of the kingdom, and healing all kinds of sickness and all kinds of disease among the people" (Matt. 4:23).

In my ministry, I teach my disciples, "Power first, then the Word. Go in and prophesy first, or demonstrate the power of God first in some way."

In the church, there's been such a lack of the demonstration of God's power. Our preaching won't be effective in the church today because so many people's attitude is, *Been there, done that, bought the T-shirt.* Their minds and hearts are often already closed five minutes into the service:

> *How shall we escape if we neglect so great a salvation, which at the first began to be spoken by the Lord, and was confirmed to us by those who heard Him, God also bearing witness both with signs and wonders, with various miracles, and gifts of the Holy Spirit, according to His own will?* (Hebrews 2:3-4)

We see it here again. God backs up the salvation message with signs, wonders, and various miracles. That is the Gospel message:

> *I have become a fool in boasting; you have compelled me. For I ought to have been commended by you; for in nothing was I behind the most eminent apostles, though I am nothing. Truly the signs of an apostle were accomplished among you with all perseverance, in signs and wonders and mighty deeds* (2 Corinthians 12:11-12).

> *For it is impossible for those who were once enlightened, and have tasted the heavenly gift, and have become partakers of the Holy Spirit, and have tasted the good word of God and the powers of the age to come, if they fall away, to renew them again to repentance...* (Hebrews 6:4-6).

As the last biblical reference suggests, when the Word of God enlightens us, we are supposed to taste the powers of the age to come—

these powers now. Ask the Lord to give you a taste of Heaven now. We don't have to wait until we die to see angels or to experience Heaven.

When John the Baptist was in prison, he sent two of his disciples to ask Jesus if He was the one or if he should look for another. I love Jesus' answer. Nowhere in His answer does He ever say "yes." He just describes His actions and lets John draw his own conclusions. Jesus could have said, "Of course I am, John. I was born of a virgin. Don't you know the Scriptures?" He could have keyed in on many aspects of His divinity, but look how He chose to describe His Messiah-ship:

> *And when John had heard in prison about the works of Christ, he sent two of his disciples and said to Him, "Are You the Coming One, or do we look for another?" Jesus answered and said to them, "Go and tell John the things which you hear and see: The blind see and the lame walk; the lepers are cleansed and the deaf hear; the dead are raised up and the poor have the gospel preached to them. And blessed is he who is not offended because of Me"* (Matthew 11:2-6).

Note also that Jesus didn't just say that He preached the Gospel to the poor and stopped at that. He set an example of what we should do. We are the generation that should enter into "greater works than these" (John 14:12). In the church today, we have limited the Gospel to only preaching, but it shouldn't be isolated from these other Kingdom manifestations. According to Jesus and Paul, preaching, healing, and miracles are a package deal.

If you want to know if the Kingdom has come to your life or your church, just ask these questions: "Do the lame walk? Do the blind see?

Are AIDS sufferers healed? Are the dead raised? And do the poor hear the Gospel?" Look for the signs and wonders of the manifestation of His Kingdom.

REAPING THE HARVEST WITH MIRACULOUS SIGNS

God is about to reap a great end-time harvest. "Thrust in Your sickle and reap, for the time has come for You to reap, for the harvest of the earth is ripe" (Rev. 14:15b). I believe that healings and miracles are the sickle that God is going to use to reap the end-time harvest. The world is hungry for the supernatural realm. Unfortunately, in the world's eye, the church has no power. That's why all the psychic hot lines are busy and why the New Age movement is growing dramatically today. The church appears weak in comparison to the works of darkness. God has spoken to me, from Scripture, that by His great power He is going to eat up the devil's counterfeit signs and wonders:

> *Then the Lord spoke to Moses and Aaron, saying, "When Pharaoh speaks to you, saying, 'Show a miracle for yourselves,' then you shall say to Aaron, 'Take your rod and cast it before Pharaoh, and let it become a serpent.'" So Moses and Aaron went in to Pharaoh, and they did so, just as the Lord commanded. And Aaron cast down his rod before Pharaoh and before his servants, and it became a serpent. But Pharaoh also called the wise men and the sorcerers; so the magicians of Egypt, they also did in like manner with their enchantments. For every man threw down his rod, and they became serpents. But Aaron's rod swallowed up their rods (Exodus 7:8-12).*

The world today is looking to false religions, cult leaders, and ungodly doctrines, but the true God is going to send His serpent into the world to eat up the counterfeit. There will be a great outpouring of God's healing power and prophetic words, and the victorious Church will eat up the false by the true signs and wonders. Then the world will know that healing for their body is in the Church. Hospitals and clinics will close. The Spirit of Truth will be seen overcoming the spirit of error (see 1 John 4:6), and the world will finally know what is true and what is false.

I see leaders of occult movements turning to the truth of Jesus Christ because of the signs and wonders the Church will work. They will see, like Simon the Sorcerer saw, that we flow in real power (see Acts 8:17-19). The outpouring of power will be so great, that the baals of today will be "shown up" by the genuine miracles of the Church, such as the account of Elijah on Mount Carmel. Let's remember that the power of God came because the "fervent prayer of a righteous man avails much" (James 5:16b). Pray fervently that this same great anointing of boldness and power would rest upon God's people today.

THE SIGNS-PROPHETS

Signs-prophets are those who carry two dimensions: First, their whole life becomes a sign as they live out the message that God has called them to bring to the church. Hosea married a prostitute to illustrate God's relationship to His unfaithful people. Ezekiel had to act out the siege of Jerusalem and then lie on his left and right sides to bear the sin of the house of Israel and Judah for 390 and then 40 days (see Ezek. 4:1-7).

Second, these prophets carry with them the reality of miracles, signs, and wonders—this is so with signs-prophets of the Bible and their contemporary counterparts. Watch the news. When the signs-prophets come to town, often you'll see a change in the weather patterns—freak storms, floods, tremors, plagues, or other signs and wonders. It's happened with several of my prophet friends and colleagues. Today, signs-prophets are again beginning to partner with God in fulfilling this verse: "I will show wonders in heaven above and signs in the earth beneath: blood and fire and vapor of smoke" (Acts 2:19).

I believe that God is releasing this signs and wonders dimension in the earth today to validate the visions and dreams of the prophets. He is increasing the authority of true prophetic words in the midst of all the prophetic fluff, and He is granting signs through true healing ministries. For example, in Seattle I said to a woman, "You've got hepatitis C. As a sign to you that the Lord will heal you tonight, I'm going to tell you the name of your husband. His name is Danny." She just came undone, and onlookers cried out in amazement. Then I said, "Don't be impressed with the detail, just receive your healing." Yes, there's a new dimension coming to the healing ministry, in which we not only call out a person's condition but, as a sign that the Lord is going to heal someone, we may share other information He gives us.

The signs and wonders ministry will even go beyond this prophetic dimension. For instance, you may hear a word like: "Revival is going to come to your city, and as a confirmation a comet will pass over your house on December 14th." Then you'll go home, look out your window, and go, "Aaah, there it is!"

I was in Birmingham, Alabama, in April 2005, and on the first night of the conference, I was caught up into the spirit and saw three major highways that led into the city. I saw revival arrive from the north, and then I gave a specific word over the region. The Lord told me to tell the people that they would know His words were true when tornadoes and floods hit Birmingham. Those arrived the day after we left.

In July 2004, I was in a meeting in Vacaville, California, when I had an open vision. I saw a massive archangel (who was assigned over a continent), with one foot on Indonesia and one foot on Malaysia. Next, I saw a tsunami wave rise up out of the sea, and in the crest of the tsunami wave I read the word *REVIVAL*. Then I saw the wave hit Indonesia, Malaysia, and Southeast Asia. After I delivered the word, I asked if there was anyone from Malaysia and Indonesia in my meeting. Four Christian leaders from Malaysia stood up as well as a major leader from Southeast Asia who ministers widely in the region.

These five people took the prophecy back to Indonesia and Malaysia and printed it out. Many Christians and leaders read the word. When Charlie Robinson (an associate minister of FFM and seer prophet) visited Indonesia and Malaysia that December, they told Charlie they believed every part of the prophecy I gave about revival coming to Indonesia, Malaysia, and Southeast Asia, except for one part: "Natural disasters don't happen in Malaysia." They told Charlie that they didn't believe the tsunami part of the prophecy for their region of Asia. Charlie replied, "God will judge the seas," because he had received a revelation from God about the seven thunders and how God will judge the seven seas (see Rev. 10).

Then, on December 4, in downtown Jakarta, the Lord showed Charlie that God would judge a demonic principality over the region that would cause a violent catastrophe in the ocean off the coast of Indonesia. He shared his revelation with one of the Christian leaders there, saying that this disaster would affect all of Southeast Asia. Later, in one of his meetings in Indonesia Charlie felt led to have everyone roar, and it lasted for half an hour!

Sometimes the Lord calls us to roar just as He does (see Joel 3:16; Hos. 11:10). At God's leading, we can release a roar by faith just as we would a victory shout (see Josh. 6:5). A roar like this often releases a holy indignation within our spirits, as a declaration to the enemy that "enough is enough!" Roaring not only looses tied-up promises, but it also tears down demonic principalities. When we roar like a lion, something happens in the spirit realm. Jesus is the Lion of the Tribe of Judah, and sometimes He causes His Spirit to rise up in our hearts with a groan or a roar of judgment on principalities.

The Lord told Charlie there would be an earthquake after he left Indonesia, and six days after his departure, on December 26, the earthquake and tsunami struck. God was judging the seas! They called Charlie and said, "It's true. Every word of the prophecy is true!" When the tsunami hit, the entire world said, "Destruction! Oh God, why? Why would God allow this to happen? Three-hundred thousand lost their lives." But listen! The crest of the wave in my vision said "REVIVAL"! Who would have thought revival would follow a tsunami and an earthquake?

First, we must realize that God does not cause natural disasters. However, when God wants to bring change or to release revival, there will always be spiritual war in the heavens as demonic principalities in the second heaven resist God's advancing plans. When there's war, there are casualties. We don't always understand why people get hurt. When Jesus cast the demon out of a child in Luke 9:42 (KJV), "The devil threw him down, and tare him." In the same way, when God deals with demonic forces in the heavens, a tearing takes places in the spiritual realm that sometimes manifests in destructive ways on earth. The enemy desires to bring destruction and to prevent God's plans for revival. However, in spite of the battle, God's plans will come to pass.

Even with all the devastation in Indonesia and Malaysia, there was a tremendous expectancy among the churches there that God was about to do something powerful. Today He is sending signs of revival in Christian meetings in the form of gold dust, diamonds, and feathers, and the people are growing in passion for the Lord as well as faith for the coming wave of revival. Indeed we visited Kota Kinabalu, Sabah, Malaysia, in May 2007 and found Malaysia marked and ripe for revival! We saw many miracles, signs, and wonders, and an outpouring of the greater glory! Every meeting was charged with Holy Ghost electricity!

Please understand that God releases judgment as answers to prayer, ultimately to bring blessings and to fulfill His promises. God reveals future events—secrets—to His friends and to His prophets (see Amos 3:7). Because of repentance and travailing prayer by God's people, the Lord will judge demonic principalities over areas. Often those supernatural judgments are manifested in the natural through disasters.

Let's remember that in the shaking—in the earthquake in Japan and in the disaster in Indonesia—God is saying: "REVIVAL!" The Lord is making His name known against His adversaries and releasing blessings on His people in those areas. He wants us "in the know" about what He's doing, so He gives us signs on the earth of what He is doing in the spiritual realm.

We win the world with power encounters and by moving in the realm of revelation as we hear His secret plans and declare them. Yes, God created His children as well as the signs-prophets for signs and wonders. The prophets may walk in a greater dimension of power than the average believer may, but we are called to start living in the reality of the super-natural realm in these end-days.

We are to be a sign, a living epistle, and a prophetic picture in the earth, a manifestation of the supernatural realm spilling over and break-ing into the natural realm everywhere we go—the marketplace, work, business, school, the mall, or the hospital. We should be carrying signs and wonders because we carry the reality of the Kingdom of Heaven within us (see Luke 17:21). Though I am on the earth, in my mind I am in Heaven. I am operating in that realm in the anointing of the Spirit of wisdom and revelation. God wants to give us the anointing of the super-natural. Later in this book, I'll teach more about signs-prophets, as well as seer-prophets and now-prophets.

WILLIAM BRANHAM AND THE "VOICE OF HEALING" REVIVAL

The Church has experienced healing revival since the Book of Acts, but the full manifestation of healings, miracles, signs, and wonders has yet to come. The "Voice of Healing" revival in America took off in the 1950s and '60s with Oral Roberts, Jack Coe, A.A. Allen, R.T. Ritchie, and Gor-don Lindsay, and the distribution of *The Voice of Healing* newsletter. Tens of thousands of people packed into tents all across America. William Branham was a forerunner of signs and wonders ministry seen in that day. In 1946, an angel visited this poor, uneducated, stuttering man and imparted a healing anointing, but it wasn't just a healing anointing—they called William Branham a "prophet of notable signs and wonders."

It is widely known that a great deal of controversy surrounded the final days of Branham's ministry. I believe that he stepped out of his grace, the sphere of influence God had called him to (which just goes to show the importance of character, accountability, and staying within your specific calling). However, during his healing ministry days, he moved in more accurate realms of revelation than almost anyone else of his time did. Some say his gifting was 100 percent accurate.

At Branham's meetings, people would receive a numbered card and wait in healing lines for hours. Branham would wait for an angel to come and stand behind him. He would do nothing until the angel arrived, and when the angel did, he would yell, "The angel is here!" It was as though the angel appeared to raise people's faith and stir God's healing waters—just as the angel in Jesus' day did at the pool of Bethesda (see John 5:4). People would line up according to their number and Branham would go into visions and tell people many details of their lives. He spoke out these words of knowledge only as a sign that the Lord would heal them. Often Branham wouldn't even pray for these people, yet they would walk out of the meeting healed.

On one occasion, Branham received a vision of a boy who would be raised from the dead after a car accident. He even described the boy's appearance, including his clothes and type of haircut. Gordon Lindsay wrote the vision down in the flyleaf of his Bible (Lindsay was Branham's travel companion and the co-founder of *The Voice of Healing* magazine). Two years later, during a ministry trip to Finland, a car right in front of the ministers struck two boys. One boy was taken to the hospital in a vehicle ahead, while the other child was placed into Branham's arms. The boy appeared dead, with no pulse, heartbeat, or signs of breathing and, according to Branham, had been that way for a half hour.

Branham remembered the vision and that prompted Lindsay to look at the entries he'd previously made in his Bible. The description he'd written from Branham's vision was identical to that of the Finnish boy in Branham's arms. Then Branham knelt in the car and asked the Lord for mercy, and others joined him in prayer. Minutes later the boy opened his eyes. As the men carried the youngster into the hospital, he cried, and they realized they'd witnessed a powerful miracle.[3]

These miracles, signs, and wonders in Branham's ministry, released through visions, validated Branham's ministry as people received dramatic healing signs in their bodies. I believe that the Holy Spirit is beginning to release this same supernatural dimension through believers today.

PROPHETIC NAMES FROM GOD

As God increasingly releases His people into supernatural ministry, He will also begin to reveal prophetic names to them to confirm that they are to be signs and wonders in the earth. Isaiah's natural children had names of prophetic significance to Israel and its destiny (they were signs and wonders). In a similar way, God has a name of prophetic significance for each of His people. Throughout the Bible God renamed people to reflect their destiny. He changed Abram's name to *Abraham*, which meant "father of many nations," and changed Sarai's name to *Sarah*, calling her a princess or queen who would be "a mother of nations" (Gen. 17:4-5,15-16). The Lord also has a prophetic name for you, and your name has significance in the spirit realm. This name assigns your nature.

In Genesis, we see Adam in the garden naming the animals. As an intimate friend, God gave Adam the authority to call them whatever he wanted. Whatever he named them is what they would be called forever. I believe that Adam gave each creature a name that reflected and released their respective natures and that each animal species today still lives out the prophetic nature Adam gave it those thousands of years ago. Thus, it would make sense that when Adam spoke the name of the animal, God bestowed upon the creature its nature and position in the "animal" kingdom.

We too have a prophetic name. In the Book of Revelation, we see an example of the overcomers' prophetic names, which God actually wrote on white stones: "…And I will give him a white stone, and on the stone a new name written which no one knows except him who receives it" (Rev. 2:17). I believe that, as the overcomers, the Lord gives each of us a prophetic name. This name may not be what your parents called you (like Melanie or Tyler), but God has a name for you in the spirit realm, which releases you into your spiritual destiny. When the Lord speaks your prophetic name to you directly, or through a prophetic person, it actually releases you into your nature and into the dimension of signs and wonders. That's why it's so important to find out what your name is, so you can fully step into your nature. As you continue to read this book, I believe the Holy Spirit will begin to release your prophetic nature. Why don't you ask the Lord what your prophetic name is?

A FIERY ANGELIC VISITOR

Now let me further illustrate the kind of revelations, signs, and wonders that God wants to give today. Once while ministering in Seattle, Washington, at a healing conference where Bill Johnson was speaking, I had a profound visitation. It was about 10 o'clock at night and while Bill spoke, an angel appeared in front of me. Nobody else saw him. His feet were like pillars of fire. With my spiritual eyes, I saw a portal about 4 feet by 4 feet that the angel had opened in the spirit realm. The rip was like a black hole in the sky.

A pillar of smoke and a pillar of fire appeared, and energy filled the room. I stuck my hand out to touch it and it felt as if my hand was going into an electrical force field. My whole body shook, and I asked the Lord, "What do You want me to do?" He said, "Climb in, climb in. Just soak."

So that's what I did. I lay down at the altar, and the Lord took me up into visions. I first entered a scene from ancient Roman times. There were seven huge pillars around me. "These are the seven pillars of revelation," said the Lord. Revelation 10:1-2 describes the same scene: "I saw still another mighty angel coming down from heaven, clothed with a cloud. And a rainbow was on his head, his face was like the sun, and his feet like pillars of fire. He had a little book open in his hand...." Later in the chapter, the angel tells John to eat the little book. He says the book would be "sweet" to the prophet's mouth and "bitter" to his stomach.

The Lord then illumined another Scripture to me: "Wisdom has built her house, she has hewn out her seven pillars" (Prov. 9:1). This verse described the pillars in my vision as "pillars of wisdom." "They're also the seven pillars of Isaiah 11:2, the seven Spirits that rested on Jesus," said the Lord. "The Spirit of the Lord shall rest upon Him, the Spirit of wisdom and understanding, the Spirit of counsel and might, the Spirit of knowledge and of the fear of the Lord" (Isa. 11:2). Suddenly I realized that this experience was a sign of a new dimension of revelation God is about to release in the Church.

As I came out of this experience the Lord said, "Get back to the hotel room. I'm going to visit you in power for one hour." I grabbed a couple of my team, including my father, and we rushed back to Charlie Robinson's hotel room. We ran into the room at one minute before 11 P.M. Everybody lay on the carpet at 11 o'clock on the nose. The power of God fell, and everyone started screaming, shaking, and vibrating as the angel with the legs like fire reappeared. We all went into a simultaneous vision. I had a vision of a fire and I started yelling, "My God is a consuming fire! My God is a consuming fire!" As I saw the fire come down I screamed, "The fire, the fire! Burn up my flesh! I want to feel the fire!"

HOLY SMOKE AND FRAGRANCE

In the natural realm, the whole room filled with smoke, and everybody smelled it. "Todd, I'm in a room in Heaven right now, and there are filing cabinets everywhere," said my dad. "The Lord opened a filing cabinet and He brought out a little book." The moment Dad spoke that, in my vision, I was already ripping a page from a book and eating it. I screamed out, "I'm in a room full of spices." I saw little jars of spices, like cinnamon, garlic, and oregano. The scene went farther than my eyes could see; the room was wall-to-wall spice jars. "The spices…the fragrant spices…oh the aromas!" Then the entire room filled with the fragrance of the Lord. In that moment, in the natural, everybody smelled burning cinnamon.

Are you thinking: *This is too much… I've heard of people having visions, Todd, but everybody being caught up into the same vision?* I'm just sharing a profound, unusual, prophetic encounter that shows us that God is about to visit us in a completely new dimension of revelation and wisdom. God usually surprises everyone when He shows up, especially the theologians.

Now, back to our hotel encounter. "What do all this fire, smoke, and fragrance mean for the Church today, God?" He directed me to the Song of Solomon where the Shulamite asks:

Who is this coming out of the wilderness like pillars of smoke, perfumed with myrrh and frankincense, with all the merchant's fragrant powders?... Solomon the King made himself a palanquin: he made its pillars of silver, its support of gold, its seat of purple, its interior paved with love... (Song of Solomon 3:6,9-10).

I asked this same question: "Who is this in the hotel room like pillars of smoke?" I realized that, like Solomon, our Bridegroom-King had come to visit us in intimacy with all His fragrant aromas. It was part of a prophetic invitation to the Church to enter a new dimension of intimacy with Jesus.

Signs Lead to Intimacy

At 12 o'clock midnight, the presence of the Lord lifted and everybody emerged from the prophetic encounter. Our experience, I believe, was part of God's release to the Church of a dimension of signs in the heavens above and wonders on the earth beneath (see Acts 2:18-19). This new dimension is not only to be connected to evangelism, but also to intimacy and friendship with God.

The next day, in what I believe to be a validation of our vision and also perhaps the Lord's judgment on a principality that hindered the move of His Spirit in that region, we'd learned through hotel staff that a woman in a room above ours had called the front desk at 11:20 P.M.—on the same night and approximate time of our vision of God's fire coming down—to complain of a crackling and burning sound in the walls. The hotel people checked things out but didn't find anything. However, at around midnight, the power went out in that area of the hotel, but our power stayed on.

Twelve hours later at 11 A.M. both rooms burst into flame. We'd been at a meeting and when we returned the entire hotel smelled of smoke.

Through this experience, I believe the Lord is saying He's going to validate the prophetic words and the visions and dreams of the prophets by releasing signs in the heavens above and wonders on the earth beneath. It's going to become commonplace in the Church today. As you read this book, I really believe the Lord wants to bring you into fresh encounters and to release a new anointing for revelation as the Spirit of the Lord rests on your life afresh. The Holy Spirit wants to give you a continual sense of what the Father is doing. He wants to pull back the curtain and let you see into the heavens.

In describing the two end-time witnesses, Moses and Elijah, Revelation chapter 11 paints a picture of two things: authority and power. God wants to release the same anointing on His people as He did these two prophets, so the Church can operate in the same kinds of signs and wonders. Look at the description of these witnesses:

> ...fire proceeds from their mouth and devours their enemies. ...These have power to shut heaven, so that no rain falls in the days of their prophecy; and they have power over waters to turn them to blood, and to strike the earth with all plagues, as often as they desire (Revelation 11:5-6).

These are awesome signs and wonders, and they can do them "as often as they desire"! When I read this passage, I had some serious questions. "Oh, come on, God. You're going to trust the Church with that kind of power as often as they choose? We can't be trusted with that kind of power just because we desire it…can we? There are corrupt people in the Church today; we can't even trust them with the power to heal the sick. Lord, in the last great healing revival, so caught up were the evangelists with envy, jealousy, and competition that they competed with one another to see who had the world's largest meeting tent. God, You're not going to trust us with power as often as we desire, are You? How could that possibly work?"

FRIENDSHIP WITH GOD

Then the Lord showed me that His secrets and His power are for those who have sweet, satisfying companionship with Him. "The secret of the Lord is with those who fear Him, and He will show them His covenant" (Ps. 25:14). He's only going to trust His friends with this signs and wonders ministry: "No longer do I call you servants, for a servant does not know what his master is doing; but I have called you friends, for all things that I heard from My Father I have made known to you" (John 15:15).

God came down and visited Moses. He would speak to Moses as a friend speaks to a friend, face-to-face. I believe that today, God is calling His people into an intimate friendship with Him, in which He can begin to speak to them in trust, face-to-face. In a restaurant one day I found that I knew things about people whom I'd never met. I knew that a man there was gay. I looked at the waitress and I could feel she had some kind of sickness in her belly. Later in the day on a flight, my spiritual *antenna* picked up signals and I heard people's thoughts. I prayed,

"What do You want me to do with this, God? Tell me who this is for and I'll just tell everybody on the airplane their destiny and lead them all to You."

Then the Lord said to me: "No, Todd, you're My friend and I'm just sharing things with My friend. I don't want you to tell just anybody about what I'm showing you. You don't have to do anything. We have sweet, satisfying companionship together, and so I'm sharing the secrets of what's going on in My heart, but that doesn't mean you need to tell everybody. Those who are My real friends, I trust and I give them understanding of what I'm doing in the earth today. I'm going to trust My friends with end-time power in the earth. It's going to be based on intimacy and friendship."

The Father wants us to enter into a friendship with Him so He can just tell us things, like: "I'm going to let you in on what I'm doing right now in the South. An earthquake will shake that area tomorrow—I'm sharing this with you because we're buddies and I trust you." Signs, wonders, and prophetic insights are all going to come through friendship; but it's not just about signs and wonders; it's about intimacy with God. Although the visitation in the hotel room was a profound supernatural encounter, the Father's greatest message to me was that He wanted to be my intimate friend. I believe that as we all enter this place of friendship with Him, the Father will also release us into the fullness of our destiny.

If reading this chapter has imparted a desire to demonstrate the supernatural and a craving for more intimate relationship with God, the next chapter will help you begin to activate this spiritual inheritance that is yours in Christ.

Chapter Four

Developing a
Kingdom Mind-set

Ionce took a team to Monterrey, Mexico. We split up and ministered in different churches on the Sunday morning. Not only did the Lord heal people in the services, but hospitals in the area also reported patients who awoke healed. Healings coincided with the same times that we preached in the churches. We had made God known to the principalities and powers of the air. The Kingdom came to earth as it is in Heaven and the spiritual climate of the city shifted.

Most Christians don't understand the spiritual realm, neither do they hear, see, and experience God in the many ways described in the last chapter. The problem is that most believers don't understand the Kingdom Jesus talked about. People ask me all the time, "What is the Kingdom of Heaven?" I answer, "The Kingdom of Heaven is as it is in Heaven now, coming to the earth now." Jesus taught His disciples to pray this prayer: "In this manner, therefore, pray: Our Father in heaven, hallowed be Your name. Your kingdom come. Your will be done on earth as it is in heaven" (Matt. 6:9-10).

I believe Jesus taught us two things in this passage: The first is that it's not on the earth as it is in Heaven. Second, He wants it to be on the earth *now* as it is in Heaven. He was telling them, in essence: "I want you to pray and invite the realm of 'as it is in heaven' into your world. I want My world to come so that your life begins to take on the image of 'as it is in heaven' now."

When you pray, "Your Kingdom come," you are actually welcoming Heaven on earth. What is it like in Heaven right now? If you died today and were present with the Lord, wouldn't you expect to see angels and seraphim, to walk on golden streets, or to talk to saints and apostles? We know there won't be sickness there, so we can be sure it's God's will to heal the sick now. Remember that Jesus told us to pray that it would be on earth as it is in Heaven. That was His mission on earth. Jesus went about doing good and healing every sickness and disease (see Acts 10:38; Matt. 9:35) because it was the Father's (Heaven's) will. Pray that it would be on the earth now as it is in Heaven.

We have a *Kingdom later* mentality and we need a *Kingdom now* mentality because Jesus said that the Kingdom of Heaven is at hand; and "at hand" means *near*. I am praying, "Let God's Kingdom invade this present evil age—NOW." The earth doesn't look much like Heaven nowadays.

As Christians, we are to establish the Kingdom, dominion, and authority of God so that what's already in Heaven now can come to earth. The Lord is on the throne and the earth is His footstool—we are the conduit that connects the two. If we don't release God's Kingdom on earth, the devil's kingdom will continue to torment us. I don't know about you, but I'm sick of the disease, fighting, death, and destruction that come with the devil's kingdom.

When God's Kingdom comes, the devil loses his hold on lives. That's what happened when Brian, a worship leader (Bill Johnson's son), some friends, musicians, and dancers visited a mall in Redding, California, to worship. Bill told me his son and the entourage took a break, and just as they sat down, a man walked by the area where they'd just worshiped. The man took some drugs out of his pocket, threw them on the ground, and kept walking. Why do you think this happened? A heavenly portal had opened, and the man encountered "Heaven now." Since drugs don't exist in Heaven, the enemy lost his grip in that atmosphere of Heaven. That's the Kingdom of Heaven in action!

SEEING, ENTERING, AND INHERITING THE KINGDOM

This Scripture passage suggests that *entering* the Kingdom is different from *seeing* the Kingdom:

> *Jesus answered and said to him, "Most assuredly, I say to you, unless one is born again, he cannot see the kingdom of God." Nicodemus said to Him, "How can a man be born when he is old? Can he enter a second time into his mother's womb and be born?" Jesus answered, "Most assuredly, I say to you, unless one is born of water and the Spirit, he cannot enter the kingdom of God. That which is born of the flesh is flesh, and that which is born of the Spirit is spirit"* (John 3:3-6).

I believe that entering God's Kingdom is first about our heavenly eternal residence, the place we'll go to live one day if we are born again. When we die, we will *enter* the Kingdom. However, according to Jesus, you need to be born again in order to *see* the Kingdom. When we enter into and become citizens in the spiritual Kingdom of Heaven, we gain a powerful authority, a rich inheritance, and new spiritual sight. Are you born again of the Spirit? "That which is born of the flesh is flesh, and that which is born of the Spirit is spirit." The Strong's Concordance definitions highlight the differences between seeing and entering:

See:

> #1492 Eido, ειδω (pronounced, *i'-do*): a primary verb; used only in certain past tenses, the others being borrowed from the equivalent οπτανομαι—optanomai #3700 and οραω— horao #3708; properly, to see (literally or figuratively); by implication, (in the perfect tense only) to know:—be aware, behold, X can (+ not tell), consider, (have) know(-ledge), look (on), perceive, see, be sure, tell, understand, wish, wot. Compare οπτανομαι—optanomai #3700.[4]

Enter:

> #1525 Eiserchomai, (pronounced *ice-er'-khom-ahee*): from eis #1519 and erchomai #2064; to enter (literally or figuratively):—X arise, come (in, into), enter in(-to), go in (through).[5]

Although the definitions of these words are clearly different, the qualification for both entering into and seeing the Kingdom of Heaven is to be born again, or born of the Spirit, which I believe are the same. While we who are believers can look forward to *entering* the Kingdom when we physically die, we don't have to wait to *see* the Kingdom. We are allowed to see into that heavenly Kingdom, that spiritual world, NOW.

When I realized that I am not a human being trying to get my spirit stronger, I had to change the way I thought. I started seeing myself, according to Scripture, as a spirit being in a human body, not a physical being trying to exercise my spirit. I realized that I am a spirit first, then a natural being. The truth is that I am spirit right now, and don't have to wait until I die to become a spirit. When we die, yes, we'll receive a new body, but we already have our eternal recreated spirit that enables us to see the Kingdom now.

God made us for two different worlds, yet, during our allotted 80 years or so on earth, we live and operate mostly in the visible world and enter the spiritual world later. Nevertheless, seeing Heaven is something that we are invited to do *now*. I want to touch, taste, hear, and see into the invisible, spiritual realm. Why did God create an invisible realm? I'm certain that this was so we would learn to see with our spiritual eyes and that we would live by faith.

"The Kingdom of God" and the "Kingdom of Heaven" refer to the same place. Everything that Heaven has to offer, therefore, is available now on earth for those willing to take it.

The concepts in Scripture, of *entering* the Kingdom and *inheriting* the Kingdom, are two different things. Galatians speaks of inheriting the Kingdom: "Now the works of the flesh are evident, which are: adultery, fornication, uncleanness, lewdness…those who practice such things will not *inherit the kingdom of God*" (Gal. 5:19-21).

I used to think that the people described in this passage, those who didn't inherit the Kingdom, actually lost their salvation; but now I have a different understanding. I believe the phrase used in this passage, and in similar passages, suggests that some will *enter* the Kingdom but won't *inherit* it. Inheriting the Kingdom speaks of God dealing out a certain inheritance that we have a right to at the point of salvation.

Scripture says that we are "joint heirs" with Jesus, which means we will rule and reign with Him. "The Spirit Himself bears witness with our spirit that we are children of God, and if children, then heirs—heirs of God and joint heirs with Christ, if indeed we suffer with Him, that we may also be glorified together" (Rom. 8:16-17). In Heaven, some will rule, reign, and be a part of the administration of His justice, peace, and judgment—that's an inheritance! We can enter the Kingdom and still not gain this inheritance. However, we have the opportunity to share in ruling and reigning with Jesus. I want to enter, see, and inherit the Kingdom (see Rev. 20:6).

Some Christians believe that we all work out our salvation and maturity individually on earth and then go into eternity at different stages of maturity. Others are of the mind-set that we all arrive in Heaven on the same page, and that we leave behind our different places of maturity on earth. Some theologians actually believe that we still learn in Heaven. As you examine the church today, have you noticed that some believers have allowed Christ to be fully formed in them while others have just started on that journey? When we enter the Kingdom of Heaven, I believe, we will all have different functions and ranks. We won't all arrive there with the same level of spiritual knowledge as others either. Some will have great understanding of Heaven because they have regularly looked into Heaven while on earth, while others will need to progress in their knowledge of God.

The apostle John's experience in Heaven suggests that some will have a more privileged place in Heaven: "To him who overcomes I will grant to sit with Me on My throne…" (Rev. 3:21). This implies that some will actually sit with the Lord on His throne, while others will not. Later in Revelation, after John saw a great multitude before the throne, we read this: "Then one of the elders answered, saying to me, 'Who are *these* arrayed in white robes, and where did they come from?'" (Rev. 7:13). The elder is speaking of a group of people before the throne; they are close to the throne, ministering to the Lord day and night. Thus, we suppose that there are others in Heaven who are not before the throne.

In his book, *The Final Quest*, Rick Joyner (a widely recognized teacher, prophet, and author) tells about the different ranks in Heaven. He writes about a vision he had of an encounter with someone in Heaven who spoke of himself as "the least of those here." This person described the different places and positions for those in Heaven:

> There is an aristocracy of sorts here. The rewards for our earthly lives are the eternal positions that we will have forever. This great multitude are those whom the Lord called "foolish virgins." We knew the Lord, and trusted in His cross for salvation, but we did not really live for Him, but for ourselves. We did not keep our vessels filled with the oil of the Holy Spirit. We have eternal life, but we wasted our lives on earth.[6]

He went on to tell Joyner how the Lord had removed all grief and remorse from each one.

> Only here can you remember such things without continuing to feel the pain. A moment in the lowest part of heaven is much greater than a thousand years of the highest life on earth. Now my mourning at my folly has been turned to joy....[7]

Then Joyner's companion began to describe the various ranks in Heaven:

The next level of rank here is many times greater than what we have. Each level after is that much greater than the previous one. It is not just that each level has an even more glorious spiritual body, but that each level is closer to the throne from where all of the glory comes.[8]

I believe that after we enter the Kingdom, some will have the privilege of coming before the throne, while others will live in other parts of Heaven. Some will live in the New Jerusalem, the capital city of Heaven, while others will live in other parts of this new world called the Kingdom of Heaven.

Even without this idea of ranks in Heaven, the biblical concept of rewards alone should be a huge motivation to make our life count for the Kingdom of God every day. Even though different levels may exist in Heaven, we will all continue to progress in Kingdom knowledge. We will continue to plumb the depths of God and His glory forever. Won't this be an exciting adventure, growing in our knowledge of God for eternity?

ASCENDING AND DESCENDING

Examine John 3:13: "No one has ascended to heaven but He who came down from heaven, that is, the Son of Man who is in heaven." Where was Jesus when He said this? He was on the earth speaking to human beings. He told them that even though He was physically with them on the earth, He was still in Heaven. How could He be in Heaven while He was on earth? Can someone literally be in both places? Yes, I believe Jesus was talking about a place in the Spirit where, from earth, you receive an invitation to ascend into Heaven and get revelation, and then bring it back down to earth, a going in and out of Heaven on a spiritual "Jacob's Ladder."

Jesus had an open Heaven—free access into the spirit realm. When you ascend, you partner with what the Father is doing in Heaven. I call this "synchronizing Heaven and earth." When this connection of the two places happen, you begin to see the invisible:

> *Then Jesus answered and said to them, "Most assuredly, I say to you, the Son can do nothing of Himself, but what He sees the Father do; for whatever He does, the Son also does in like manner. For the Father loves the Son, and shows Him all things that He Himself does; and He will show Him greater works than these, that you may marvel"* (John 5:19-20).

Jesus only did what He saw the Father doing. Is there a realm where you can *see* what the Father is doing before it happens? In Heaven, I believe, my next crusade has already taken place in the eternal predestination of God. We have an invitation into a realm where we can be in Heaven while on earth. I learned years ago that the greatest tool for me to minister in the power of Heaven was to wait on the Lord and ask Him to pull back the curtain. I asked Him to let me see the people who were going to be in the meeting and what their afflictions were. God wants to show us the plans of Heaven in advance.

Too much of what we do now is based on what someone else saw or what we saw 20 years ago. We need to see daily and hear daily. Most church services are very similar; the order of service is the same each week. However, I never know what my meetings are going to look like from service to service—because I'm waiting on the Lord all the time to see His model for the service in Heaven. Oftentimes, God will pull back the veil and give me a glimpse of the meeting five hours or five days early—He's very creative!

Can you imagine an invitation into this realm of John 5:20? "The Father loves the Son, and shows Him all things." What if you really "got" the revelation, "I'm a beloved son" or "I'm a cherished daughter"? Imagine "seeing all things" as opposed to hearing once a month or once a year. Through Isaiah the prophet, the Lord shows us that we can hear His voice often: "He awakens Me morning by morning, He awakens My ear to hear as the learned" (Isa. 50:4b). Although considered a messianic message, we know that, as God's children, we have the same inheritance to hear our Father as Jesus did. We are also His sheep who hear His voice.

Let me pause and put something in perspective before we go further: I'm not just after encounters for the sake of encounters. I'm after encounters because they bring more intimacy with the Lord and because He gives me divine strategies to defeat the enemy's kingdom and bring more of the Kingdom of God to earth. I meet people who have many encounters because they are super-sensitive in the spiritual realm and discern everything that's going on. However, I want to know why they aren't bringing souls into the Kingdom and why quadriplegics aren't being healed. I want to see the *fruit* of people's heavenly encounters...I want to see Heaven touch earth! An encounter only for the sake of an encounter means nothing.

KINGDOM NOW

We have a "Heaven in the future" mind-set, but we need a "Kingdom now" mind-set. That's what Jesus had:

Now when He was asked by the Pharisees when the kingdom of God would come, He answered them and said, "The kingdom of God does not come with observation; nor will they say, 'See here!' or 'See there!' For indeed, the kingdom of God is within you" (Luke 17:20-21).

Don't look for a day in the future as the Pharisees did! Here's our mind-set: "We've got our PDAs ready, Jesus—tell us when the Kingdom is coming!" However, Jesus replies, "No. It's in you."

Don't wait to enter the Kingdom later. The Kingdom of Heaven is at hand (see Matt. 10:7) and the Kingdom of Heaven is within you NOW. God wants us to act now. How far can we take that? I'm on my way to filling as much of the earth with as much of the Kingdom as I can. I'm a beloved son and I'm willing to push as far as I am able until the Lord says, "No more." Funny though, in all of the meetings I've done, I've never heard the Lord say to me, "Hold on, Todd, I think way too many people are coming into the Kingdom tonight. Cut the altar call short," or "Back off, son, I don't want to see any more cripples healed tonight; you've reached your limit." The Kingdom is here! Just get out there and go for it! "The kingdom of heaven suffers violence, and the violent take it by force" (Matt. 11:12b).

Living in Heaven on earth—that's my ministry. I ascend because there's an invitation. In Genesis 28:12, we have the story of Jacob's dream: "Then he dreamed, and behold, a ladder was set up on the earth, and its top reached to heaven; and there the angels of God were ascending and descending on it." The "Jacob's Ladder" anointing for believers today we see in the New Testament, in John 1:51: "And He said to him, 'Most assuredly, I say to you, hereafter you shall see heaven open, and the angels of God ascending and descending upon the Son of Man.'" Notice that Jacob's Ladder is *set up on earth* and *extends into Heaven*. The Lord has extended the invitation to us on earth to "come up here."

Jesus is Jacob's Ladder reaching to the heavens, and we have free access just as the angels did. That's our inheritance under the New Covenant. The angels of God ascend and descend via Jesus. We have access through Him. Heaven has issued an open invitation to come boldly before the throne (see Heb. 4:16), to ascend into Heaven. We're invited to come as often as we want; Christ's blood has given us free entrance. It's unrestricted access for believers because we're no longer under the old Law. Under the New Covenant, the high priest no longer needs to enter the Holy of Holies once a year. Rather, we are all spiritual priests who can enter any time we want.

Do you know how to access "every spiritual blessing in the heavenly places in Christ" that Ephesians 1:3 claims we have? We know in our minds that Scripture promises us these blessings, but how do we experience the fullness of these promises? We experience the fullness by being with Christ Jesus in heavenly places. You can't lay hold of the inheritance of Heaven from the physical realm on earth. It's only when you're experiencing the realm of Heaven that you can access its supernatural blessings and inheritance. The realm of Heaven has such tremendous riches stored up, and God wants to open that supernatural treasure chest for us. I pray that He opens your spiritual eyes and ears so you can hear and see heavenly things:

> *"The wind blows where it wishes, and you hear the sound of it, but cannot tell where it comes from and where it goes. So is everyone who is born of the Spirit." Nicodemus answered and said to Him, "How can these things be?" Jesus answered and said to him, "Are you the teacher of Israel, and do not know these things? Most assuredly, I say to you, We speak what We know and testify what We have seen, and you do not receive Our witness. If I have told*

you earthly things and you do not believe, how will you believe if
I tell you heavenly things?" (John 3:8-12)

Jesus told Nicodemus that he needed to understand spiritual things now. Being born again is about seeing and hearing heavenly things, understanding heavenly things, and being heavenly minded now on the earth. When we die and go to Heaven, we'll get no points for being ignorant of the Kingdom while we were here.

THE KINGDOM OF HEAVEN IS WITHIN YOU

Our idea of Heaven is a little messed up. Heaven is a real, tangible place we enter when we die, but it's more than that. The born-again encounter is all about living in the Kingdom now—seeing the Kingdom, hearing heavenly things, as well as ascending and descending so we can partner with Heaven to minister heavenly things on the earth now. I emphasize again: It's all about synchronizing Heaven and earth.

We always think about the first chapters of Genesis as the creation of earth and mankind, but I believe God also created Heaven, or many heavens, when He created everything else: "In the beginning God created the heavens and the earth" (Gen. 1:1). The creation account talks about the "heavens of heavens"—that means that Heaven has heavens or heavenly places like the third Heaven (which is just one of the places in Heaven). Heavenly places include the first, second, and third heavens, the abyss, heavenly courts, Hades, and hell. (We will examine these places in more detail in the following chapter.)

What about the citizens of these heavenly places? When God completed His creation work, Scripture says, "Thus the heavens and the earth, and all the host of them, were finished" (Gen. 2:1). As the apostle Paul writes: "For by Him all things were created that are in heaven and that are on earth, visible and invisible, whether thrones or dominions or principalities or powers. All things were created through Him and for Him" (Col. 1:16). It seems that when God created the earth and man, He created the heavens and the angels too. Where did God dwell before He created Heaven? We're not sure, but we do know that the Bible says the Heaven of heavens cannot contain God (see 2 Chron. 2:6). So, really, Heaven is not for God; Heaven is for us.

God created an invisible realm so that you would learn to see with your spiritual eyes. We usually don't take the Bible literally when it invites us to come boldly before the throne. Should you really be surprised if God opens your spiritual eyes and you see a sea of glass like crystal, or you see angels?

How would you like to experience a throne-room encounter, or have Heaven come down to you? These are only a few of the many potential heavenly encounters you can contend for. Here's a key of understanding for opening up this realm to you.

First, consider that you are a temple of the Holy Ghost. Next, consider that the throne of God is in Heaven. Could it be that you carry heavenly places within you? I don't access the heavenly realm with the natural body or with my soul. I access that realm with my spirit-man and the eyes of my understanding. By faith, I make myself available for the Holy Spirit to take me into that place. Then I cultivate a lifestyle of disengaging from my own understanding and looking through my spiritual eyes.

I believe God wants us to become still and quiet, turn our heart inward, and use our spiritual eyes. Since the Kingdom of God is within every believer, entering into the spirit can happen as quickly as you can turn your heart to the Lord and allow Him, by faith, to speak to you through promptings, word impressions, visions, dreams, spiritual experiences, and your sanctified imagination. We are God's children, and He wants to speak to us; it's His will. He will give us heavenly encounters when we access and receive them by faith.

Where does Jesus dwell? According to Paul in Colossians, Christ dwells in you. "The mystery which has been hidden from ages and from generations, but now has been revealed to His saints...Christ in you, the hope of glory" (Col. 1:26-27). The Kingdom of Heaven is within you. How close is the Kingdom? Jesus said, "Repent for it is at hand." Where does Jesus sit? In heavenly places. Where does Christ dwell? Christ in you the hope of glory. Where is Heaven? It's within you. Think about that.

Do you want to go to the throne? Close your eyes and go to the throne of grace. Before you try to get God to take you up or get Heaven to come down, develop a consciousness of Heaven within you. Change your worldview. Start thinking, *I am carrying Heaven with me when I walk into the coffee shop. I am carrying Heaven with me on the airplane. I'm in heavenly places right now, hallelujah.*

Have you ever been in the presence of God, your telephone rang or something interrupted you, and suddenly you were *out* of the presence? Did God really leave that quickly? No, you left. The *door into the presence* is your mind, and the door out of the *presence* also is your mind. Are you ready to ascend Jacob's Ladder? Jesus is the ladder, and He extends an invitation to come boldly. Close your eyes and focus on Him...there He is; He lives inside you. It's time to think like a spiritual being: *Heaven is within me. There I am at the throne. I carry heavenly places, and I rule and reign from here. I can access every spiritual blessing from here.*

God's Kingdom Is Power

If Heaven, the Kingdom of God, is within us, perhaps we should examine the characteristics of this Kingdom more. Scripture clearly defines our Kingdom inheritance: "But if I cast out demons with the finger of God, surely the kingdom of God has come upon you" (Luke 11:20). According to this verse, the Kingdom of God is casting out devils and setting the captives free. Wherever Jesus went He told people that the Kingdom of Heaven was at hand; where Jesus went, God's Kingdom rule touched earth. What did that look like? The Kingdom of God, through Jesus, turned sinfulness into holiness, poverty into wealth, sickness into health, and darkness into light. In the same way, Christ in us wants to manifest the Kingdom in power.

However, His Kingdom comes from another world: "Jesus answered [to Pilate], 'My kingdom is not of this world. If My kingdom were of this world, My servants would fight, so that I should not be delivered to the Jews; but now My kingdom is not from here'" (John 18:36). As a Christian, I am also a citizen of Heaven now; I am not always subject to the natural laws and limitations of the world in which I dwell. Though I live in my body, I am really an alien. I'm from "planet Heaven," and I live by another law and another order. The restrictions of a natural body don't limit me. God has made me a representative of His government and His world. The Kingdom of Heaven is within me and the Kingdom of Heaven is at hand. Remember, God's Kingdom is not in word only, but the Kingdom of God is in power. Because of that truth, I can taste the power of the world to come.

Chapter Five

REALMS OF
THE SUPERNATURAL

As I spent time with the Lord while on a ministry trip in Georgia, I suddenly felt myself caught up into the spiritual realm. As I passed through the second heaven, I heard the sound of shattering glass. Floating before me, opposing me, was a Tibetan Buddhist monk with his legs crossed. As far as my eyes could see there was only darkness, yet a shaft of light surrounded me. Fear washed over me and the monk's presence kept me from getting into the third Heaven.

This experience reminded me of the story of Gabriel eventually getting through to Daniel after the Prince of Persia held him up for 21 days (see Dan. 10). Sometimes we face spiritual warfare before we can enter into the supernatural world because the devil and his demons don't want anyone to have visions, dreams, or any supernatural experiences. They don't even want you to hear God's voice and will do everything they can to keep you from living in the supernatural realm of God.

I described my experience to Bob Jones, a mature prophet and friend of mine. "Was it that old Tibetan monk guy? That's the spirit of the Dalai Lama. He opposes people all the time," he said.

I asked Bob what I should do, and he said, "Before you make yourself available, take authority over any demonic powers that want to come against anything that God wants to give you."

Now I take authority over demonic hindrances before I wait on the Lord and enter into the experiences He has for me. If I do come across an opposing spirit, I rebuke it in Jesus' name.

This experience is one of many I've had in the second heaven as the Lord teaches me how to live as a naturally supernatural being. In Scripture, Joshua had a similar experience to mine where satan opposed him in the third Heaven as he came before the Lord: "Then he showed me Joshua the high priest standing before the Angel of the Lord, and Satan standing at his right hand to oppose him. And the Lord said to Satan, 'The Lord rebuke you, Satan!'" (Zech. 3:1-2a). Here we see Joshua, a human being like us, allowed into the heavenly court system before God the Judge and satan the accuser. I believe that we too can come "boldly to the throne of grace" (Heb. 4:16). We can participate in the proceedings of Heaven and have free access into God's council room as friends of God.

In this chapter, we'll take a whirlwind tour of the supernatural world and examine the different realms or places that exist there. Heaven and hell will become more real to you, and I believe that God will give you a greater passion for intimacy with Him, as well as a greater compassion for the lost. Get ready to walk in a deeper reality of life as a supernatural being residing in a natural body.

Heaven

When we read the first chapters of Genesis, we think about God creating the earth, animals, and humans. When did He create Heaven?

In Genesis 1:7-8 God created the firmament, and I believe He created the heavens and the earth at the same time:

> *Thus God made the firmament, and divided the waters which were under the firmament from the waters which were above the firmament; and it was so. And God called the firmament Heaven. So the evening and the morning were the second day.*

Note that the heavens and the earth were created simultaneously. "Thus the heavens and the earth, and all the host of them, were finished" (Gen. 2:1). In addition to creating Heaven and earth at the same time, God created all the heavenly hosts at this time too. God created the angels at the same time He created the earth, animals, and people.

Do you know why God created Heaven? Was it for His benefit? Remember, the Heaven of heavens can't contain Him. "But who is able to build Him a temple, since heaven and the heaven of heavens cannot contain Him?" (2 Chron. 2:6a). (Notice that this verse differentiates between "heaven" and the "heaven of heavens," which we will examine later.) The earth was originally an earthly Paradise created for us. God visited Paradise to fellowship face-to-face with Adam and Eve. At that time, He didn't speak in parables and was never far away; however, when the pair fell into sin, everything changed. Death entered in, defiling the earth, so no longer could it be called "Paradise." Heaven therefore became the dwelling place for believers after death.

Heavens Are Supernatural Realms

Heaven is more than an eternal residence we will go to one day, for the heavens are also supernatural realms. The Bible refers to "heavenly places." Notice it's plural, more than one heavenly place: "In the beginning God created the heavens and the earth" (Gen. 1:1). Often people think that "heavenly places" refers to the second heaven where the demons dwell. Yes, the phrase can refer to this realm, but it's more than this, because Scripture tells us that Jesus is seated in the heavenly places (plural) (see Eph. 1:20), and He's not dwelling with the demons.

I believe that in Genesis, God created the sky and atmosphere of the universe (the visible realm), the second heaven where demons and angels operate (the invisible realm), and the third Heaven where God rules on His throne (also the invisible realm). Apostle Paul says this: "For by Him all things were created that are in heaven and that are on earth, *visible and invisible*, whether thrones or dominions or principalities or powers. All things were created through Him and for Him" (Col. 1:16). Paul also speaks of these invisible heavenly places in Ephesians 6:12: "For we do not wrestle against flesh and blood, but against principalities, against powers, against the rulers of the darkness of this age, against spiritual hosts of wickedness in the *heavenly places*." Although *heavenly places* in this verse refers to the second heaven, the phrase can't always refer to just the second heaven. Earlier in Ephesians we read that God "made us sit together in the *heavenly places* in Christ Jesus" (Eph. 2:6). In this case, "heavenly places" speaks of the third Heaven. It seems that in Scripture *heavenly places* refers to the many places in the invisible realm, including second and third heavens, the abyss, Hades, and Paradise. We will examine these different places in this chapter.

GOD'S KINGDOM IS OUT THERE AND WITHIN

Many in the church view Heaven as a nice piece of real estate, possibly the size of the United States. They live for the day when they will die and go there permanently. Heaven is more than a place, although it is that too. Until we understand what Heaven is and where it is, we'll never gain access now. This "one day in the future" mind-set is one reason we don't have prophetic visions today. We're waiting until we die.

The only things that separate you from Heaven now are your physical body and however many years you have left in your life. If you were dead right now, where would you be? In Heaven. And what would you be doing? Seeing angels, talking to the apostle Paul, and basking in the glory. So why do we get nervous when someone who is still in his or her earthly body catches a glimpse of that now?

IT'S BIBLICAL

Is it biblical to go to the throne? There's no place in the Bible that doesn't make Heaven available now. The flesh, the mind focused on the things of the earth, "cessationist" theology (belief that God stopped speaking or doing miracles after the Bible was written), traditions of man, and fear make Heaven unavailable now, and are responsible for creating obstacles to accessing the spiritual realm. The Bible gives us a free invitation in Hebrews 4:16. Actually, it's more than an invitation; it's a command to "come boldly to the throne." Most of us are OK with that verse until someone actually sees the throne or has an encounter and describes what it looks like; then controversy erupts. We're OK with Paul, John, and Ezekiel seeing the throne, but the idea of having our eyes opened and seeing the throne seems a little *out there*. Nevertheless, we have the invitation/command in Hebrews 4.

It's OK for me to say, "Holy Spirit, come now and let me touch what's in Heaven with my spiritual senses." That's where my expectation and my heart are, and where I'll live for all eternity! I make myself available for God to communicate with me based on the scriptural truths I am sharing with you. Maybe some day I'll see you there!

Not everyone will have these types of experiences, but I believe that many more can have their eyes opened now. Many people have limited their faith based on what they have or haven't seen; artificial, self-imposed ceilings kept in place by fear, religious attitudes, and the traditions of men.

Look Inward

We're shifting gears now so we can look inward. Christ is seated in heavenly places and I'm seated in heavenly places, but God's Kingdom is also at hand and living in me. The word *kingdom* means the *king's domain*. Christ dwells in me, so the Kingdom is inside me. You and I, as believers, are the temple of the Holy Ghost. The Ark of the Covenant is gone, and the veil ripped from top to bottom in the temple when Jesus died. You're the present-day Holy of Holies. It is fine to expect to be taken up to Heaven, but know that you can also have a heavenly encounter by looking within, because the throne and the King are in your heart. You're close to Heaven; look within, and enjoy these supernatural realities of God.

Heavenly Realms

I believe that Heaven has different geographical locations and climates of its own. Heaven is a world very much like earth, but without sin, sickness, disease, death, and poverty. It isn't just about 24-hour, 7-days-a-week worship around the throne. John went to the throne, but he was also caught up into a place called "the temple": "Then the temple of

God was opened in heaven, and the ark of His covenant was seen in His temple" (Rev. 11:19a). We can journey to different geographic locations in the heavenlies. In my visits to heavenly places, I've been all over. Heaven is huge like a planet or a world. Just as the earth has seven continents, many countries, and numerous cities, so I believe, Heaven has a capital city, the New Jerusalem, and many other cities and regions. Will everyone live in New Jerusalem, or will people live in other parts of Heaven outside this city?

Charlie Robinson, our Fresh Fire seer prophet, spent some time with Dr. Percy Collett, who for 30 years has served as a medical missionary in South America. Dr. Collett had a supernatural visit to Heaven. In this experience, says Charlie, Dr. Collett saw different regions of Heaven outside of the throne zone where he visited villages, towns, and areas of Heaven. Like earth, different areas and regions had different physical characteristics, but far more beautiful than those on earth. In different parts of Heaven, he saw mountain ranges, valleys, and even waterfalls.

Most people think that Heaven consists solely of a throne room with eternal worship. But look at how diverse God created the world we live in now, with mountains, rivers, canyons, and numerous continents, each with different climates. Could it be that in Heaven we will experience the same diverse beauty but in greater glory and splendor? Think of all the activities you enjoy today: horseback riding, hiking in the mountains, or a vacation to Hawaii. Is it not possible that we will enjoy some of these same activities in Heaven?

William Booth (1829–1912), founder of the Salvation Army, had a visionary experience in Heaven that was to inspire his ministry, instill in him a blazing passion for the lost, and ultimately birth millions into the Kingdom. Here's his description of Heaven:

No human eyes ever beheld such perfection, such beauty. No earthly ear ever heard such music. No human heart ever experienced such ecstasy, as it was my privilege to see, hear, and feel in the celestial country.

Above me was the loveliest of blue skies. Around me was an atmosphere so balmy that it made my entire physical frame vibrate with pleasure. Flowing by the bank of roses on which I found myself reclining was the clearest and purest water of a river that seemed to dance with delight to its own murmurings. Along the riverbank, I saw trees covered with the greenest foliage, and laden with most delicious fruit— sweet beyond all earthly sweetness, and I lifted my hand, plucked and tasted of it. In every direction above and around me the whole air seemed not only to be laden with the sweetest perfumes coming from the fairest flowers, but filled with the fairest forms. For, floating around me were beautiful beings whom I felt by instinct were angels and archangels, seraph and seraphim, cherub and cherubim, together with the perfect blood-washed saints who had come from our own world. They were sometimes far, and again coming nearer.

The whole sky at times seemed to be full of white-winged, happy, worshiping, joyous beings. And the whole country, apparently of limitless extent, was filled with a blissful ecstasy that could only be known by being experienced.[9]

The Bible also refers to specific realms of Heaven: "...such a one was caught up to the third heaven" (2 Cor. 12:2). Obviously if there is a third Heaven, there must be a second and a first heaven.

There's also a forecourt of Heaven, an outer perimeter. William Booth, after his visionary glimpse of Heaven, realized he was standing there, where his life was about to be evaluated:

> Nevertheless, a further glance at my record appalled me, for there was written therein—leaving out, as I have said, the sins of commission—there was written the exact daily record of the whole of my past life! In fact, it went much deeper, because it described in full detail the object for which I had lived. It recorded my thoughts, feelings, and actions—how, and for what I had employed my time, my money, my influence, and all the other talents and gifts which God had entrusted me with to spend for His glory and for the salvation of the lost.
>
> They wrung my soul with sorrow and self-reproach, because on the *Record of Memory* I saw how I had occupied myself during the few years that I had been allowed to live amidst all these miseries, after Jesus Christ had called me to be His soldier. I recalled how, instead of fighting His battles, instead of saving souls by bringing them to His feet, and so preparing them for admission into this lovely place, I had been on the contrary, intent on earthly things, selfishly seeking my own, spending my life in practical unbelief, disloyalty, and disobedience.
>
> I didn't know which way to look. Again and again I remembered my life of ease and comfort. What could I say?

How could I appear with the record of my life before these waiting ones? What was there in it except a record of self-gratification? I had no martyr stories to tell. I had sacrificed nothing worth naming on earth, much less in heaven, for His dear sake! (In this place, Booth met a heavenly being who explained his experience to him.)

"Where you find yourself is not actually heaven," he said, "but only its forecourt, a sort of outer circle. Presently, the Lord Himself, with a great procession of His chosen ones will come to take you into the Celestial City itself. There is where your residence will be if He deems you worthy; that is, if your conduct on the battlefield below has pleased Him." (Later, he met a widow in heaven who posed a sobering question to him.) She said: "My daughter lived near you. You know her. Have you saved her? I don't know much about her, but I do know that one earnest and determined effort would save her, and win her to Christ."

And then again she asked me, "Have you saved my child?" What I felt under that look and those words, no heart or mind could possibly describe. They were mingled feelings. First, came the unutterable anguish arising out of the full realization that I had wasted my life, that it had been a life squandered on the paltry ambitions and trifling pleasures of earth—while it might have been filled and sown with deeds that would have produced a never-ending harvest of heavenly fruit. My life could have won for me the approval of heaven's King, and made me worthy to be the companion of these glorified heroes.[10]

Booth's experience in Heaven shook his being to the core and formed the foundation for a Salvation Army movement that would spread around the world. It's interesting to note, however, that this experience happened in a specific part of Heaven, the outer perimeter. Again, it's evident that when we begin to think about Heaven, we need to change our thinking to include multiple realms and heavenly places.

The First Heaven

The first heaven is the realm we live in right now. This realm includes the sky, the stars, the moon, the planets, and the universe. This was one of the realms referred to in the creation story: "Then God said, 'Let the waters under the heavens be gathered together into one place, and let the dry land appear'; and it was so" (Gen. 1:9).

The Second Heaven

Remember in Colossians 1:16 that God created the visible realm and the invisible realm? "For by Him all things were created that are in heaven and that are on earth, visible and invisible, whether thrones or dominions or principalities or powers…." God hid things from your eyes. The second heaven is also called the *invisible realm*; it overlays the first heaven and you can't see it without spiritual eyes, but it's here. If your spiritual eyes were suddenly opened now you'd see angels and probably demons.

> *For we do not wrestle against flesh and blood, but against principalities, against powers, against the rulers of the darkness of this age, against spiritual hosts of wickedness in the heavenly places* (Ephesians 6:12).

Notice that this verse uses the plural, heavenly *places*, again. The second heaven is the realm of angels and demons—the battleground where the angels and archangels operate. It's a huge world in itself with high places, and it contains the demonic hierarchy. Somehow, we have the idea that the first heaven is ours, that the devil owns the second heaven, and that God dwells in the third Heaven or Paradise. However, God actually owns the second heaven, and He allows the devil to operate there. Scripture tells us that "the heaven, even the heavens, are the Lord's; but the earth He has given to the children of men" (Ps. 115:16). It's clear—God has given the earth to people but the second and third Heaven belong to Him.

The Third Heaven

The third Heaven is the abode or dwelling place of God, translated as "Paradise." It's not an experience, but a place or realm, just like the other heavens, where you may have a dream or a vision while being caught up. Usually in these experiences, one is "caught up," and it's quite the experience. In my visits, it felt as though a huge vacuum cleaner just sucked me up through a roof—yep, a roof! I first saw blue sky, then a black sky with stars and planets, flashing lights and a g-force atmosphere, vibrations, and tremendous speed. The first thing I thought as I "landed," was: *Where am I?* Like Paul, I wasn't sure if my body went, or not. I'm of the impression that our body doesn't leave, but our spirit travels. Here's more of Paul's awesome experience:

> *It is doubtless not profitable for me to boast. I will come to visions and revelations of the Lord: I know a man in Christ who fourteen years ago . . . was caught up into Paradise and*

heard inexpressible words, which it is not lawful for a man to utter (2 Corinthians 12:1-4).

Often third Heaven experiences are so intimate and private that it's almost criminal to speak of them, because it seems to cheapen the experience, much like a husband or wife exposing what goes on in their secret union. I think Paul felt that way about his experience. I've shared some of these times with others, and then regretted it. Sometimes though, it's because people just aren't ready to hear about them, so my recount of the experience was very much like casting my pearls before swine (see Matt. 7:6)!

So too, an experience like this might make one seem boastful. Remember Joseph telling his brothers about his dreams? Select the right people and the right time to tell about these experiences. Ask God whom you should tell, and how much you should tell, and discern wisely, because some details are just between you and the Lord. People may have difficulty receiving because third Heaven experiences aren't exactly common fare! Trust though, that a third Heaven visit will leave a divine mark on you forever!

All spiritual experiences originate in the third Heaven, but usually they come to us and we experience them on earth, like the times we fall into a trance or have a vision. These *earthly revelations* are just as profound, and we must dispense of assumed hierarchy. Any revelation from God comes from the third Heaven, and no matter the experience or encounter, all are to be tested. It comes down to knowing the character of the person sharing his or her testimony, and ensuring that what they say lines up with Scripture. In the next chapter, we'll unpack the third Heaven in more detail.

Paradise

Paradise is another name for Heaven or third Heaven—it's the same thing. It is the dwelling of God. In Greek, Paradise means Eden, park, a place of future happiness, a state of ecstasy. [Strong's Concordance #3857 (Greek) paradeisos, par-ad'-i-sos of Oriental origin (compare 6508); a park, i.e. (specially), an Eden (place of future happiness, "paradise")—paradise.][11] The Garden of Eden was an earthly Paradise:

> And Jesus said to him, "Assuredly, I say to you, today you will be with Me in Paradise" (Luke 23:43).

> How he was caught up into Paradise and heard inexpressible words, which it is not lawful for a man to utter (2 Corinthians 12:4).

> He who has an ear, let him hear what the Spirit says to the churches. To him who overcomes I will give to eat from the tree of life, which is in the midst of the Paradise of God (Revelation 2:7).

The Paradise of God is the *heavenly model* God used in creating the Garden of Eden, in the same way the heavenly temples were used as patterns for the earthly ones in the Old Testament:

> Who serve the copy and shadow of the heavenly things, as Moses was divinely instructed when he was about to make the tabernacle. For He said, "See that you make all things according to the pattern shown you on the mountain" (Hebrews 8:5).

I've had profound third Heaven encounters where I was taken to Paradise and walked in the Garden of Eden. I've actually tasted fruit from the Tree of Life. I believe that we can all taste of that fruit in some way. The Bible tells us, "To him who overcomes, I will give to eat from the tree of life, which is in the midst of the Paradise of God" (Rev. 2:7b).

THE REALMS OF HELL

The whole earth and the heavens belong to God. The devil doesn't own the second heavens. The devil doesn't even own hell. God created the whole universe and it's under His control. Here are other realms under the earth described in Scripture:

Sheol

In the Bible, *Sheol* refers to natural death or the grave. From there souls make their journey into Heaven or Hades depending on whether they are saved or not. The word is defined as "grave, pit, the world of the dead and the subterranean retreat." [Strong's Concordance #7585 (Hebrew). sh'owl, sheh-ole' or shol, sheh-ole'; from 7592; hades or the world of the dead (as if a subterranean retreat), include its accessories and inmates:—grave, hell, pit.][12] Here is what Scripture says about this place:

> ...In the prime of my life I shall go to the gates of Sheol; I am deprived of the remainder of my years (Isaiah 38:10).

> Whatever your hand finds to do, do it with your might; for there is no work or device or knowledge or wisdom in the grave [Sheol] where you are going (Ecclesiastes 9:10).

For You will not leave my soul in Sheol, nor will You allow Your Holy One to see corruption (Psalm 16:10).

Drought and heat consume the snow waters, so does Sheol those who have sinned (Job 24:19 NASB).

If I ascend to heaven, You are there; if I make my bed in Sheol, behold, You are there (Psalm 139:8 NASB).

If I look for Sheol as my home, I make my bed in the darkness; if I call to the pit, "You are my father"; to the worm, "my mother and my sister"; where now is my hope? And who regards my hope? Will it go down with me to Sheol? Shall we together go down into the dust? (Job 17:13-16 NASB)

Hades/Abraham's Bosom

Hades means "the place or state of departed souls, the grave, the unseen." Before Jesus' death and resurrection, people who died all went into holding places—the righteous to Abraham's Bosom and the unrighteous to a place called Hades, which means the "abode of the dead." [Strong's Concordance #86 (Greek) haides hah'-dace from 1 (as negative particle) and 1492; properly, unseen, i.e. "Hades" or the place (state) of departed souls:—grave, hell.][13]

Hades and Abraham's Bosom are geographically in the same region; a huge gulf or chasm separates them, but souls on one side can see others across the divide. The Catholic Church got the idea of purgatory from Abraham's Bosom:

There was a certain rich man who was clothed in purple and fine linen and fared sumptuously every day. But there was a certain beggar named Lazarus, full of sores, who was laid at his gate, desiring to be fed with the crumbs which fell from the rich man's table. Moreover the dogs came and licked his sores. So it was that the beggar died, and was carried by the angels to Abraham's bosom. The rich man also died and was buried. And being in torments in Hades, he lifted up his eyes and saw Abraham afar off, and Lazarus in his bosom. Then he cried and said, "Father Abraham, have mercy on me, and send Lazarus that he may dip the tip of his finger in water and cool my tongue; for I am tormented in this flame." But Abraham said, "Son, remember that in your lifetime you received your good things, and likewise Lazarus evil things; but now he is comforted and you are tormented. And besides all this, between us and you there is a great gulf fixed, so that those who want to pass from here to you cannot, nor can those from there pass to us" (Luke 16:19-26).

Notice that before the cross Abraham wasn't in Heaven. He was there with Lazarus; they, along with all the others who died in righteousness, were waiting until Jesus came to release them. Abraham's Bosom was *emptied at the cross*. Jesus' blood made a way to open Heaven for them and for us: "...when He ascended on high, He led captivity captive..." (Eph. 4:8).

The people who were in Abraham's Bosom were those saints that came out of the graves and were seen walking around after Jesus' resurrection. They were on their way to Heaven with Him.

And the graves were opened; and many bodies of the saints who had fallen asleep were raised; and coming out of the graves after His resurrection, they went into the holy city and appeared to many (Matthew 27:52-53).

Can you imagine? There's a knock on the door and it's Uncle Amos who has been dead for ten years. "Hi, just in the neighborhood for the afternoon, thought I'd drop by on my way to Paradise."

Since the cross, the dead in Christ are not in Abraham's Bosom any longer; they are actually in Heaven. Today when Christians die, they immediately go into God's presence. "We are confident, yes, well pleased rather to be absent from the body and to be present with the Lord" (2 Cor. 5:8). The cross did away with the holding place for the righteous. The unrighteous before and after the cross are still being held in Hades.

We have this idea that hell is a present-day home for the devil and his structured hierarchy. That structure, however, is what operates in the second heaven. The devil and his demonic spirits are not in hell now; they are in the second heaven—*a holding place*—until after the judgment. They also have access to Hades to torment the ones who are waiting there, as we see in the story of the rich man. Demons are like the wardens and prison guards there. Unsaved people who die now don't go straight to hell; they are in Hades waiting for the judgment at the Great White Throne where they will be sentenced to hell. Hitler (assuming he did not accept Jesus as his personal Lord and Savior) is not in hell right now, but tormented in Hades.

"For You will not leave my soul in Hades, nor will You allow Your Holy One to see corruption" (Acts 2:27). This verse quotes King David as he prophesies about the coming Messiah. Although Jesus was to be killed, Hades could not hold Him because the Father had promised to raise Him. Jesus must have meditated on this verse as a source of encouragement to prepare for His crucifixion.

After He died at crucifixion, Jesus went to Hades and took back the keys to Hades and Death that the devil had stolen from Adam and Eve. Hallelujah, Jesus is the Victor forever! As Christ said, "I am He who lives, and was dead, and behold, I am alive forevermore. Amen. And I have the keys of Hades and of Death" (Rev. 1:18).

More Bible passages speak of Hades. See if they make more sense to you now in light of what you just learned.

The Abyss

"'Who will descend into the abyss?' (that is, to bring Christ up from the dead)" (Rom. 10:7). The Bible uses the term *abyss* several ways. In the Greek, it means "deep bottomless pit, depthless." [Strong's Concordance #12 (Greek) abussos ab'-us-sos from 1 (as a negative particle) and a variation of 1037; depthless, i.e. (specially) (infernal) "abyss":—deep, (bottomless) pit.][14] Scripture also calls the abyss "*the shaft of the bottomless pit*," or "the shaft of the abyss," and they appear to be the same dark place.

Did you know that not all the demons are free on the earth right now? The Book of Luke describes a prison for disobedient spirits. It's like Alcatraz for demons. When Jesus was about to cast the legion of demons out of the demoniac, "…they begged Him that He would not command them to go out into the abyss" (Luke 8:31). When they are released, demons are freed from deeper levels of the abyss.

Demons on earth need a body to inhabit and express their evil nature. If demons are in the second heaven they can look for a body to inhabit, but if they are in the abyss they no longer have freedom to roam.

That is why the demons begged Jesus to send them into the pigs, not the abyss. Demons want to inhabit a body so they can stay in the earth realm. In begging Jesus, the demons essentially said: "We know You've come to set humans free, but can we live in the pigs? Just don't send us back to that place!" The abyss is horrible, and devils suffer too. The bigger ones pick on the smaller ones because they hate each other, not just people. There's no unity among the demon, they only cooperate with each other if it furthers their own purposes.

To them, inhabiting a pig seemed a better option than the bottomless pit. Scripture tells us that some devils are restrained in chains in the abyss waiting for the judgment. "And the angels who did not keep their proper domain, but left their own abode, He has reserved in everlasting chains under darkness for the judgment of the great day" (Jude 1:6). Other demons await release during the tribulation. Revelation 9:1-5 (NRSV):

> *And the fifth angel blew his trumpet, and I saw a star that had fallen from heaven to earth, and he was given the key to the shaft of the bottomless pit; he opened the shaft of the bottomless pit, and from the shaft rose smoke like the smoke of a great furnace, and the sun and the air were darkened with the smoke from the shaft. Then from the smoke came locusts on the earth, and they were given authority like the authority of scorpions of the earth. They were told not to damage the grass of the earth or any green growth or any tree, but only those people who do not have the seal of God on their foreheads. They were allowed to torture them for five months, but not to kill them, and their torture was like the torture of a scorpion when it stings someone.*

The star that fell is satan. The bottomless pit is the realm containing grotesque, demonic forces that we haven't seen yet. Some interpret this passage as saying that demonic forces are locked away and reserved for the tribulation. However, others believe that the Book of Revelation records many past events and that the release of demonic hosts from the pit in this passage took place before the cross. Either way, it's obvious that even though Jesus took the keys to Death and Hades, the devil possesses the key to the bottomless pit. I believe that many of these demonic locusts have already been released to torment the human race, but that many more are being held in the pit and will be released as the world darkens. But don't sweat it! These evil hordes won't be able to harm Christians hidden in Christ—we have the seal of God on our foreheads!

Perversion, homosexuality, lust, war, alcohol—we're seeing more of these demons. Although none are new, we're seeing a strengthening of these sinful strongholds. Today, as in Bible days (i.e. Noah's day), it seems that as a generation's lust for carnality and evil increases, the devil has license to release more demonic hordes from the abyss to work their dark power on earth. The Book of Romans tells us that as unrighteousness increases, God gives people over to uncleanness and lust (see Rom. 1:24). Today, "sheep" or "goat" nations and cities are forming as people's appetite for righteousness or sin grows.

In Revelation 20:1-3 we see that satan will be restrained in this pit during Jesus' 1,000-year reign and then released briefly before he's thrown into hell:

Then I saw an angel coming down from heaven, having the key to the bottomless pit and a great chain in his hand. He laid hold of the dragon, that serpent of old, who is the Devil and Satan,

and bound him for a thousand years; and he cast him into the bot-
tomless pit, and shut him up, and set a seal on him, so that he
should deceive the nations no more till the thousand years were fin-
ished. But after these things he must be released for a little while.

Hell

In ancient times, the Valley of Hinnom was Jerusalem's garbage dump. People discarded and burned waste of all kinds there, even dead animals and executed criminals! The fire never went out, and when the wind blew the wrong way, the stench in the city was unbearable. Hinnom became the symbol for the place of eternal punishment. In Greek, "Valley of Hinnom" becomes *Gehenna*, which is translated *hell* (see Luke 12:5). Jesus spoke of hell 11 times. Gehenna was a visual aid that Jesus used to help the people grasp the torments of hell. Hell is the eternal holding place for the wicked. It's also called "the lake of fire" and "the second death."

Kenneth Hagin (1917–2003), pastor of Rhema Bible Church and considered the father of the modern-day faith movement, had a near-death experience at the age of 15. Lying on his bed, dying from a mal-formed heart, Hagin had an actual visitation to a place he describes as hell (possibly the abyss?), which led to his dramatic conversion and helped birth his ministry (which inspired the planting of hundreds of churches, a Bible training center, and the spread of powerful teachings on healing, prayer, and faith). Here are excerpts of Hagin's description of his experience, during which he descended into the pit three times:

I began to descend—down, down, into a pit, like you'd go down into a well, cavern or cave. And I continued to descend. I went down feet first. I could look up and see the lights of the earth. They finally faded away. Darkness encompassed me round about—darkness that is blacker than any night man has ever seen. The farther down I went, the darker it became—and the hotter it became—until finally, way down beneath me, I could see fingers of light playing on the wall of darkness. And I came to the bottom of the pit.

When I came to the bottom of the pit, I saw what caused the fingers of light to play on the wall of darkness. Out in front of me, beyond the gates or the entrance into hell, I saw giant, great orange flames with a white crest. I was pulled toward hell just like a magnet pulls metal unto itself. I knew that once I entered through those gates, I could not come back…

I was conscious of the fact that some kind of creature met me at the bottom of that pit. I didn't look at it. My gaze was riveted on the gates, yet I knew that a creature was there by my right side. But then I thought, "This is the third time. I won't come back this time! I won't come back this time!" Darkness encompassed me round about, darker than any night man has ever seen.

And in the darkness, I cried out, "God! I belong to the church! I've been baptized in water." I came again to the bottom of that pit. Again I could feel the heat as it beat me in the face. Again I approached the entrance, the gates into hell itself. That creature took me by the arm. I intended to put up a fight, if I could, to keep from going in. I only managed to slow down my descent just a little, and he took me by the arm. Thank God that voice spoke. I don't know who it was—I didn't see anybody—I just heard the voice. I don't know what he said, but whatever he said, that place shook; it just trembled. And that creature took his hand off my arm.

It was just like there was suction to my back parts. It pulled me back, away from the entrance to hell, until I stood in the shadows. Then it pulled me up head first.[15]

After this experience and knowing his life had been saved and his soul preserved from hell, Hagin made a personal decision for Christ, searched the Scriptures, and eventually laid hold of a Scripture (see Mark 11:24) which led to his complete healing and subsequent teaching ministry.

THE GREAT WHITE THRONE JUDGMENT

Romans 14:11-12 tells us that every knee shall bow and every tongue shall confess to God; that every one of us shall give account of himself/herself to God. It is appointed unto us once to die, but after this "the judgment" (Heb. 9:27).

There will be two specific judgments conducted by Christ Jesus. One is for repentant believers—those who have accepted Him as Lord and Savior, the *Judgment Seat of Christ*: "For we must all appear before the judgment seat of Christ, that each one may receive the things done in the body, according to what he has done, whether good or bad" (2 Cor. 5:10). The other is for unbelievers, those who have chosen to reject Christ's sacrifice made on their behalf at Calvary, the devil, and his demons, the *Great White Throne Judgment*.

Then I saw a great white throne…And I saw the dead, small and great, standing before God, and books were opened. And another book was opened, which is the Book of Life. And the dead were judged according to their works, by the things which were written in the books. The sea gave up the dead who were in it, and Death and Hades delivered up the dead who were in them. And they were judged, each one according to his works. Then Death and Hades were cast into the lake of fire [hell]. *This is the second death. And anyone not found written in the Book of Life was cast into the lake of fire* (Revelation 20:11-15).

All the unrighteous dead who have been contained in Hades will stand at the Great White Judgment Throne. Notice that more than one book will be opened. Unbelievers' names will not be found in the Book of Life so their deeds will be examined in the other books, and of course be found lacking.

As well as his visionary experience in Heaven, William Booth also had a vision that further emblazoned an awareness of the reality and compassion for lost souls dying and going into eternity without Christ. While thinking of the millions of people around him engrossed in drink, dance, business, and in the pleasures of life, unconcerned for their spiritual condition, God gave him a vision. He saw multitudes in an ocean during a storm struggling to get to shore, yet perishing before they were able to make it to the rock. Many on shore, on the safety of the rock, continued about their business and pleasures, unconcerned for the perishing. However, a few were doing everything they could, even risking their lives to rescue the drowning souls. This vision so stirred him that Booth began to recruit thousands into his Salvation Army to rescue the lost with words like this:

You have enjoyed yourself in Christianity long enough. You have had pleasant feelings, pleasant songs, pleasant meetings, pleasant prospects. There has been much of human happiness, much clapping of hands and shouting of praises—very much of heaven on earth.

Now then, go to God and tell Him you are prepared as much as necessary to turn your back upon it all, and that you are willing to spend the rest of your days struggling in the midst of these perishing multitudes, whatever it may cost you.

You **must** do it. With the light that is now broken in upon your mind and the call that is now sounding in your ears, and the beckoning hands that are now before your eyes, you have no alternative. To go down among the perishing crowds is your duty. Your happiness from now on will consist in sharing their misery, your ease in sharing their pain, your crown in helping them to bear their cross, and your heaven in going into the very jaws of hell to rescue them.[16]

William Booth had such a revelation of hell; it caused him to be consumed with soul-winning and greatly influenced his preaching. Here is one impassioned plea to his hearers:

Put your ear down to the Bible, and hear Him bid you go and pull sinners out of the fire of sin. Put your ear down to the burdened, agonized heart of humanity, and listen to its pitiful wail for help. Go stand by the gates of hell, and hear the damned entreat you to go to their father's house and bid their brothers and sisters and servants and masters not to come there. Then look Christ in the face—whose mercy you have professed to obey—and tell Him whether you will join heart

and soul and body and circumstances in the march to pub-
lish His mercy to the world.[17]

Although people are enduring the lesser torments of Hades right
now, only after the White Throne Judgment will souls be sent to hell. At
that time, the devil, his angels, unbelievers, as well as Hades and Death,
will be thrown into hell, the lake of burning fire. When people go to hell,
in addition to the physical torment, they will be in constant mental
anguish living with the knowledge that salvation was a free gift, which
they rejected, and they are now eternally separated from God and His
love. Hell won't be as cartoons portray it, nor will the devil torment people, because he'll be burning in hell, too, screaming out in his own pain.

When lucifer fell, God created hell for him and for his demons. God
has offered us the free gift of eternal life, but unfortunately many people
have refused His love and many will end up in hell. God has done everything to make salvation available for free—He's sent prophets and evangelists and has revealed His goodness and love in many ways. If a person
chooses to reject His gift, it's not because God hasn't provided the way.
Once people go to the place called hell; that's it for them for all eternity.

REVELATION OF HEAVEN AND HELL

What we've just covered are some of the realms that the Bible refers to
when it speaks of the heavens or of hell's regions of darkness below the
earth. Understanding these realms gives you a foundation to help you
understand the spirit world. We need to receive a revelation of Heaven, so
we can walk in our authority in Christ and receive continuous third Heaven
revelation to overcome the works of darkness in the second heaven.

Continually ask the Lord to increase your awareness of, and vision into, the supernatural realms. I hope that by learning about these realms that your "ceilings" will be removed and you can reach for more in the supernatural realm. As we experience heavenly encounters, we will grow in deeper intimacy with the Father and experience more of Heaven, so we are filled with His presence and glory, heavenly riches that we can take to the lost.

Imagine if every believer received the same type of revelation of the terrible reality of hell as William Booth and Kenneth Hagin have. Our passion for evangelism and God's Kingdom would grow dramatically. Let's cry out for God to make us more aware of the sobering truths about the realms of darkness. Let's ask Him to give us a new compassion for the lost and a desire to snatch souls from hell into the Kingdom of heavenly light.

Jonathan Edwards (revivalist and theologian, 1703–1758) conveyed the seriousness of our apathy, and the greatness of God through his sermon titled, "Sinners in the Hands of an Angry God." Before he preached this message, he spent the whole night prior in prayer. While he delivered the message to his congregation, the Spirit of God was so mightily poured out—God so manifested His holiness and majesty during the preaching of that sermon—that the elders threw their arms around the pillars of the church and cried, "Lord, save us, we are slipping down into hell."[18]

I'll close this chapter with a quote from Nelson's New Illustrated Bible Dictionary:

> Because of the symbolic nature of the language, some people question whether hell consists of actual fire. Such reasoning should bring no comfort to the lost. The reality is greater than the symbol. The Bible exhausts human language in describing heaven and hell. The former is more glorious, and the latter more terrible, than language can express.[19]

Chapter Six

THIRD HEAVEN

Have these teachings helped shed light on some of the Scripture you see day-to-day in your devotion time? I pray they become alive to you as you learn to think outside of the traditional box as it relates to living in the supernatural realms of God. Some of the ideas I'm sharing with you are radical for the church today, however, they are also normal spiritual truths. I hope that as I've unfolded these powerful realities of Scripture with you, that God is opening your eyes to the new, exciting, supernatural world that He lives in and that we can live in.

As you continue to read these pages, not only will you become more aware of spiritual things and become available for encounters with God, you will find yourself coming into a deeper place of intimacy with the Father. You will also become more aware of the eternal realms and notice a growing compassion for the lost. So, keep reading, asking the Holy Spirit to guide you into all truth—that's part of His job description and you can trust Him to do His job. I'm going to crank it up another spiritual notch now as I discuss the third Heaven.

Discovering Third Heaven Experiences

During my three-month soaking shortly after my conversion, I discovered the powerful and awesome reality of this dimension! I had several dramatic third Heaven experiences. One time in prayer, I felt the sensation of being pulled out of my body and flung into space. It was as if I was caught up into a giant vacuum cleaner, but I was still in my living room. It was similar to the feeling one gets on a roller coaster. My body vibrated and the g-forces caused my face to contort. I was traveling through the stars and I wasn't even in a spaceship!

Then I entered into another dimension where my whole being filled with a brilliant white light. I landed suddenly on a mountain. Even though I was lying on my carpet, I felt a cold wind on my face. I freaked out. This had never happened before. Dark, thick clouds and thunder and lightning filled the sky. My senses responded to what I saw, but I could still feel the carpet under me. Farther than I could see, in all directions, was a desert wasteland, with the exception of one river, which flowed out from the mountain's base.

In the distance, from every direction, I occasionally saw a horse and rider or sometimes two or three. My sense was that they were all being called to the mountain, but each assumed they were the only one. The riders were drinking from the river in preparation for the battle to come. I sensed the Lord was gathering His end-time army, girding their loins and anointing their shields.

As the vision changed, I was on my face before the King of Glory, the Lord of Hosts. I sensed that I was receiving strategy for the hour to come, just as Joshua did before the Commander of the army of the Lord (see Josh. 5:13-15). During the encounter, I was aware that the Church was protected from the battle, seated in heavenly places with Christ, and that God's mighty release of His end-time harvest would come upon the kingdom of darkness suddenly and unexpectedly. I sensed that this battle strategy was hidden from the world; it was God's secret weapon. Harvest was about to break out in the earth in such a great way that the enemy would be caught off guard, as if under siege in a night ambush. Simultaneously, money, resources, power, and laborers would be commissioned and released into the harvest.

In the vision, I felt the Lord was saying that the Church had moved from a season of equipping and preparing for the battle to a season of the revealing of secret faithful *nobodies* who have never bowed a knee to the world's idols. These faithful servants of God would be part of a new commissioning of fivefold ministers with an Ephesians 4:11 calling as apostles, prophets, evangelists, pastors, and teachers.

THE HIGHEST OF PROPHETIC EXPERIENCES

As the Body of Christ prepares for the end-time battle, third Heaven revelation—as in my vision—will become more and more common for fivefold ministers as well as for ordinary believers. We will need to receive regular strategy from Jesus, our Captain, for the role He's called us to assume. Some of that strategy will come through various forms of divine communication like visions and dreams, but sometimes the Lord will open up the third Heaven to us.

Third Heaven revelation is the highest level of prophetic experience where you're actually in the spirit realm and walking around Heaven. Even though your body may be back on earth, it's "Hi, Enoch. Hey, Moses. What's up, Peter?" You are talking to the saints who are a part of the great cloud of witnesses and you are on the streets of gold; you see Jesus and you see the throne. It's life changing, and not a casual experience that someone would get over right away!

You may wonder if my physical body ever went into the third Heaven on one of my spiritual adventures. Never that I know of. I'm usually physically in my house, or at church, yet still aware that I'm in another place. Even apostle Paul couldn't figure out if his body went or not, so I guess it really doesn't matter (see 2 Cor. 12:2). The most important thing is the experience itself; it's not vital to know every detail of how it happened. The Lord will reveal to you anything that is important for you to know. Don't miss God's whole purpose for giving you the experience by trying to dissect each detail. It's a spiritual experience that the carnal mind can never fully understand (see 1 Cor. 2:14).

In this chapter, we're going to examine the third Heaven from a biblical perspective. I want to remove the spookiness from the idea of a third Heaven visitation and give you a few keys to activate your spiritual senses.

BIBLICAL EXAMPLES

As I wrote in the last chapter, the third Heaven is the immediate presence, abode, and dwelling place of God. It includes the throne room, but I believe it is more than that. I think Heaven is a lot bigger than we believe it is. We'll start by examining some third Heaven experiences listed in the Bible.

Paul

The only place in the Bible where we find the term "third heaven" is in Paul's writing in Second Corinthians, which you have probably memorized by now!

*It is doubtless not profitable for me to boast. I will come to visions and revelations of the Lord: I know a man in Christ who fourteen years ago—whether in the body I do not know, or whether out of the body I do not know, God knows—such a one was caught up to the **third heaven** . . . and heard inexpressible words, which it is not lawful for a man to utter (2 Corinthians 12:1-2,4).*

Later in the chapter, we discover the man that Paul was speaking of was actually himself. In verse 7, he tells of a thorn in the flesh given him, to keep him from getting proud because he received so many revelations. Notice that Paul had visions (plural) and revelations (plural).

Let me give you some other scriptural examples of what I believe are also the third Heaven. Below is another familiar passage, this time from the Book of Revelation.

John

After these things I looked, and behold, a door standing open in heaven. And the first voice which I heard was like a trumpet speaking with me, saying, "Come up here, and I will show you things which must take place after this." Immediately I was in the Spirit; and behold, a throne set in heaven, and One sat on the throne (Revelation 4:1-2).

In this passage, the Lord actually invited John through a door into Heaven where he saw God on a throne and received divine revelation. That same door of revelation that stood open for John never closed. It's still standing open for you and me. That is the word of the Lord right now. God has extended an invitation for us to come boldly before the throne of grace. As blood-bought sons and daughters, we have free access into the things of the Spirit.

Isaiah

The prophet Isaiah also had a third Heaven vision of the Lord on a throne:

> *In the year that King Uzziah died, I saw the Lord sitting on a throne, high and lifted up, and the train of His robe filled the temple. Above it stood seraphim; each one had six wings: with two he covered his face, with two he covered his feet, and with two he flew. And one cried to another and said: "Holy, holy, holy is the Lord of hosts; the whole earth is full of His glory!" And the posts of the door were shaken by the voice of him who cried out, and the house was filled with smoke* (Isaiah 6:1-4).

Isaiah saw the Lord on His throne, so he had to be seeing Heaven. Then he watched as an angel came down with a coal and touched his lips to commission him into his office as a prophet.

You've probably heard this story often—possibly, since you were a child in Sunday school. Don't let these supernatural biblical experiences lose their impact just because you are familiar with them. Think about Isaiah's experience again and try to picture it in detail. How would you feel if an angel carrying a glowing hot coal headed straight for your lips? You need to read the Bible with new eyes to look for supernatural events. Picture them happening in the present, and picture them manifesting through your life.

Following Jesus Into Heavenly Realms

Let's now examine a revelation in John 20:17. Jesus is speaking to Mary after His resurrection, but before He has ascended. "Jesus said to her, 'Do not cling to Me, for I have not yet ascended to My Father; but go to My brethren....'"

Why couldn't Mary touch Jesus before He ascended? Jesus now had a heavenly body. I believe Mary would have had illegal access to the heavenly realm because God had yet to issue an invitation to come boldly to the throne. In addition, Jesus was about to complete the work of redemption and bring His holy blood before the Father. Mary's sinfulness might have compromised His holy sacrifice. Hebrews 9:12 describes the redemptive work that Jesus was about to complete: "Not with the blood of goats and calves, but with His own blood He entered the Most Holy Place once for all, having obtained eternal redemption."

Hebrews 10:12 continues to describe Jesus' work: "But this Man, after He had offered one sacrifice for sins forever, sat down at the right hand of God." When did Jesus complete this act of redemption? When He ascended into the holy place, He obtained eternal redemption once and for all. In that place, He sat down for a moment at the right hand of God, and that's when it was finished. I believe that only after Jesus completed His work in Heaven did He come back and stay with the disciples for 40 days. That's when they were able to touch His physical body for the first time. In John 20:19,26-27, we see that He appeared to the disciples later that evening (after seeing Mary, ascending into Heaven, and returning) and they touched Him.

God showed me that because of what Jesus did, now we can ascend too. We can follow Him into the heavenly realm because He went before us and prepared the way. Now we can follow Jesus into the place of revelation. I remember several different times waiting on the Lord with my prophet friend, Bob Jones, and several others. Bob would say to us, "I'm going to take you into the heavens with me." He would just touch us and somehow, in the anointing, a transfer would happen and we would be taken up into the spirit realm with him, following him into the places he had visited often before. Recently I wanted to confirm that this ability to go into the spiritual realm could be transferred. "Let's see if this thing works," I said. After praying for Jill Austin and a couple of my team members, I released the anointing and said, "Let's ascend." All of a sudden the visions started.

Now before you start to get worried about this idea of transference of prophetic anointing, let me remind you of an Old Testament story that may help you understand. Do you remember the two occasions that King Saul prophesied when he met a group of prophets and came under their mantle? (See First Samuel 10:10-11; 19:24.) He didn't even want to prophesy, but he couldn't help it. This is the same principle. Jill, the rest of the team, and I all ascended together under the same mantle.

Throne Room Encounters

I remember my first third Heaven experience. I was in my living room worshiping and praying with a group of people. All of a sudden, I was taken into the spirit. With my eyes open, I saw a river flow out of the kitchen. I watched my carpet get wet. I didn't realize I was seeing in the spirit so I screamed, "Who left the water on?" I thought the bathtub was overflowing. No one else could see the vision, so I described it. When I told them that the river had become a few feet deep, one guy, who was on the couch, jumped to the floor so he could get in the river. I saw the river flow over his back. Soon riverbanks appeared, and I could no longer see my living room.

I didn't have socks on and I felt the grass brush over my feet like waves of God's presence. It was alive; everything was alive because of the glory. Then I remembered that in Heaven there is no sun and no moon; the glory makes everything alive and bright there. The grass moved in the wind of the Spirit. There was so much of God's glory that the grass seemed to have its own personality. I was getting drunk in the Spirit just looking at it. I realized I was in the Garden of Eden. The tree of life appeared. It was massive and covered in gold, bronze, and silver colors woven together. The fruit was so large that the branches bowed to the ground under the weight.

During this encounter, another friend in my apartment who couldn't see what I was experiencing, lay on the carpet going, "Mmm, yumm, yumm," as if he was enjoying something delicious from the tree. In the spirit, I saw a big piece of fruit hanging off a branch right in front of his mouth. He had no idea what was going on in the spirit, and yet he was acting it out in prophetic intercession. In fact, every person in the room acted completely as if they were in the vision with me, although none of them could see it. They would do something and I was able to see why they did it because I was in another dimension.

Next, I heard the sound of the Lord God walking in the garden as He did in Eden with Adam and Eve in the cool of the evening. I can't even describe it to you. I ran around the apartment shouting, "I hear the Lord walking in His garden." I could hear the sound of the glory moving. I had all the sensations as if I was there. I felt the wind blow. I smelled the grass. All my senses functioned, but I knew that I was still in my apartment. The experience changed my life. After that, I knew, without a doubt, that there was an unseen realm more real than the natural realm I lived in.

Since then, I've had many other experiences in which I felt all of my senses heightened, as I was totally caught up in the experience. I'd shake as I felt myself hurled through space and time. In these experiences, I could actually look down and see my house below. As I arrived at the end of the black universe, I saw a flash of bright light and a tunnel.

Here are some other third Heaven experiences that I've had (which should give you greater understanding as to how God can speak during such an encounter):

At My Mother's Death

My mother died while I was ministering in Albany, Oregon. On the drive home to attend the funeral, I asked the Lord if my mom was with Him. Immediately I saw my mother as a young girl dancing with the Lord. She was so happy.

Two years later, while in Latvia, as I remembered that wonderful vision of her, the Lord took me back to Heaven. Off in the distance, I saw the Son of Righteousness. He appeared as a rising sun. Rays of light hit me and my entire body vibrated with His love toward me. It broke off fear and rejection and I understood that God accepted me. Each ray shone the healing revelation of the Father's love into my soul. It pushed out the darkness.

Standing on the Sea of Glass

I also had a similar vision in which I was standing on a sea of glass like crystal. Shafts of light from the Son of Righteousness hit the sea of glass and ricocheted off, like light rays refracted through a prism; a kaleidoscope of vibrant, brilliant colors: red, blue, green, emerald, and more. The beams, traveling at the speed of light, arrived first; then the sounds of Heaven followed. The healing rays of light from the Son of Righteousness hit me and transmitted physical healing.

My very being vibrated and thundered with sound, as if 50,000 voices sang different songs at the same time, yet they were in perfect harmony. With my natural mind, I couldn't identify any one song, but my spirit-man was able to understand and feel the love and acceptance. Healing rays touched my heart's broken places. Every time one of those beams hit me, I heard the voices of the heavenly choir sing of the Father's love. "I love you; you are accepted; you are beautiful; you are worthy"—I heard all the words that the Father sings over His children. I knew the Father was assuring me of my cherished place in His heart, as He declared that I was worthy, accepted, loved, and beautiful.

HINDRANCES TO REVELATION

Do you see now that third Heaven experiences are not just for the pages of the Bible? As you've seen from the stories of Dr. Percy Collett and William Booth in the last chapter, other Christians in recent history have had these experiences. And, in reading about my third Heaven experiences and the many testimonies of others within these pages, I'm sure you're seeing that third Heaven visitations are for all of us today. They're for me, and for you—for all believers. You may still be saying, "OK, Todd, I am with you on all these things, but I'm still not hearing and I'm not seeing."

Realize this: Understanding, seeing, and perceiving is all connected to the heart. If your heart is hardened, you don't see. If you don't see, you don't understand. The key to seeing and understanding is the same key to unlock a dull heart. Hebrews 5:11 describes Christians of that day, saying they have "become dull of hearing." It seems clear that becoming dull is a process. Look at Matthew 13:14-15:

> *...Hearing you will hear and shall not understand, and seeing you will see and not perceive; for the hearts of this people have grown dull. Their ears are hard of hearing, and their eyes they have closed, lest they should see with their eyes and hear with their ears, lest they should understand with their hearts and turn, so that I should heal them.*

According to this passage, when people see and hear spiritually, their hearts begin to understand, and then they are positioned to receive healing from the Lord. Hearing, seeing, and understanding are also the keys that release healing revival. How do the hearts of people grow dull? Let's examine the causes of a dull heart, unseeing eyes, and deaf ears.

1. Forgetting God's Past Faithfulness

God has called us to a lifestyle of thankfulness. When we don't remember the good things He has done for us, our hearts become dull and the enemy prevails:

> *The children of Ephraim, being armed and carrying bows, turned back in the day of battle. They did not keep the covenant of God; they refused to walk in His law, and forgot His works and His wonders that He had shown them* (Psalm 78:9-11).

Why would anyone who was armed and ready for battle turn back?

This is where most Christians live because they do not remember or consider the past.

You may have been at a meeting where you witnessed the blind receive their sight and a myriad of others receive healing from the Lord, but now you are the one who needs to be healed. If we forget about all the times that God has brought healing in our past, our hearts grow weary and we begin to turn back in the day of battle. However, remembering God's goodness and His promises puts a renewed fight in our spirits that says, "I am going to press on to the mark of the high calling of God in Christ Jesus. It doesn't matter how much of hell comes against me! God has proven Himself faithful in the past and He will prove Himself faithful again. The Lord has spoken! Regardless of what I see, I am going to fight and war and contend; I'm going to ask, and seek, and I will triumph with His anointing!"

Sometimes as I prepare to minister, I wonder, *What if God doesn't show up tonight?* When that happens I encourage myself in the Lord by remembering His mighty works. I lie on my bed and I dream about every miracle that I've ever seen God do in any crusade I've ever been in. By the time I'm done, I'm like, "Take me to the crusade now!"

You limit what God can do in your life when you forget His power. That's what the Israelites did: "Yes, again and again they tempted God, and limited the Holy One of Israel. They did not remember His power..." (Ps. 78:41-42a). Many Christians feel restraints and limits on their lives because they haven't dreamed about what God has done in the past. Sharing testimonies and making His deeds known keeps you fresh in the anointing and keeps your faith high.

This New Testament story also shows us how seeing, hearing, and understanding are hindered by not remembering:

Now the disciples had forgotten to take bread, and they did not have more than one loaf with them in the boat. Then He charged them, saying, "Take heed, beware of the leaven of the Pharisees and the leaven of Herod." And they reasoned among themselves, saying, "It is because we have no bread." But Jesus, being aware of it, said to them, "Why do you reason because you have no bread? Do you not yet perceive nor understand? Is your heart still hardened? Having eyes, do you not see? And having ears, do you not hear? And do you not remember? When I broke the five loaves for the five thousand, how many baskets full of fragments did you take up?" They said to Him, "Twelve." "Also, when I broke the seven for the four thousand, how many large baskets full of fragments did you take up?" And they said, "Seven." So He said to them, "How is it you do not understand?" (Mark 8:14-21)

Jesus tried to teach the disciples about the leaven of the Pharisees, and they said, "It's because we forgot to take bread." Jesus replied (paraphrased), "You guys are not seeing! You are not hearing the revelatory truth that I am bringing you." Jesus even prompted the disciples with a question about leftovers from the feeding of the 4,000 and the 5,000. They had lost the power of their understanding, and they were seeing in the natural, not with their spiritual eyes.

Some of you limit God financially because you have forgotten the testimonies of His power of provision throughout Scripture. If you can't think of a specific instance in the area of finances where the Lord has intervened on your behalf, then remember times that He delivered someone out of a situation that was a whole lot darker than yours was. Meditate on a relevant passage of Scripture. Can you imagine the shocked look on the disciples' faces when there were 12 baskets of food left over? I can imagine Him giving one basket to each of them and saying with a laugh, "Boys, there's more where that came from!"

Many in the church today forget so quickly. God brings a miraculous breakthrough of provision or healing in their lives and they say, "God, forgive me for ever doubting You. I'll never do it again." Then they find themselves in that same battle again, making plans just in case He doesn't come through. They have ears but do not hear because they do not remember.

Sometimes I battle with unbelief while praying for the deaf. Do you know whom God holds responsible? Me. Why? Because I've already seen thousands of deaf healed. God expects a little bit more from me.

We all have to learn to meditate in our hearts on His past faithfulness. We have to encourage ourselves. We don't always get to run to another prophetic conference and get another word; we just have to pull out what we've already gotten! Some of us can't even get anything else from God because we haven't done anything with what He has already given us! Forget about more! Dream! Stir up past words! Remember the anointing the prophets prophesied. We must remember how we moved in it before. Stir up the gift and release it by remembering God's goodness. I went into a church and the preacher said, "Todd, preach on healing, but don't share testimonies of anything that you've seen God do, because I want all their faith to be in Jesus. If healing is real it will work because of the Word." I said, "That's not biblical brother. When we forget, we lose the power of understanding and our hearts get hardened." I'll tell you how to get faith and strength for tomorrow's battle—remember what God did yesterday.

2. Not Exercising Your Spiritual Senses

If you haven't learned how to activate your spiritual senses, you've probably grown dull and your heart is hard, which makes it hard to hear and see. For the most part, Christians have no experience using their spiritual eyes, seeing in the invisible realm, having prophetic experiences, or even hearing the still small voice of God and feeling the nudging of the Holy Spirit.

It's interesting that people understand you can't become good at things in the natural without practice; no one expects to become competent at tennis or piano without dedicating a lot of time to that pursuit. However, when it comes to the things of the Spirit, people don't understand that it takes time and practice also.

Sensitivity comes by using what God gives us. It's by exercise and practice or, as Hebrews 5:14 calls it, "reason of use," that we hone our giftings. That phrase, in the Greek, means *habit* or *practice*. It's the old principle of *use it or lose it*. Practice hearing the Lord's voice by giving prophetic words at the mall or at your home group, by soaking, being heavenly minded, and by waiting, expecting that God will show you what He wants to do.

3. The Deceitfulness of Sin

Another reason for dull hearts? Sin in your life. "Aw, just one little sin tonight isn't really going to hurt me. It's not like I do it every day; I can repent later." That attitude comes from a hardened heart. "But exhort one another daily, while it is called 'Today,' lest any of you be hardened through the deceitfulness of sin" (Heb. 3:13).

If you have a sin in your life that you've been playing around with, you need to get serious and repent. The longer you toy with it, the harder your heart will become. Eventually, as the following passage shows, you become captive:

Now the word of the Lord came to me, saying: "Son of man, you dwell in the midst of a rebellious house, which has eyes to see but does not see, and ears to hear but does not hear; for they are a rebellious house. Therefore, son of man, prepare your belongings for captivity, and go into captivity by day in their sight" (Ezekiel 12:1-3a).

Maybe you aren't committing sins of commission, but rather, sins of omission. For instance, many people haven't acted on the last prophetic word they received and yet they are trying to get another one. Maybe you aren't giving the way He told you to, or the Lord may have said, "Pray an hour a day," and you didn't do it—then start again. The heart gets hard every time you disobey any word, unction, vision, prophecy, or dream. If you are not obedient to what the Lord has already revealed to you, that's rebellion, and He won't trust you with more.

Some of you have too many prophetic words; you don't know who you are—apostle, prophet, pastor, teacher, evangelist, or youth pastor? You are everything, yet you are nothing. Start being something. You need to ask where you have missed God or failed to act, then repent and get back to His plan.

The Lord has nudged me pretty good about some things; I had every intention of getting to them but I didn't. That's a dangerous place. I don't even want more prophecy unless it is a confirmation on something I've already received.

4. Failure to Remain in the Word

If you don't stay teachable under the hearing of the Word, your heart will remain dull and calloused. Don't go a day without reading the Bible or your well will dry up, and empty wells don't get revelation or grow in character. "So then faith comes by hearing, and hearing by the word of God" (Rom. 10:17). We need to meditate on God's Word and allow Him to speak revelation to our hearts. Remain connected and stay submitted under the Word and the anointing.

5. Failure to Hear His Voice Today

Not hearing from the Lord regularly will make your heart hard:

> *Therefore, as the Holy Spirit says: "Today, if you will hear His voice, do not harden your hearts as in the rebellion, in the day of trial in the wilderness, where your fathers tested Me, tried Me, and saw My works forty years"* (Hebrews 3:7-9).

How often should I be hearing God's voice? I expect to hear from the Lord every day. Every day is today. Sometimes it's a small nudge or an impression through a Scripture. You shouldn't expect third Heaven visitations each day, but you should hear from your Father each day.

It's the same with any discipline. Have you ever been in a place where it was easy to enter into the presence of the Lord, and then you didn't pray for a week? Then the next time it was like plowing hard ground? It's always easier to stay connected than to get re-connected.

Shortly after my dad's salvation, and while traveling with me, he said, "If I go home for more than four days it takes forever to get going again!" It's the same with me. The first time I preach after taking a two-week break, it's like "urgggh, urgggh, urgggh," but if I come to your church and I've preached 50 sermons already that month, I'm cookin'!

6. The Cares of This World

I think this is the number one reason hearts get dull: "…and the cares of this world…choke the word, and it becomes unfruitful" (Mark 4:19). You can't engage the revelatory when you are too caught up in the things of this world. When you are too focused on the temporal, you can't focus on the eternal realm. Scripture says that where your treasure is that is where your heart is (see Matt. 6:21). If your heart treasures the things of the world, then you will have a hard heart. We are foolish people to concentrate on what is passing away and ignore the Kingdom that God says will last forever.

HOLY DESPERATION LAYS HOLD OF REVELATION

Before I started experiencing spiritual encounters, I arrived at a place in my heart where I said, "I can have that too!" Some of you already believe that. Others are not sure whether God wants you to have visions, revelation, or hear audibly from Heaven. Could God want to transport or translate you? Some people think: *Everyone else but me.* God has changed my thought life. Now I think, *Why not me?*

God *sovereignly* releases visitations, but I believe we can take hold of God's promises through holy desperation and hunger. David understood the power of desperation:

> *How lovely is Your tabernacle, O Lord of hosts! My soul longs, yes, even faints for the courts of the Lord; my heart and my flesh cry out for the living God….For a day in Your courts is better than a thousand. I would rather be a doorkeeper in the house of my God than dwell in the tents of wickedness. For the*

Lord God is a sun and shield; the Lord will give grace and glory; no good thing will He withhold from those who walk uprightly (Psalm 84:1-2;10-11).

God wants us to seek Him first, but He also wants us to seek for the gifts He has for us: "Pursue love, and desire spiritual gifts, but especially that you may prophesy" (1 Cor. 14:1). In this verse, *spiritual gifts* in the original language actually means "spiritual" or "spirituals." God wants us to live as spiritual beings, to practice the gifts He has made available for us, and to learn to hear His voice. Early in my Christian walk, I started praying, "God, I want You to communicate with me the way that You communicated with Elijah." If John can get revelations and if Paul can go into the third Heaven, then I can have that too. If it happened to them, it can happen to me. If it happened to them, it *should* happen to me! These divine encounters are all through the Bible. I've said to the Lord, "If angels can come to Abraham's house, God, they can come to mine."

I can't find anything in the Scriptures that indicates that we can't have frequent supernatural experiences. The Bible says that Elijah was a man just like us (see James 5:17). Don't think of these people in their office as prophets; think of them as faithful Christians who have gone to be with the Lord. Who is the Moses, Daniel, Gideon, or Paul of today? Who is the Smith Wigglesworth, Maria Woodworth-Etter, Kathryn Kuhlman, Evan Roberts, or Charles Finney of today? We are! Those saints are gone. We are the saints today! We need to learn from what they walked in, but their ceiling should be our floor. We need to expect to go higher than they did.

Engage in Revelation: Eight Keys

People ask me, "Todd, is the depth of the experiences you receive because of the mantle on your life?" Though I probably get these experiences more frequently because of the call on my life, on most occasions I'll say "no." You might not speak to 100,000 people in a meeting or have a word for the head of state. There is a favor that comes with the office, but that doesn't mean that trances, visions, angelic visitations, and dreams are beyond you. It doesn't mean that you can't begin to hear the voice of the Lord on the same level as I do. Here are eight simple keys that I have used and that have helped me engage in revelation:

1. Learn to See With the Correct Eyes

In Ephesians, the Bible talks about our spiritual eyes. Paul prays that "…the eyes of your understanding being enlightened; that you may know what is the hope of His calling, what are the riches of the glory of His inheritance in the saints" (Eph. 1:18). What are the eyes of your understanding? In the original Greek language, *understanding* translates as "the mind and imagination." Let's learn to see in the spirit. Our Father wants us to learn how to disengage our understanding and begin to operate in the inner man with our inner eyes.

What I am about to say I have touched on briefly before, but I think it is worth repeating. Some of you cannot see because you're trying to look through the wrong eyes. If you hear someone say, "I saw an angel," do you look around the room with your natural eyes? When you hear a prophet say, "I saw," most of the time they're describing what has taken place on the inside, on their inner movie screen. When you're trying to see in the spirit, you should be looking inside. Quite often, the Holy Spirit will initiate visions, revelations, and experiences in the imagination. Have you ever just lain on your bed, started to daydream, and then realized that a movie is playing in your mind? This mental imagination is very closely linked to the "spirit of your mind" (Eph. 4:23) or the "eyes of your heart" (Eph. 1:18 NASB).

There are times when I'll wait on the Lord's presence in a posture of surrender. Then the Holy Spirit will come and initiate a thought pattern. A series of scenes will come, and I'll see myself, for instance, in Africa. I yield to this image by making a conscious decision to cooperate as it unfolds instead of writing it off as my own thoughts or too much pizza. If the Lord has initiated these thoughts, then they start growing into a prophetic experience.

God doesn't want you to be spiritually blind. He wants you to have vision and revelation. He wants to visit you. I don't know if you'll receive an impression or an angelic visitation, but I know God will come to you. We'll cover more ground about the eyes of the heart a little later, because it's vital to understand this principle, or you'll constantly be frustrated trying to *see*.

2. *Don't Wait for a Sovereign Move*

"OK, Todd, I believe in the supernatural realm, but it's got to be sovereign," people sometimes say. I tell them to read Romans 5:1-2:

> *Therefore, having been justified by faith, we have peace with God through our Lord Jesus Christ, through whom also we have access by faith into this grace in which we stand, and rejoice in hope of the glory of God.*

We have access through faith. *Sovereignty* is when God initiates, and *faith* is when I initiate. Sovereignty will take place regardless of what you are or are not doing. The question is: Can I initiate the revelatory realm, or do I have to wait for God's sovereignty to initiate?

How do you access other promises in the Bible? If you are stressed, do you think, *Well, I guess if God wants me to have peace, He can sovereignly drop it in my lap?* How do I access healing? By faith. How do I access any promise of God? By faith. Why should receiving revelation be any different?

It's OK for you to begin to seek and make yourself available for God to visit you. I can't go into a prophetic experience at will or dictate what kind of encounter I want, but I can make myself available through the model of soaking, waiting, and contemplative prayer. God always allows me to enter when I do that. That may not be your testimony, the way it's going to be for you. As for me, I've come to the place where I'll take one to three hours to wait before the Lord every day, and every time I will receive revelation. It's not third Heaven all the time, but God speaks to me every day.

3. *Understand Open Heavens*

Even though I'm devoting a chapter of this book to examining open heavens, I'm going to lay a little groundwork. An important step to activating our spiritual senses is to understand an open Heaven, a brass heaven, an open door, and a gateway. If we don't have an open Heaven, an open door, or a gateway, we are not going to enter into the revelation God has for us. When Heaven opens, the most common manifestation is the word of the Lord and revelation:

> *Now it came to pass in the thirtieth year, in the fourth month, on the fifth day of the month, as I was among the captives by*

the River Chebar, that the heavens were opened and I saw visions of God (Ezekiel 1:1).

Only after Heaven opened did God take Ezekiel out into visions. We see this same sequence of events again in Revelation 19:11: "Now I saw heaven opened, and behold, a white horse...." After Heaven opened, John saw Jesus riding on a white horse and the saints in white linen following behind.

Everybody wants to have prophetic encounters and experiences, but we can't have them without an open Heaven. Notice the same thing in Acts 10:9-11 with Peter's trance. It happened after Heaven opened.

In the same way that we can have an open Heaven, we can also have what the Bible calls a *brass heaven*. Have you ever just felt like God was a million miles away, your prayers bounced off the ceiling, and everything was dead and lifeless? Has the Bible become a boring history book? Have you cried out like the psalmist David, "Where are You, God? Don't be far from me or turn a deaf ear to my cry?" Some people live under a heaven that's like that all the time.

One thing that I want to be clear about is that I also believe that God will allow us to walk in the wilderness, and He will hide His presence from us to see how desperate we are to search for Him. However, that is not always the case. Sometimes you live, or your ministry lives, under a heaven that is brass. It's like hard ground; you can't get a breakthrough. The earth beneath your feet can be like iron. If you are sowing seed, iron ground just isn't productive. You will not be very fruitful if the ground is iron. If Heaven isn't open, you are not going to have fruit.

While listing the curses of disobedience, Scripture speaks of a brass heaven: "The heavens over your head shall be brass and the earth under you shall be iron" (Deut. 28:23 AMP).

Now look at Revelation 4:1. We see John here taken up into a prophetic experience, taken up into a realm of the spirit before the throne: "After these things I looked, and behold, a door standing open in heaven." Then there was a voice like the sound of a trumpet and an invitation to "Come up here."

That's what we all want in the church today—a door standing open in Heaven, His door to His realm. I want to be there; I want to see; and I want to encounter the realm of "as it is in heaven" now. How about you?

In the next chapter, I am going to give you some keys on how to open Heaven. If you can get Heaven open, if you can get the door open, if you can get the gate open, then revelation is going to happen and the spirit realm is going to come in your life.

4. *See the Supernatural Through Other's Eyes*

In Second Corinthians 4:16-18, Paul writes about looking at the unseen realm. If you don't have any unseen things happening in your life, then look at somebody else's vision. Find every biblical encounter with the unseen world and study every one, over and over, until they become real to you, until they almost become your visions. Get yourself saturated with and exposed to the supernatural through someone else's eyes. It's a good way to exercise your spiritual senses.

Jacob had his experience with God in Genesis 28, but it wasn't Jacob's own righteousness and faithfulness that caused him to enter in. His encounter was based on the encounter that Abraham and Isaac had before him. Isaac spoke the blessing of Abraham over Jacob. It was that prophetic blessing that allowed Jacob to come into his own encounter with God. Then he entered in. In every testimony, there is a prophetic invitation; even in sharing prophetic encounters, there's a realm where those encounters become available to the person who is listening. It opens up the spirit realm.

Frequently when I share about an open Heaven experience that I've had, other people will start to enter into the same experience. That's because my experience is an open door for others to walk through and follow me into the heavenlies. Also, if you're struggling to enter into a spiritual experience, use one that you've had before as a springboard. Remember it. Even a quick glimpse of the glory will mark your life forever; it's imprinted on your spirit so you can get back there. It's called "from glory to glory." So God sometimes uses those encounters as an access point to get you from glory to glory.

Many people in the church today can't enter into a prophetic experience because they have no language for it. Get language from others who have been there and fill your life with that. Picture scenes that you read about in the Bible. How could it be wrong to visualize the stories that God sovereignly recorded for us in Scripture?

If God hasn't given you a sovereign vision or dream or isn't sovereignly bringing angels into your life or taking you up into the heavens, how can you look at the eternal realm? Look into the unseen world by asking, "What is it like in Heaven now?" Look at the prophet's revelatory experiences and then the door will open for you.

I want you to read the Book of Revelation, especially chapter 4:1-11, not as an end-time story, but so you can get heavenly glimpses. Forget about all the things happening on earth; just see what is going on in Heaven. What is the throne room like? What does Jesus look like in Revelation 1:9-18 and 19:11-16? Then study the Ancient of Days, the glorified Son of Man, in Daniel 7 and 10. You can also find out what the glory looks like by reading Ezekiel 1 and 10 as well as Isaiah 6.

I want you to fill your mind and spirit with what Heaven looks like by reading different encounters between men and Heaven. Get the description of the Ancient of Days in your spirit—the glory, the fire in His eyes, the white hair, His bronze feet, the amber, the living creatures, and the streets of gold. The more acquainted you become with Heaven the easier it will be to open up your heart and mind so you can receive from the Holy Spirit. The more you meditate on heavenly things, the more you will see the unseen. Start praying these Scriptures aloud, cry out for them to manifest in your life. Read aloud, over and over again, the descriptions of the glory, of the angels, of the throne, of Jesus, and of the Ancient of Days.

Close your eyes right now and let the Lord show you heavenly things. See the throne. See the sea of glass like crystal. We develop our spiritual senses when we see what is recorded in the Bible. See the heavenly lamp burning, the living creatures, the elders, and the rainbow. Imagine the thunder and lightning. Just go to the throne in your mind right now, according to John's description. See yourself walking on the sea of glass. See yourself before the throne. As you see and picture these things, you are exercising your spiritual eyes and getting language written into the DNA of your spirit.

5. *Set Your Mind on Heavenly Things*

Who told you that it was wrong to seek those things that are from above—healing, miracles, provision, and the other things that God gives? You must have heard the saying, "You're so heavenly minded that you are no earthly good"? That's wrong! If I am heavenly minded, I am going to be operating in wisdom and revelation. Actually, those who are no earthly good are probably not heavenly minded!

Seek those things that are from above. Where is the heavenly world that we seek? Above. Where am I seated with Christ? In heavenly places. That's the realm above. Start seeking the experience of what you have positionally, as an inheritance, in Christ. Make yourself available every day for heavenly encounters.

In the first few early months after my salvation, I would cry out, "God, open my eyes. I want to see in the realm of the invisible. I want to ride in the chariots. I want to see the angels." I would pray every day for those kinds of encounters. Why? The Bible says, "Set your mind on things above" (Col. 3:2a).

A mind set on the earth is a mind not focused on the Kingdom of God. A mind that turns itself to Heaven walks in the Kingdom of God. The Kingdom of Heaven is at hand. The veil, the membrane, between these two worlds is so thin. I can enter into the Kingdom realm right now by changing my mind and turning my heart to the Lord. That act removes the veil. The minute my mind returns to think on the things of the earth the veil is replaced.

6. Overcome Fear of Deception

The fear of deception prevents many Christians from engaging in the supernatural realm. People think, *What if I start to wait on the Lord and I leave my body—isn't that astral travel?* Or, *What if it's a devil that comes to deceive me because I make myself vulnerable?* We need to trust in our Father's ability to keep us. If you ask the Father for the Holy Ghost, is He going to give you a stone? "If you then, being evil, know how to give good gifts to your children, how much more will your Father who is in heaven give good things to those who ask Him!" (Matt. 7:11). What a wonderful promise.

If you are waiting in the presence of the Lord and you say, "I ask You to come. Holy Ghost, open up the eyes of my heart and take me into visions of Heaven," do you think God is going to let the devil slip in and show you something else? If we are living right, studying the Word, praying, and keeping our life accountable to others, then it is reasonable to put our trust in God's ability to keep us. We need to overcome the fear that we won't hear from God or have authentic encounters. God wants to give us the good gifts we ask Him for. Living in fear can prevent us from receiving God's spiritual gifts; we can hinder God or miss an encounter. We have to trust Him as a trustworthy Shepherd who speaks to us, His sheep.

7. *Increase Your Level of Faith*

"Todd, lift the expectancy of how much of Me My children can receive and manifest in the Church today," God once said to me. Most people don't even think about the reality of the supernatural or, if they do, they think it's for the great prophet or that such experiences are so rare that people are fortunate ever to have one in a lifetime. Those ungodly mind-sets hinder Christians from having prophetic encounters.

After the Lord challenged me to stretch my faith to believe for more of Him, I searched through the Scriptures. I began to realize that everybody in the Bible, even ordinary men and women like Mary, Joseph, and Elijah, had encounters with Heaven and angels and had dreams from God to guide them.

I believe that I can have access every day. How about free access? Tell me why not. How much more now that the veil is torn, and we have access by the blood of Jesus and an invitation in Hebrews 4:16 to come boldly before God's throne:

And Jesus cried out with a loud voice, and breathed His last. Then the veil of the temple was torn in two from top to bottom (Mark 15:37-38).

Let us therefore come boldly to the throne of grace, that we may obtain mercy and find grace to help in time of need (Hebrews 4:16).

We've been led to believe all this *positional Christianity* stuff. People say, "Well, I come before the throne of God positionally." Who told you that? Why can't you see the throne with the eyes of your understanding? Why can't you approach the throne of God at will, right now by faith, to confess your sin at the throne of grace? Is the throne available for free access to confess sin but for nothing else? Why can't I see or hear things happening in the throne room or in Heaven? It's surprising to me that when someone says, "I saw the throne," everybody goes, "Wow!" So what? You too are invited to the throne—every day! Why aren't you seeing anything?

I have developed a faith level so that I now believe I should be having encounters every day and that if God wants to keep me out of heavenly places, He will—but most of the time He doesn't. By faith, I gain access. If I took ten minutes right now to wait on the Lord, I would go into some spiritual experience. Would it be third Heaven? Not necessarily—what's important is that I see with spiritual eyes. Not every experience need be in the third Heaven. I am just teaching about spiritual sight. God wants to give us a seer anointing. (The seer prophet is one who usually *sees* things in the future, like Daniel and Ezekiel, particularly in the realm of imagination, visions, and dreams.) We need to overcome our fear and grow our faith. Why? Because God created us to be spiritual beings and to have fellowship with Him.

There is going to be a day in the Church where every single believer will prophesy and have dreams and visions, not just the prophets. In Joel 2:28-29, God promises that He will pour out His Spirit on all flesh. What is *all flesh* going to do? Prophesy. Who is going to have dreams and visions? Everybody! I believe that we can activate all flesh and that it is God's will to do so. How are you going to prophesy the heart and mind of God if God isn't communicating with you? God communicates in dreams and visions. We have to let our faith increase and change our thinking until we can say: "OK, I can experience this now, not once every five years." Don't let your old beliefs or the traditions of men rob you of your spiritual inheritance.

8. *Don't Rank Prophetic Experiences*

Some people think that an out-of-body experience lends more creditability to their word. All revelation has to be tested the same way. I don't care if it was the still small voice, a vision, a quickened Scripture, or a trip into the third Heaven, if it's the word of the Lord, it's the word of the Lord. It doesn't have to come through an angel.

If I say, "I saw an angel," people often respond, "Let's clarify that. Was it your mind's eye or did you really see it here?" I usually respond, "I saw an angel. Does it matter whether it was on the inside or the outside? It was an angel." For some reason, we tend to think that an experience is more valid if it was on the outside. When you learn to use your spiritual senses, it won't matter. It will be real to you whether it is in or out.

What I've tried to do in this chapter is to use simple language to show that it's OK to enter into heavenly things with the eyes of the heart. How real is Heaven to you right now? Say to the Holy Spirit, "Come, I want to know You more." Don't seek a certain kind of experience—just seek Him. Say, "God, I make myself available for whatever way You want to come to me." Then let Him initiate. You see in faith and make yourself available, but He is still sovereign and chooses the kind of encounter He will take you into. When you have an experience, don't be so quick to write it off as your mind. Just go with it.

PREPARE FOR YOUR ENCOUNTER

If these insights about heavenly visitations have created a desire in you to experience more of the supernatural, begin to position yourself to see in the spirit. Pray that the Lord would remove any veil over your life that has caused hardheartedness or blindness. Ask Him to release the Spirit of understanding so that you will know by revelation that the Kingdom of God is within you. You can carry within you the realm of what it is like in Heaven right now. Believe that the Lord will open the Revelation 4:1 open door for you. Encounters in the heavenly realm are your inheritance because you are a citizen of Heaven today. You are a spiritual creation with spiritual senses to see, smell, hear, touch, and taste the heavenly realm. So enter in by the blood and receive whatever God desires to give you!

Chapter Seven

MINISTERING UNDER AN OPEN HEAVEN

"Please, God, turn it off, and let me go to sleep!" Exhausted after hours and hours of receiving revelations, holy visitations, and being caught up in heavenly experiences, I finally had to beg God to let me rest. I was so tired I had trouble absorbing everything. There was so much stuff happening, I couldn't write it all down. God had opened up the windows of Heaven, and His presence came down and saturated me—so much so I could hardly contain it all. This was one of my experiences under the waterfall of Heaven.

Can you imagine having a moment like that—when you're simply overwhelmed by the presence of God? When the heavens open and God's glory falls upon you and all you have to do is position yourself to receive Him, to soak in His presence? Are you ready for God to pour out favor and open Heaven all over you like that?

IT CAN HAPPEN TO YOU

I have a friend, who, whenever asked how he's doing, always responds with, "Truly blessed and highly favored of the Lord." Isn't that a great answer? How about you? If someone asks you the same question, what is your usual response? "Fine," "OK," "Ho hum," "Could be better," or "No comment"? If so, then you're not living the victorious life God intended for you. What if I told you that the Father desires to tear open the heavens for you? To bathe you in the fragrant waters of His glorious presence too?

You are highly favored of the Lord, and He wants you to experience the fullness of Him in all realms. Are you thinking, *Who—me?* Yep—you! In fact, God favors *all* of His saints. That means you, me, your children, parents, John at the corner store, and sweet, old Aunt Martha, too. If God opened heavens for Elisha, Mary, Elijah, Philip, Moses, Sarah, Joseph, Jacob, Enoch, and other men and women of the Bible, He'll do it for you. Let me also tell you that, *especially* if God did it for me, He'll do it for you! One day, if we're still alive when Christ returns, we'll ultimately experience the supernatural here on earth. After the dead in Christ are raised, we'll be "...caught up together with them in the clouds to meet the Lord in the air" (1 Thess. 4:17). In the meantime, God wants to *rend the heavens* so that we can experience the fullness of His presence and power *now*.

It is because God highly favors His children that He wants to release the extraordinary into our lives, bless us mightily, and surround us with His abundant favor:

> But let all those rejoice who put their trust in You; let them ever shout for joy, because You defend them; let those also who love Your name be joyful in You. For You, O Lord, will bless the righteous; with favor You will surround him as with a shield (Psalm 5:11-12).

Imagine a good soak in God's presence! Under an open Heaven, God can saturate an entire nation with revival, miracles, signs, and wonders.

He can bathe saints with a fresh anointing and fresh fire, and drench ministries with immense favor. Pray now for the Holy Spirit to open the heavens and the eyes of your understanding, so that your life and ministry may experience His presence, and increase in the blessings of the supernatural in Christ Jesus.

In this chapter, I'm going to share some keys that will open up Heaven in your life. An open Heaven is the secret to living as one truly blessed and highly favored. As God opens up the windows of Heaven, we can freely receive not only material blessings, but a host of supernatural ones as well. He meets all of our needs—those of our ministries and families—when His presence comes down. Miracles, signs, wonders, revelation, as well as material and supernatural treasures abound when we learn how to tear open the heavens and position ourselves to receive all God has for us. Under an open Heaven, God will do the impossible in our lives. Imagine it! Believe it!

WHAT IS AN OPEN HEAVEN?

When the heavens are open, we have free access to everything in heavenly realms, a free flow of God's abundant graces and ministry power. Ministering under an open Heaven is like toiling the soil without labor or sweat on the brow. When Heaven is open for you, God will be near and Heaven will be manifest in the natural "as it is in heaven" (Matt. 6:10). When heavens open, God's presence comes down. Do you desire greater power and revelation in your life? Then you need to cry out to God as Isaiah the prophet did. He prayed that God would tear open the heavens, come down, and shake his world!

Rending the Heavens

Have you ever cried out like that? Have you ever prayed that God would invade your world and bring revival, healing, miracles, signs, and wonders? Isaiah knew that in order for the abundance of God's grace and power to come down, first the heavens had to *tear* open:

> *Oh, that You would rend the heavens! That You would come down! That the mountains might shake at Your presence— as fire burns brushwood, as fire causes water to boil—to make Your name known to Your adversaries, that the nations may tremble at Your presence! When You did awesome things for which we did not look, You came down...* (Isaiah 64:1-3a).

The word *rend* means to "tear," and Isaiah, trusting God's faithfulness, positioned himself under Heaven as God tore it open and moved mightily. Isn't it exciting to know that God will rip open the heavens in His eagerness to commune and spend time with us, and then shower us with earthly and spiritual blessings?

Don't Leave Home Without It

Jesus ministered under His own open Heaven, and He carried the open Heaven wherever He went. It didn't get any harder than living in Israel 2,000 years ago, and although Jesus faced opposition, people were saved from sin, healed of disease, and delivered from devils. The power of God began to function in His ministry shortly after Heaven opened over His life when He stepped into the waters of baptism with

John. From that moment on, the heavens remained open over Jesus wherever He went.

> *When He had been baptized, Jesus came up immediately from the water; and behold, the heavens were opened to Him, and He saw the Spirit of God descending like a dove and alighting upon Him. And suddenly a voice came from heaven, saying, "This is My beloved Son, in whom I am well pleased"* (Matthew 3:16-17).

The fruit of this open Heaven was the power of God. This window stayed open during the rest of Jesus' life on earth. Jesus ministered in some of the hardest soil in history. He battled constantly with a tough spiritual climate dramatically affected by the religious spirit. This demonic invader contaminated the people's mind-sets with unbelief and skepticism. So how did Jesus overcome? What was His secret in ministry? It was the open Heaven that He carried everywhere. Remember that open heavens can be anywhere. If one heaven is closed, and the heaven over your own life is open, then you possess a *platinum* card that sets no limit to the *supernatural* funds you can access for any type of ground-breaking opportunity. God wants to give us an open Heaven of His limitless power!

WE BROUGHT HEAVEN WITH US

In one of our meetings in Latvia, a nation that at that time wasn't under an open Heaven, people were skeptical that our being there would have much affect on the nation. In this country, where only 2 percent of the people are saved, miracles, signs, and wonders were seldom experienced.

However, we carried an open Heaven—our open Heaven—with us into the country, and God showed us immense favor. He opened doors never before thought possible. The government allowed us to conduct a number of crusades, to broadcast on television and radio, and to minister in the second largest church in the country—and it became even more miraculous. They invited me to meet with 30 government officials, including two of the highest government officials in Latvia *and* the mayor. Business people and senators even visited me in my hotel room. God tore open the veil and gave us a great harvest—over a thousand souls saved! Others had tried before us, but our Heaven was open, and the nation received an abundance of miracles, signs, and wonders, because we *brought* Heaven with us.

CARRY A BLUEPRINT

Yes, we can carry our own open heavens into churches, cities, nations, peoples, and regions where there are no open heavens. Everywhere we go we can bring a blueprint of "as it is in heaven":

> *The Lord will open to you His good treasure, the heavens, to give the rain to your land in its season, and to bless all the work of your hand. You shall lend to many nations, but you shall not borrow* (Deuteronomy 28:12).

PURSUE AND PRACTICE GOD'S PRESENCE

At the beginning of my ministry, God tore open the heavens and came, and I shook and trembled in His presence. Out of that particular visitation of God's presence came blessing, favor, miracles, revelation, and healing. However, I sought an open Heaven not for the blessings that come with it, but I longed for, hungered for, and desired so desperately to see His face and for Him to visit with me. As I began to pursue God's presence, it happened. God tore the heavens open and invaded my realm. Every day, for three months, I entered into His presence freely, without resistance. It happened because God opened the heavens.

Are you familiar with Brother Lawrence and his writings in *The Practice of the Presence of God*? According to author Gary Thomas, after years of much suffering and spiritual anguish, this monk suddenly found his life transformed, as deep peace and a powerful manifestation of God's presence invaded his life. It was like a revelation when I finally understood what Brother Lawrence had experienced by practicing the presence of God. Thomas says that from the day of his first *open Heaven* experience, Lawrence was overcome with an "unusually intense awareness of the presence of God"[20] very similar to my own experience.

It was so strong that sometimes he consciously kept himself from laughing in the company of others. No longer dreading work in the monastery kitchen, he now felt as close to God peeling potatoes as he did kneeling at the altar. He learned to live so deeply in God's presence that people would even come to see him wash dishes—people were drawn to him as he lived under an open Heaven.

OPEN HEAVEN BLESSING

When Heaven opens, we have visions of God. When Heaven opens, material and financial blessings come. When Heaven opens, we're showered with the bread of His presence. When Heaven opens, we're filled with the Spirit of wisdom and revelation. When Heaven opens, angels visit. Prosperity, abundance, favor, increase, fruit of the Spirit, harvest, and revival, as well as God's power which releases the ability to heal, cast out demons, and preach under the anointing of the Holy Ghost—all these things burst forth when God tears Heaven open. Pursue the open Heaven and the blessings will come. The first 12 verses of Deuteronomy 28 give us a better glimpse into God's myriad of blessings available to us. I've numbered the verses, because you'll want to refer to them often:

1. *Now it shall come to pass, if you diligently obey the voice of the Lord your God, to observe carefully all His commandments which I command you today, that the Lord your God will set you high above all nations of the earth.*

2. *And all these blessings shall come upon you and overtake you, because you obey the voice of the Lord your God:*

3. *Blessed shall you be in the city, and blessed shall you be in the country.*

4. *Blessed shall be the fruit of your body, the produce of your ground and the increase of your herds, the increase of your cattle and the offspring of your flocks.*

5. *Blessed shall be your basket and your kneading bowl.*

6. *Blessed shall you be when you come in, and blessed shall you be when you go out.*

7. *The Lord will cause your enemies who rise against you to be defeated before your face; they shall come out against you one way and flee before you seven ways.*

8. *The Lord will command the blessing on you in your storehouses and in all to which you set your hand, and He will bless you in the land which the Lord your God is giving you.*

9. *The Lord will establish you as a holy people to Himself, just as He has sworn to you, if you keep the commandments of the Lord your God and walk in His ways.*

10. *Then all peoples of the earth shall see that you are called by the name of the Lord, and they shall be afraid of you.*

11. *And the Lord will grant you plenty of goods, in the fruit of your body, in the increase of your livestock, and in the produce of your ground, in the land of which the Lord swore to your fathers to give you.*

12. *The Lord will open to you His good treasure, the heavens, to give the rain to your land in its season, and to bless all the work of your hand. You shall lend to many nations, but you shall not borrow.*

HOLY VISITATIONS

As I recounted earlier, God tore open the heavens, and every day for three months, I soaked in His presence. It wouldn't have happened if I had not pursued an open Heaven, and then positioned myself to receive Him, and to receive His blessings. Deuteronomy 28:2 reveals that the blessings will *overtake us and make us rich.*

I wanted to see God's face and desired a holy visitation, and I got what I asked for. Oh yeah, He overtook me, big time.

Prosperity and Abundance

An open Heaven is the Lord's *"good treasure"* (Deut. 28:12). The storehouses in Heaven open wide when we listen to Him. He blesses our provision, our bank accounts. How would you like to have an open Heaven in your business, in your ministry? In an open Heaven over our finances, we will not borrow, but lend! Our baskets will overflow just as the baskets overflowed with loaves and fishes and fed the multitudes under the open Heaven where Jesus walked. In verse 11, God promises that He "will grant you plenty of goods." When we have Heaven open above us, we prosper in the earth beneath and receive abundance for others and ourselves. However, the greatest treasure of all is not material prosperity, but eternal treasure. Now, read over those Deuteronomy blessings again. Excited? It gets even better. He protects those treasures, too.

So, we now know that when God opens the windows in Heaven, treasures, both eternal and material, are released. However, He not only releases those treasures, but He offers protection for all of our goods and storehouses in the natural and spiritual as well. He says:

> *"Bring all the tithes into the storehouse, that there may be food in My house, and try Me now in this," says the Lord of hosts, "If I will not open for you the windows of heaven and*

pour out for you such blessing that there will not be room enough to receive it. And I will rebuke the devourer for your sakes, so that he will not destroy the fruit of your ground, nor shall the vine fail to bear fruit for you in the field," says the Lord of hosts (Malachi 3:10-11).

Not only will God cause an overflow of blessings, He'll protect even the surplus!

REVIVAL AND HIDDEN MANNA

Part of that surplus is hidden manna. God is the true hidden manna of Heaven, and we should desire the bread of His presence. When God gives us an open Heaven, we get revival and hidden manna.

Now we know from the previous Scripture that Heaven has windows (see Mal. 3:10), but do you know that Heaven also has doors? Doors release greater measures of *goods*. Imagine the doors of a barn, swelling to capacity with stores from an abundant harvest. The big, high doors burst open and the tons of produce pour out:

Yet He had commanded the clouds above, and opened the doors of heaven, had rained down manna on them to eat, and given them of the bread of heaven. Men ate angels' food; He sent them food to the full (Psalm 78:23-25).

When we have an open Heaven and the doors of Heaven open, the first thing that happens is that God rains down manna. As we'll see later, the Bible mentions more manifestations of manna than almost any other kind of open Heaven. When this Heaven opens, people have dreams, trances, and visions.

Some who desire to go deeper into the prophetic can't, because Heaven isn't open. You see, if it opens, it can close as well. Some may think they are living under an open Heaven, when they're not. Some live in a partially open Heaven. I want the Heaven that's open all the time—the Heaven that brings down revival and manna. Don't you?

The manna and the bread was a taste of what was to come. God opened the windows of Heaven for His people in the wilderness and rained manna, a special bread that would bring them life. This miracle foreshadowed the *Bread of Life* who was to come hundreds of years later (see John 6:48). The true and hidden manna today is Jesus Christ, and that means *revival!* When the doors of Heaven are open, the Bread comes down, revival bursts forth, and the bread of His presence saturates and fills us. It is the true and living bread that satisfies. When the heavens above open, God rains down the hot, fresh, heavenly manna, His presence, revelations, secrets of the Lord, and wisdom! Jesus is the Bread of Life; "Taste and see that the Lord is good" (Ps. 34:8).

RIVERS IN THE DESERT

In Genesis 7:11-12, two things simultaneously happen when Heaven opens. First, the fountains of the deep open, and then the flood comes:

> *In the six hundredth year of Noah's life, in the second month, the seventeenth day of the month, on that day all the fountains of the great deep were broken up, and the windows of heaven were opened. And the rain was on the earth forty days and forty nights.*

The fountains of the deep opened up at the same moment that Heaven opened, and *then* we see in verse 12 that it rained "on the earth forty days and forty nights." Yes, I realize that this story is about God's judgment, and the waters are floodwaters. However, in a similar way, if we are in a wilderness and God wants to release rivers, springs, and pools of living water, then guess what happens. The very fountains of the deep break open and those waters flow through the wilderness. Look, He even promises floods of blessing on our deserts: "For I will pour water on him who is thirsty, and floods on the dry ground; I will pour My Spirit on your descendants, and My blessing on your offspring" (Isa. 44:3). Do you want a pool of revival? I do!

How would you like to experience a flood of the Holy Ghost? It happens simultaneously when the heavens open. I want deep fountains. I don't just want to go drink out of somebody else's well. I don't just want to run to a revival meeting or conference for spiritual refreshment. I want a well of my own. I want the fountains that are down deep in my life to break open, and I want heavenly rain of spiritual blessing and revival to come down on my life. When there are no wells to drink from, then you have to be the well. You have to learn to dig, dig, and dig down deep. Keep pressing in to get breakthrough for yourself and for others. Be a fountain—be a well! If there is no rain, renewals, or revival, then break open the fountains of the deep! When they open, the rain will come and everyone will drink.

THE POWER OF GOD

This is the manifestation we all desire—the power of God. Jesus ministered under an open Heaven for healing, miracles, and signs and wonders. God's grace and power are available for you to bring about miracles wherever you go.

I once ministered in a small Vineyard church in Albany, Oregon. For several months, we experienced an open Heaven and a tremendous outpouring of healings and miracles. For months, the church had been preparing for an open Heaven through prayer and servant evangelism. When revival ignited, people traveled to Albany from all over the United States and around the world. We witnessed healings, miracles, a great number of salvations, and the return of many prodigals. Every evening, we baptized dozens of new converts. Pastors returned home after sitting under that outpouring and had miracles break out in their meetings. It was an amazing open Heaven of God's power, healing, and deliverance over that church, and the spiritual shaking and trembling continues there today.

In one of those services, I saw Heaven open. It was like a hole in the air above the pulpit and it tore open. A glory cloud resembling a pillar flowed out of the hole and then an angel appeared. The Lord told me that this angel was like the angel in John 5:1-4 that came to stir the waters of the pool of Bethesda, where the lame, blind, sick, and paralyzed came to be healed. God revealed to me that the angel's name was *Healing Revival.* Tremendous healings took place that evening. Here are excerpts from Albany healing revival reports written by Steve Shultz, publisher of *The Elijah List,* January 2001:

> So many baptisms have begun happening at the Albany Healing Revival, on *the spur of the moment*, that a large horse watering trough has now been set up and remains in place, at the ready—as many are being healed, saved, and baptized—

all in one night. "Is it a salvation revival or is it a healing revival?" The answer to that question seems to be, "Yes, it is!"

On Friday evening, a call was made for anyone who came prepared to be baptized. Only one came forward, but before he was baptized, more came forward and soon there were approximately 15 who came to be baptized, wearing only what they had on.

Already, at least three or four groups are reporting revival and healing outbreaks in their own spheres immediately upon returning home from Albany. In the last 17 weeks, some 25 states have been represented as those eager to receive a healing touch have traveled to this small, previously "unknown" town of Albany. Just as was hoped by those who prayed this anointing in, the anointing is transferable to other homes, churches, and home groups. One young man has taken to the streets and is seeing dramatic healing results in Gresham, Oregon. Another group of teens has taken the anointing to their on-the-street ministry.

But it's not just teens. One pastor is suddenly seeing revival break out in his church. He came for healing. He is now getting revival in his church.

This healing movement—apparently launched when 25-year-old Todd Bentley came to Albany, Oregon from Canada (at the invitation of Pastor Denny Cline)—now continues even when Todd is not present. There is what is being called a *corporate anointing*, according to Pastor Denny Cline. The anointing remains and other healing ministries are preparing to come and impart even more healing.

The following are some healing testimonies from the Albany meetings, as reported by Steve Shultz:

> Last August Todd anointed and prayed over prayer cloths for healing, and people sent them out all over the country.
>
> Debbie sent one to her step-dad in California who had colon cancer. This week she received word there is no trace of cancer in his body. Her brother, who had cancer in his prostate and urinary tract as well as in his bones, also received a prayer cloth. He has been given a report from his doctor this week that he, too, is cancer free.
>
> Twenty-five-year-old Adrianne had been an addict for ten years. She testified Friday night: "There hasn't been a day where I haven't craved drugs. I've been in and out of jail and prison for seven years. Pastor Denny prayed for me on Wednesday night; I haven't had a craving since."
>
> Phil, a young man with an incurable condition (and an unpronounceable name), came for prayer. There was chronic pain in his knees for three years due to the disease. Todd laid hands on him and immediately the pain left, mobility returned, and he was able to run for the first time in two years.

Nothing's changed: There were open heavens 2,000 years ago, and there are open heavens today! Throughout history, believers followed open heavens of God's power as they affected geographic regions and entire nations. Consider the Welsh revival, Azusa Street, the Jesus Movement, and the healing outpouring called the Voice of Healing of the 1940s to the 1960s as examples.

Do you want to lay hands on the sick and see them healed? Cast out demons? Preach under the anointing of the Holy Ghost? Do you want to see city transformation and revival? All of these things come with an open Heaven and the power of God in our lives.

REVELATION

If you can get the heavens open over your life, what I am about to share is going to happen to you. In another chapter of this book, we delve deeper into revelation, but I want to make a few points as it relates to open heavens.

Revelation is one of the most common manifestations of living under an open Heaven. When we receive revelation, we are tasting "the powers of the age to come" (Heb. 6:5). Hello? God *invites* us to *taste* of the powers of the age to come! It's what happens when we access heavenly realms and receive revelation! He communicates with us supernaturally by speaking truth to our minds. His revelation uncovers and sheds light on things that are hidden, misunderstood, and hard to believe, in the past, present, or future.

As you live and breathe, and walk and talk, under an open Heaven, God releases revelation and it becomes constant. One of the first and most frequent experiences we encounter are *visions*: visions of God, angels, things to come, Heaven, and the word of the Lord. When the heavens opened, Ezekiel the prophet saw visions of God (see Ezek. 1:1); Jacob saw angels (see Gen. 28:12); Peter went into a trance and received a vision and words that brought revival to Cornelius's house (see Acts 10:13-20); John saw Heaven and things to come:

183

After these things I looked, and behold, a door standing open in heaven. And the first voice which I heard was like a trumpet speaking with me, saying, "Come up here, and I will show you things which must take place after this." Immediately I was in the Spirit; and behold, a throne set in heaven, and One sat on the throne (Revelation 4:1-2).

Now I saw heaven opened, and behold, a white horse. And He who sat on him was called Faithful and True, and in righteousness He judges and makes war (Revelation 19:11).

The first passage goes on to describe the throne room. All of the visions of Jesus in the Book of Revelation came out of that one particular open Heaven. John experienced one big, massive revelation. He first received an invitation to "Come up here." After that invitation, John said he was immediately in the Spirit and shown visions of the future. But look at chapter 4:1: "After these things...." After what things? After the first three books of Revelation. "Immediately I was in the Spirit..." (Rev. 4:2). But, according to Revelation 1:10, John was already in the Spirit on the Lord's Day. So when John said, "after these things," it's not like he came out of the vision, waited a few days, and then went back in. He was already in the Spirit when he saw a door standing wide open. He was already in a vision, caught up in Revelation 1. It seems that John actually went up another level within the spiritual realm than the one he was already in, and not into a separate open Heaven. He was already receiving revelation when the voice invited him up into higher revelation.

God promises that we'll receive "rain from heaven and fruitful seasons" as well as "food and gladness" to fill our hearts as the Spirit witnesses to us (Acts 14:17). Are you ready now for a revival? Are you hungry enough for the bread of His presence? Is your spirit willing to soak in the *rain from Heaven*? When you position yourself to receive under an open Heaven, you'll receive fresh fire revelations, and it *will* spread. An open Heaven—you know you want it!

FAVOR

An open Heaven is the secret to living as one who is truly blessed and highly favored. "The Lord your God will set you high above all nations of the earth" (Deut. 28:1b). Remember that meeting in Latvia? God showed us immense favor by opening the country to us. We went in under the open Heaven that God gave me, and Latvia opened to the Gospel, even though it was closed for other Christians. God favored Cornelius and saved his entire household, because he lived under an open Heaven and positioned himself to receive from the Lord.

7 KEYS THAT OPEN THE DOORS AND WINDOWS OF HEAVEN

Jesus saw Heaven open, and then the Holy Spirit descended. As I've discussed in a previous chapter, the Holy Spirit and the Kingdom lives within us as believers. However, at certain times, the Spirit visits us in a manifest, visible, or tangible way, as He did in Jesus' life. We have to get the heavens open, so that God's manifest presence can come down and rest on us—to do that, we need a few keys:

Key #1: Pray for Holy Hunger

My own open Heaven experiences began with a holy hunger. We have to hunger for God's presence. It's pretty hard, though, to develop that hunger through your own determination or willpower. Instead, in fervent prayer, ask God to make you hungry—then press in! When that glorious holy hunger comes, God fills you with living fountains of water: "They shall neither hunger anymore nor thirst anymore; the sun shall not strike them, nor any heat; for the Lamb who is in the midst of the throne will shepherd them and lead them to living fountains of waters" (Rev. 7:16-17a). He also fills you with the Bread of His presence: "Blessed are you who hunger now, for you shall be filled" (Luke 6:21a).

Key #2: Soak and Wait

People often ask me how I came to know and draw close to the Lord. It just seemed a natural thing to do after asking Him into my heart. In my desire to know Him better, I tried what I learned from Brother Lawrence and *practiced the presence of God*, as I do today.

When I practice His presence, I stop talking and listen; I lie quiet and still. Sometimes I sit at His feet as Mary did. I practice quiet, listening prayer in a meditative, contemplative way. I worship, play worship music, meditate, gaze, and think about Jesus. I quiet my mind of all busyness, and when it wanders, I refocus my thoughts toward Him. I wait upon Him, and when His presence comes, I lie on the floor and receive. When His presence lifts, I usually want more, and so I reposition myself, and press in again the same way. Sometimes I do this up to 12 hours a day. Usually, one to three hours per day is what I'm more able to do. Now, because I've practiced His presence so often, I don't even have to press in or wait to receive and soak. I just get into position and the presence comes.

Practice First Samuel 3:1-8. *Be like the boy Samuel*, and lie where the Ark of God is. If the glory is around, I know I want to shut up and lie in it! There is a place for prayer and praise, but worship your way into His presence. The word of the Lord in Eli and Samuel's time was rare, and there was no open vision. God, however, reopened Heaven because Samuel positioned himself in a place of soaking in God's presence. He practiced the presence, and God tore open the heavens and rained down fresh anointing, prophecy, favor, and visions on him, a young man who was just getting to know the Lord.

There's an old saying, "Silence is golden—let's all shut up and get rich quick." When we quiet our racing thoughts and listen, we receive *the richness of His holy presence*. There's a time to pray and a time to listen. Listening releases Heaven into our lives. So, do as young Samuel did when God's glory surrounded him. Shush! Soak, bask, and lie in it!

Key #3: Repentance and Obedience

Repentance opens Heaven, and obedience keeps it open. Dude, that's catchy. It's truth. Let me repeat. *Repentance opens Heaven, and obedience keeps it open.* These actions act as a master key that unlocks the heavens' doors—those same doors that close as a result of disobedience.

Let's again look to Jesus as an example; for if you recall, He carried an open Heaven wherever He went and broke through some pretty hard ground. The power of God began to function in the ministry of Jesus as Heaven opened in Matthew 3:16-17:

> *When He had been baptized, Jesus came up immediately from the water; and behold, the heavens were opened to Him, and He saw the Spirit of God descending like a dove and alighting upon Him. And suddenly a voice came from heaven, saying, "This is My beloved Son, in whom I am well pleased."*

Simultaneously with this baptism experience, I believe, Jesus was anointed with power for ministry: "God anointed Jesus of Nazareth with the Holy Spirit and with power, who went about doing good and healing all who were oppressed by the devil, for God was with Him" (Acts 10:38).

His open Heaven was the power of God, anointed with the Holy Ghost and power to go about doing good and healing all those oppressed of the devil, to perform miracles, signs, and wonders, and to cast out devils.

The waters of baptism were the waters of repentance. Jesus became obedient by the things He suffered. Note here, He wasn't obedient; He *became* obedient. Jesus had every opportunity, just like us, to *choose* to disobey or to *choose* to obey. Now, let's zip back to our Deuteronomy Scripture:

> *Now it shall come to pass, if you diligently obey the voice of the Lord your God, to observe carefully all His commandments which I command you today, that the Lord your God will set you high above all nations of the earth* (Deuteronomy 28:1).

His *obedience opened the heavens.* He had constant battles to make decisions to be obedient. In every situation that arose in life, Jesus had to make this conscious decision. He didn't possess any special grace or power to help Him toward obedience. He laid that all down, took on our form, and modeled the relationship that we can have with the Father. He did everything that He did in the power of the Holy Ghost, the same Holy Ghost who can come upon our lives. However, the reason we are not moving in similar dimensions of the ministry of Jesus is that the heavens are not open the same way because *we are not living in repentance and obedience,* and yet we *still* want the power of God, and miracles, signs, and wonders. Are you still with me? God wants to give us an open Heaven of the power of God.

So, take a break, then go and review all the Deuteronomy blessings again, and repeat after me, "Repentance opens Heaven, and obedience keeps it open." Then meet me at the next important key to opening the heavens, *prayer and fasting.*

Key #4: Prayer and Fasting

When I shut up heaven and there is no rain, or command the locusts to devour the land, or send pestilence among My people, if My people who are called by My name will humble themselves, and pray and seek My face, and turn from their wicked ways, then I will hear from heaven, and will forgive their sin and heal their land (2 Chronicles 7:13-14).

Hey, what happened? This key is to be about prayer and fasting, not obedience! But it has its place here. We just learned that repentance and obedience are like a master key that opens the closed heavens. When we open the heavens again through repentance and obedience (and that involves prayer), we're told that God *hears* us from His throne in Heaven. Read the verse again. *He hears us AND forgives our sin AND heals our land!* Notice the first verse, though, "When I shut up heaven...." When Heaven is shut, there's no blessing, revival, or fruitfulness. That's NOT a good thing.

Gird yourselves and lament, you priests; wail, you who minister before the altar; come, lie all night in sackcloth, you who

minister to my God; for the grain offering and the drink offer-
ing are withheld from the house of your God. Consecrate a
fast, call a sacred assembly; gather the elders and all the
inhabitants of the land into the house of the Lord your God,
and cry out to the Lord (Joel 1:13-14).

Prayer and fasting are important Heaven openers. However, it takes desperate and fervent prayer for God to restore an open Heaven to us. In this first chapter of Joel, we find the church in a rather disgusting state. It's in such shambles, that even joy has withered away.

He has laid waste My vine, and ruined My fig tree; he has
stripped it bare and thrown it away; its branches are made
white. Lament like a virgin girded with sackcloth for the hus-
band of her youth. The grain offering and the drink offering
have been cut off from the house of the Lord; the priests mourn,
who minister to the Lord. The field is wasted, the land mourns;
for the grain is ruined, the new wine is dried up, the oil fails. Be
ashamed, you farmers, wail, you vinedressers, for the wheat and
the barley; because the harvest of the field has perished. The vine
has dried up, and the fig tree has withered; the pomegranate
tree, the palm tree also, and the apple tree—all the trees of the
field are withered; surely joy has withered away from the sons of
men (Joel 1:7-12).

It's a church in ruins. The people have separated from God, and as a result, the harvest has perished, and even the fig tree is bare. The heavens are definitely closed. The people are really in a rut because they can't make *atonement*. The pestilence had destroyed the harvest, and that included olives and grapes, the ingredients for making the oil and the wine, which were two very important offerings in their relationship with the Lord. Because of their separation, God had withdrawn an important ingredient in their relationship with Him. What a sad predicament.

But God, as the old saying goes, never closes a door without opening a window. In this dire situation, He offered the people an alternative, because of His love for them. Are the heavens closed in your life, your church, your family, your business, your ministry, or your nation? Pray and repent—fast in obedience to His Word. Lie all night long at the altar if you have to. Cry out to the Lord! Be diligent and persevere and God will restore to you the harvest, the oil, and the wine:

> *Be glad then, you children of Zion, and rejoice in the Lord your God; for He has given you the former rain faithfully, and He will cause the rain to come down for you—the former rain, and the latter rain in the first month. The threshing floors shall be full of wheat, and the vats shall overflow with new wine and oil* (Joel 2:23-24).

Everything depends on doing *the Father's will*. The open Heaven blessings are dependent on our continued repentance and obedience, especially through fasting and fervent prayer. God promises that He will restore the years even when much has been lost...if we make atonement—amends.

The locusts that the prophet wrote about not only destroyed that year's produce, but also did so completely. They ate all the buds and bark of the trees, and it took them some time to recover. So be persistent—persevere and press in. As you make your atonement offerings to the Lord, it may take a little time for total restoration, but He will restore!

Key #5: Tithes and Offerings

Wait—come back! Don't let the title scare you! There's a lot of manna in this section. Tithes and offerings are integral keys to opening heavens. OK, so we've come this far, and I haven't lost you, Hallelujah!

What does money really have to do with God and the spirit realm? It's amazing how often God draws a parallel between Heaven and blessing, and money. People think that if they tithe (give God 10 percent of their income), they are going to be blessed; but that's not necessarily true. I know people who tithe, who are *not* blessed because they tithe by *law*. But hold on a second. You may be thinking, *Isn't tithing a biblical law?* Nope. God did it with Abraham *before* the Law (see Gen. 14:20). It's by faith.

Although some may argue that there is no tithing recorded in the New Testament, it doesn't mean that Jesus excused the tithe, but He did have strong words to say to the teachers of the Law, and to the Pharisees who tithed without mercy, faithfulness, and justice:

> *Woe to you, teachers of the law and Pharisees, you hypocrites! You give a tenth of your spices—mint, dill and cumin. But you have neglected the more important matters of the law—justice, mercy and faithfulness. You should have practiced the latter, without neglecting the former. You blind guides! You strain out a gnat but swallow a camel* (Matthew 23:23-24 NIV).

We hinder the blessings of tithing when we ignore justice, mercy, and faithfulness, but we aren't to ignore tithing either. Are you stingy about tithing? Do you tithe the *obligatory* 10 percent and still not see the blessings? It could be because you haven't provided *offerings* to the Lord. In the old days, tithes *and* offerings opened heavens.

The tithe breaks up the ground so that the rest of our seed (offerings) can bring forth fruit. The Word says in Malachi 3 that when we bring our tithes and offerings into the storehouse, God will open up the windows of Heaven:

> *"Will a man rob God? Yet you have robbed Me! But you say, 'In what way have we robbed You?' In tithes and offerings. You are cursed with a curse, for you have robbed Me, even this whole nation. Bring all the tithes into the storehouse, that there may be food in My house, and try Me now in this," says the Lord of hosts, " if I will not open for you the windows of heaven and pour out for you such blessing that there will not be room enough to receive it"* (Malachi 3:8-10).

You'll recall if you studied the Deuteronomy blessings earlier in the chapter, that the Lord calls His storehouse "the heavens." Your giving is put into His good treasure, the heavens. God says, "I am going to open up the windows of Heaven to pour out blessings." We tend to use this verse and apply it to money, but it really includes all of the benefits of the open Heaven.

In Acts 2, God opened the heavens and poured out His Spirit. Three thousand got saved, and as a result, the Church foundation was laid. Two chapters later, we see that people began to sell their land and houses, and place offerings at the apostles' feet. Pentecost released generosity and extravagant giving. But why wait for the unction to give? Why wait for a revival and then give? Why not offer it as a sacrifice to the Lord now?

Do you believe that our God, Jehovah Jireh, is your provider? Would you like to operate in the heavenly system so that a stock market crash, recession, or a downturn in the economy doesn't affect you? If we want our dollars used for heavenly purposes, why not invest it there? I would much rather possess a heavenly ATM! If we want our money to be in a particular system, then we have to place our money where that system is—and that's up!

This is the reason why Abraham paid tithes to Melchizedek (see Gen. 14:20). Melchizedek was a prophetic picture of Jesus. Abraham, the Father of faith—faith as seen in the tithe—placed his money up in the heavenly realms. He became a possessor of Heaven and earth, because he chose to deposit his assets into a different system.

If we want to live in a different system, then we have to contribute to that system with tithes and offerings. We also have to practice *extravagant giving*. Why settle for 10 percent? If you want the revelatory anointing, sow extra into the revelatory anointing. In other words, sow into ministries that possess the anointing that you want. Sow seeds of faith. Sow more than you have to. Do you truly desire an open Heaven? Sow—sow into it. Sow yourself into revival; sow yourself out of bankruptcy; sow as if your life depended on it.

Can we actually sow ourselves into revival? Cornelius did. He sowed alms, and a Heaven opened over his entire household. Revival came to his house by way of Peter:

> *About the ninth hour of the day he saw clearly in a vision an angel of God coming in and saying to him, "Cornelius!" And*

194

when he observed him, he was afraid, and said, "What is it, lord?" So he said to him, "Your prayers and your alms have come up for a memorial before God" (Acts 10:3-4).

Alms are charitable giving. Our alms go to the poor, not our tithes. The angel of the Lord came to tell Cornelius, "Oh, by the way, I've heard your prayer. God is about to send revival to your house, because He's kept track of your charitable giving." Charitable giving should not be a chore:

Beware lest there be a wicked thought in your heart, saying, "The seventh year, the year of release, is at hand," and your eye be evil against your poor brother and you give him nothing, and he cry out to the Lord against you, and it become sin among you. You shall surely give to him, and your heart should not be grieved when you give to him, because for this thing the Lord your God will bless you in all your works and in all to which you put your hand (Deuteronomy 15:9-10).

In Israel, the practice of charitable giving, especially to the poor, was a very important belief and practice. Failure to give to the poor was a sin. In the New Testament, alms are referred to as an expression of a righteous life. The technical term for *alms* (Greek, *eleemosune*) occurs 13 times there. Jesus criticized those who gave for selfish purposes, such as recognition (see Matt. 6:2-3). However, Jesus did command His disciples to give alms, but to do so in order to lay up treasures in Heaven and receive a reward from the Lord (see Luke 12:33).

So to open Heaven over your life and to release revival, it's important to sow. You may be thinking, *Sow what?* Consider not only tithes and offerings, but also practice charitable and extravagant giving. When we sow in the midst of a closed Heaven, there will be no room to contain all of the blessings as the windows and doors swing open.

Key #6: Word Meditation

I'll cover this principle in greater detail later in the book, especially in Chapter Thirteen. The key is to get the Word in your heart, mind, and soul on a daily basis. Become a modern-day Brother Lawrence. Practice the presence of God and soak in His Word. Speak it, cry it, pray it, feel it, think it, bathe in it, marinate in it, eat it, live it. His Word will open the heavens over your life!

Key #7: Servant Evangelism

Earlier in the chapter, I wrote about the open Heaven revival in the Vineyard church in Albany, Oregon. People often ask me why God picked Albany for this tremendous outpouring of healings and miracles. It was because the people in that church believed that they could open the heavens through servant evangelism, and the faith of 50 people opened Heaven and revival over an entire city:

> For in Christ Jesus neither circumcision nor uncircumcision avails anything, but faith working through love....For you, brethren, have been called to liberty; only do not use liberty as an opportunity for the flesh, but through love serve one another (Galatians 5:6,13).

Love acts—it never fails. Faith works by love. For a change, let's forget power evangelism, prophetic evangelism, preaching on street corners, and tracts. Let's just go out and buy people groceries. Let's go down to the skateboard park and buy hot dogs for everybody. Let's give out gas vouchers, wash cars for free, or mow people's lawns. Loving and blessing the city opened the heavens, and God gave us an unprecedented miracle outpouring. Love never fails! Ask God today, "Whom can I love? What can I do for my neighbor? What can I do that will totally blow someone's mind?" Stand in a grocery line and tell the person in front of you who doesn't have much money, perhaps a single mom, that you're going to pay her bill. "Be blessed, and know that there is a God in Heaven who loves you." That would make her think—most likely about the Lord. And that's a good thing!

I remember as a drug addict when someone yelled out a drive-by blessing, "Jesus loves you!" I went home that night, still on dope, and I thought, *Did they say that because they are freaks, or is there really a God in heaven who told them to say that? Is God trying to get a message through to me because I am about to die? Why are they telling me that Jesus loves me?* It just freaked me out!

In prison, a guy came in and sat down on the end of my bed. I'd been listening to some satanic music; that's what I liked—death metal. He looked at the lyrics and said, "Hey, do you see what they are singing about?" I shrugged, "I just like the way that it sounds. I don't care what they are saying."

"OK," he replied. "That's cool. So, you like the sound of heavy metal! I've got some good Christian music."

"Christian? You've got to be kidding, come on!" I was thinking southern gospel, or funeral-type hymns with an organ background.

Later, he brought me some tapes of Christian heavy-metal bands. I was so impressed that when I got out of prison I'd play the tapes around my friends, not even concerned that it was un-cool Christian music, and they'd be like, "Dude, this is good." One person's kindness had begun to affect my life.

Jesus was moved with compassion and He healed every sickness and every disease. If you want to get more of God's power in your life, try some acts of compassion. The Bible says to bless your enemies. Rock their world, surprise them, do something no one has ever done for them before. Acts of kindness open Heaven.

Walking Under an Open Heaven

God created all of the heavens for us to experience, even while we are here on earth. We are not of this world; we are citizens of Heaven. Let's continue to seek God's face and cry out for Him to rend the heavens and quicken our spiritual senses. Let's also receive, by faith, the abundant earthly blessings that God has for us as the heavens over our lives open.

The Father desires that we experience intimacy with Him, that we walk in the many levels of heavenly revelation, and that we are blessed in every area of our lives. As we learn to walk under an open Heaven, God can use us to bless others and to impart the reality of the supernatural to people around us. If miracles, healings, signs, wonders, visions, and revelation are to come down, Heaven must open for us.

Seek all that the Father has for you. Ask Him to open up the windows and doors of Heaven for you. Tell Him you want to see into the spirit realm. Ask Him to heighten your spiritual senses: sight, ears, eyes, taste, smell, and touch. He'll open the treasure rooms and bring His power and revelation into your life. He'll bring revival and His power into every area. Ask Him to open the heavens wherever you go. Develop and practice the keys you've learned to unlock the secrets of the spiritual realm. Then watch as the floodgates of Heaven open!

Chapter Eight

ANGELIC
HOSTS

When you think of angels, do you picture a Renaissance-type painting of a naked baby with wings, carrying a bow and arrow? Let me see if I can give you a new picture of angels in this chapter. I once had an angel come to me who was about 6'4" tall with 24" biceps. Ripped with huge muscles, he wore a golden sash around his waist. He had blonde, shoulder-length hair and blue eyes. We are talking better than Fabio, OK? I don't know where we picked up this little, wimpy, cupid-type angel image, but I'm here to tell you they don't look like that.

I love the presence of angels, especially when I minister. I've had hundreds of people tell me that they've seen angels in my meetings or standing with me on the platform. I even received an e-mail from a group of youth who wanted to know if our ministry hired actors in white suits to walk around in the meeting! Every one of them saw angels in the back of the sanctuary, but they really didn't have a theological grid for modern-day angel sightings—so they thought they must be actors!

As you read this chapter, you'll learn about angelic activity and its place in Scripture. As a result, you are going to come under the anointing to walk daily in the supernatural that God wants to put on your life. God wants our lives to be prophetic messages that carry supernatural substance.

Believe that your eyes can be opened. Don't just collect a bunch of information and say, "Wow, this is a great teaching on angels." Be praying, "Holy Spirit, open the eyes of my heart and let the angels come right now. Let me feel their presence and let me see them." I want to pray for you before we continue:

> *Holy Spirit, come. Father, please release angelic activity. I ask for the angels—the angels of intercession and healing, the different angels we see in Your Word. I ask for angels to be released to everyone reading this. Let these ministering spirits come from Your throne, God. Let this whole angelic realm become more real to us, because we don't wrestle against flesh and blood. We need to see into the invisible realm. Thank You, Lord, for answering this prayer—in the name of Jesus. Amen.*

Remember Elisha and Gehazi? Just because Gehazi couldn't see the angels didn't mean they weren't there. Elisha, on the other hand, had his mind on the eternal things not on the temporal. He didn't seem the slightest bit upset that a massive army was coming to kill him. Until we learn to trust in the reality of the supernatural, we will be at the mercy of what we see with our physical eyes.

God also wants to reopen the spiritual realm to those who have at one time had angelic encounters but were afraid because they didn't understand that level of prophetic revelation. Some of you have had frequent heavenly experiences but didn't know who to tell. God wants to give us all a new freedom to experience and talk about supernatural encounters.

When I'm aware of the activity and ministry of angels, I become more aware of the supernatural realm. It becomes easier to release miracles, healings, and other things that God wants released. Please realize that I am certainly not talking about worshiping angels—we worship God. However, in order for the invisible realm to open for us, we need to talk about all the supernatural stuff in the Bible, because we actually call forth those things that are not as though they were. As I speak out the truths of the heavenly realm, I'm actually prophesying angelic visitation. I wouldn't be surprised if you have an angelic visitation or a prophetic dream. Angels can come in the natural, and quite often they can come in your dreams.

First, we're going to look at angels in Scripture—what they look like and various ways they have appeared to people in the Bible. Then I'm going to describe different angels and some experiences I have had.

DESCRIPTIONS OF ANGELS

Today our world has developed an increased interest in the supernatural and in angels. Think about it—how many different angels do we see around us? We've got the fat chubby little angels and angels with big wings. We can buy all kinds of angel ornaments, jewelry, and pictures in the store and then go home and watch *Touched by an Angel* on television. Even though I've never seen an angel that has ever looked anything like the world portrays them, it is interesting that people have become extremely curious about these beings. It is time that we, the Church, begin to talk about and portray the true, God-given angelic realm.

Are you wondering what angels really look like? One time, I had a muscular, buff-looking angel come to me—he appeared young, in his early 20s. With hope and expectation, I asked, "God, is that like me in the spirit?"

"No, son. It's an angel," He replied with an "in your dreams" tone. I imagine the Father rolled His eyes and got a kick out of that one.

Angels Can Look Like Men

What about the appearance of angels in the Bible? Well, the Bible tells us that the angel Gabriel looked like a man:

> *Then it happened, when I, Daniel, had seen the vision and was seeking the meaning, that suddenly there stood before me one having the appearance of a man. And I heard a man's voice between the banks of the Ulai, who called, and said, "Gabriel, make this man understand the vision"* (Daniel 8:15-16).

Many angels look like men. I once had an angelic visitation while in a convenience store with a friend. We'd parked the car in front of the store and left my wife and her girlfriend to wait while we hurried in to buy a few things. A group of guys inside laughed, mocked, and scoffed at us as we shopped. One of them, an atheist, said, "Look, it's the guy who came in here last week talking about Jesus. What do you guys think about Jesus?" They were drunk, stoned, or smoking cigarettes, and wore AC/DC and Motley Crew T-shirts.

"We don't believe in angels and God and all that crazy stuff and blah, blah, blah." Nothing besides the power of God would have convinced these hardened skeptics.

Right there and then, God's power dropped me to the floor on all fours, and a roar like a lion came out of me. The shop clerk ran with fear and dove behind the counter, and the two dope-heads followed. By now, the entire atmosphere had changed. The atheist pointed his finger at me and in a mocking tone of voice asked, "Is *that* your God?"

Just then, a dirty bum walked in with two bags of empty bottles and placed them on the counter, and just like that said, "You guys listen to what these guys are telling you. Everything they tell you is true." The clerk gave him his money and he left.

My first thought was, *That was an angel.* When we returned to our vehicle, I told Shonnah what had happened. She said she didn't see anyone enter or leave the store.

I'm convinced this bum was an angel. Often angels are at work in our lives, but they come in disguise. Unless we are spiritually in tune, we will be unaware that angels have even appeared to us. As Scripture says, "Do not forget to entertain strangers, for by so doing some have unwittingly entertained angels" (Heb. 13:2).

So, angels do come looking like men at times. Did you know that you even have an angel that looks like you? In Acts 12:15, Peter was jailed and his friends were having a prayer meeting for him. When Peter showed up at the door, they didn't think it was he, saying it was his angel. They were so casual about it that it must have been common for angels to show up looking like people in those days.

Angels Can Wear Bright Clothing

I've had angels come as shimmering pillars of light with such brightness that I couldn't make out the details; I could just see their form and presence. They appeared as white brilliant light from being in the glory of God all the time. Scripture describes angels this way too:

And out of the temple came the seven angels having the seven plagues, clothed in pure bright linen, and having their chests girded with golden bands (Revelation 15:6).

Angelic Visitation in Scripture

We forget how numerous the angelic hosts are. Scripture refers to them as innumerable or countless. If the devil were to amass every demon in hell to come against you, the angels would still outnumber them. Only one-third of the angels were kicked out of Heaven with satan, so God still has two-thirds of the angels on His side. Not only does God have far more angelic forces, His angels also have far greater power—they soak in God's glory and carry it with them wherever they go.

There are over 300 references to angels in the Bible. Below are some Scriptures describing angels coming to bring deliverance, encouragement, strength, information, and warnings. (Note that the word "angel" in "angel of the Lord," or the word "commander," is capitalized in the first three examples. So, according to many theologians, it's actually Jesus, not an angel, who appears as recorded in these passages.)

Abraham

> *But the Angel of the Lord called to him from heaven and said, "Abraham, Abraham!" So he said, "Here I am"* (Genesis 22:11).

Joshua

> *So He said, "No, but as Commander of the army of the Lord I have now come." And Joshua fell on his face to the earth and worshiped, and said to Him, "What does my Lord say to His servant?" Then the Commander of the Lord's army said to*

Joshua, "Take your sandal off your foot, for the place where you stand is holy." And Joshua did so (Joshua 5:14-15).

Gideon

Now the Angel of the Lord came and sat under the terebinth tree which was in Ophrah, which belonged to Joash the Abiezrite, while his son Gideon threshed wheat in the winepress, in order to hide it from the Midianites. And the Angel of the Lord appeared to him, and said to him, "The Lord is with you, you mighty man of valor!" (Judges 6:11-12)

Jacob

Then he dreamed, and behold, a ladder was set up on the earth, and its top reached to heaven; and there the angels of God were ascending and descending on it (Genesis 28:12).

Elijah

Then as he lay and slept under a broom tree, suddenly an angel touched him, and said to him, "Arise and eat" (1 Kings 19:5).

Daniel

My God sent His angel and shut the lions' mouths, so that they have not hurt me... (Daniel 6:22).

Zechariah

*And there was the angel who talked with me, going out; and
another angel was coming out to meet him… (Zechariah 2:3).*

Mary

*Now in the sixth month the angel Gabriel was sent by God to
a city of Galilee named Nazareth… (Luke 1:26).*

Joseph

*But while he thought about these things, behold, an angel of
the Lord appeared to him in a dream, saying, "Joseph, son of
David, do not be afraid to take to you Mary your wife, for
that which is conceived in her is of the Holy Spirit."*

*Now when they had departed, behold, an angel of the Lord
appeared to Joseph in a dream, saying, "Arise, take the young
Child and His mother, flee to Egypt, and stay there until I
bring you word; for Herod will seek the young Child to
destroy Him"* (Matthew 1:20; 2:13).

Paul

*And now I urge you to take heart, for there will be no loss of life
among you, but only of the ship. For there stood by me this night
an angel of the God to whom I belong and whom I serve, saying,
"Do not be afraid, Paul; you must be brought before Caesar;*

and indeed God has granted you all those who sail with you" (Acts 27:22-24).

John

The Revelation of Jesus Christ, which God gave Him to show His servants—things which must shortly take place. And He sent and signified it by His angel to His servant John… (Revelation 1:1).

Jesus

At His Birth

Now there were in the same country shepherds living out in the fields, keeping watch over their flock by night. And behold, an angel of the Lord stood before them, and the glory of the Lord shone around them, and they were greatly afraid. Then the angel said to them, "Do not be afraid, for behold, I bring you good tidings of great joy which will be to all people. For there is born to you this day in the city of David a Savior, who is Christ the Lord. And this will be the sign to you: You will find a Babe wrapped in swaddling cloths, lying in a manger." And suddenly there was with the angel a multitude of the heavenly host praising God and saying: "Glory to God in the highest, And on earth peace, goodwill toward men!" (Luke 2:8-14)

After His Temptation

Then the devil left Him, and behold, angels came and ministered to Him (Matthew 4:11).

In Gethsemane

And He was withdrawn from them about a stone's throw, and He knelt down and prayed, saying, "Father, if it is Your will, take this cup away from Me; nevertheless not My will, but Yours, be done." Then an angel appeared to Him from heaven, strengthening Him (Luke 22:41-43).

At His Resurrection

And she saw two angels in white sitting, one at the head and the other at the feet, where the body of Jesus had lain (John 20:12).

After the Ascension

Who also said, "Men of Galilee, why do you stand gazing up into heaven? This same Jesus, who was taken up from you into heaven, will so come in like manner as you saw Him go into heaven" (Acts 1:11).

At the Second Coming

For the Lord Himself will descend from heaven with a shout, with the voice of an archangel, and with the trumpet of God. And the dead in Christ will rise first (1 Thessalonians 4:16).

Spiritual Hierarchy in Heavenly Places

The Demonic Realm

Now let's explore the structure of the heavenly places. The spirit realm, or the second heaven, is a real physical place. Consider what the apostle Paul said about the subject: "For we do not wrestle against flesh and blood, but against principalities, against powers, against the rulers of the darkness of this age, against spiritual hosts of wickedness in the heavenly places" (Eph. 6:12).

This Scripture describes the four demonic levels in the invisible realm: First, *principalities* are like the prince of Persia that Daniel saw (see Dan. 10:20). Principalities usually preside over nations; they are geographical spirits and are the biggest demons. They take directions from satan. Second, the verse mentions *powers*; these may be ruling spirits over states, cities, or regions. They are under the direct command of the principality. Third, we see *rulers of darkness*. These rulers are like army generals—they're commanders over the troops for special operations. Finally, *hosts of wickedness*. These demons are the soldiers, the evil spirits that do what the generals tell them. These are the spirits that are most likely to torment you. For the most part you'll be attacked by devils of fear, torment, lies, lust, and other evil spirits, each boasting a different evil nature.

But, if you get an anointing to minister in the church, or if you become well known in your state or region, you'll face those governing spirits. My ministry is international, so I have to deal with principalities over nations. If I stayed in Canada, the principalities in Africa wouldn't care about me at all, but when I come to Africa, I have to do battle with them.

The Heavenly Realm

I believe the Kingdom of Heaven is structured like the demonic realm, with angels over nations, angels over cities, angels that are commanders over the troops, and angels who act as the regular troops. Satan has just copied (and perverted) God's system of hierarchy. The angelic structures exist in the second heaven. In order of command, the hosts are under the general, the general answers to the powers, and the powers take their orders from the principalities. The ones that oversee the principalities are called archangels. That is why in Daniel 10, Michael the archangel came to help another being (probably an angel) who was fighting with the prince of Persia, a demonic principality. Michael came in response to Daniel's persistent prayers, to help this unnamed angel bring his message to Daniel:

> Then he said to me, "Do not fear, Daniel, for from the first day that you set your heart to understand, and to humble yourself before your God, your words were heard; and I have come because of your words. But the prince of the kingdom of Persia withstood me twenty-one days; and behold, Michael, one of the chief princes, came to help me, for I had been left alone there with the kings of Persia" (Daniel 10:12-13).

The archangel, Michael, mentioned in this passage appears to be the highest-ranking angelic officer in the second heaven. Many Bible scholars also believe that Gabriel is an archangel and that lucifer was an archangel before he was thrown out of Heaven, however, the Bible doesn't specifically say that. The only angel specifically called an archangel in Scripture is Michael (see Jude 1:9); he is mentioned five times. He is also called "one of the chief princes" (Dan. 10:13 above) and "the great prince" (Dan. 12:1). Each time Scripture refers to Michael, he is associated with spiritual warfare. He is the ruling big chief over spiritual warfare in the heavenly places. The Book of Colossians also speaks of these structures of authority in the spiritual realm:

For by Him all things were created that are in heaven and that are on earth, visible and invisible, whether thrones or dominions or principalities or powers. All things were created through Him and for Him (Colossians 1:16).

Isn't it interesting that God created invisible things? People the world over would be saved if they saw angels and demons, don't you think? Why would people need faith? In His wisdom He created an invisible realm. He created thrones, dominions, principalities, and powers. Above all these heavenly structures sits Jesus, the Great Commander of the Hosts. He is the Lord of the armies, the Chief, the Commander of the army of the Lord. He is also the King of kings, Lord of lords, and God of gods.

ANGELS IN THE "THRONE ZONE"

Seraphim Described

Now that we've examined angelic hierarchy in the second heaven, we'll examine the angelic ranks in the third Heaven where God dwells— the glory realm. The Scripture speaks of angels called "seraphim" with six wings and full of eyes, front and back. We can read about these, the third Heaven's highest ranking angels, in Isaiah's vision of God's throne: "Above it stood seraphim; each one had six wings: with two he covered his face, with two he covered his feet, and with two he flew" (Isa. 6:2).

These are the angels with faces of an ox, lion, eagle, and man. I'll talk about these faces and their significance more in the chapter on throne room encounters. In the movies, angels are usually portrayed as having wings. I've always wondered where the scriptwriters get that idea. These seraphim angels have six wings not two, and I believe the wings have feathers. Scripture tells us that God "shall cover you with His feathers, and under His wings you shall take refuge" (Ps. 91:4). Maybe you've even seen some of those angel feathers fall in meetings. Here is Isaiah's powerful description of these angels as they worship in God's throne room in Heaven:

> *In the year that King Uzziah died, I saw the Lord sitting on a throne, high and lifted up, and the train of His robe filled the temple. Above it stood seraphim; each one had six wings: with two he covered his face, with two he covered his feet, and with two he flew. And one cried to another and said: "Holy, holy, holy is the Lord of hosts; The whole earth is full of His glory"* (Isaiah 6:1-3).

From their place above the throne, these six-winged angels appear to oversee the worship in the heavenly throne room.

Cherubim Described

In Ezekiel 10, the Bible also describes angels, called the cherubim, who live around God's throne. They are the ones who cover and protect the glory. The cherubim are found wherever the Shekinah glory of God is. We read about these angels above the mercy seat, moving with, and ministering in, God's glory. Precious stones of many colors cover them, and they have four faces and four wings with the likeness of a man's hand under each wing. The cherubim are also described in Ezekiel 1 and referred to as living creatures. However, in Ezekiel 10, it appears that the cherubim and living creatures are one and the same. These angels act as guardians of God's glory.

They also serve as celestial chariots that carry the glory of God. Just as the Levitical priesthood bore the Ark on their shoulders, the cherubim serve as four wheels on a celestial chariot that carries God's throne. In Ezekiel 10, the living creatures have eyes and wheels:

> *And their whole body, with their back, their hands, their wings, and the wheels that the four had, were full of eyes all around.... Then the glory of the Lord departed from the threshold of the temple and stood over the cherubim. And the cherubim lifted their wings and mounted up from the earth in my sight. When they went out, the wheels were beside them; and they stood at the door of the east gate of the Lord's house, and the glory of the God of Israel was above them* (Ezekiel 10:12,18-19).

So where does the throne go? Check out the first ten chapters of Ezekiel and read about the cherubim carrying God to the different cities that He is judging. Did you know that there is one throne in Heaven, but the throne is on wheels that move it to different rooms? It moves from the throne room of worship to the throne room of judgment. We'll examine that in more detail later.

Angels in Worship

> *The four living creatures, each having six wings, were full of eyes around and within. And they do not rest day or night, saying: "Holy, holy, holy, Lord God Almighty, who was and is and is to come!" Whenever the living creatures give glory and honor and thanks to Him who sits on the throne, who*

lives forever and ever, the twenty-four elders fall down before
Him who sits on the throne and worship Him who lives for-
ever and ever, and cast their crowns before the throne, saying:
"You are worthy, O Lord, to receive glory and honor and
power; for You created all things, and by Your will they exist
and were created" (Revelation 4:8-11).

When you come into a meeting where God's people are praising Him, these angels are present because God inhabits the praises of His people. These throne room angels go wherever the presence of God is. If you had the eyes of your heart opened, you would see living creatures, seraphim, and cherubim there. We need to ask the Lord to open the eyes of our heart to the throne zone, the glory realm. Every time you worship you need to say, "God, let me see the throne; let me experience Revelation 4:1." As you acknowledge the activity of angels, you will begin to experience the throne.

Earlier in the book, I described a service in Iowa where we saw lightning and the Lord took me into a prophetic experience that lasted until 11:30 at night. I wasn't even able to preach. During the middle of that service, I felt the Holy Spirit say, "Thank God for the cherubim. Thank God for the seraphim. Acknowledge their presence in your midst." And as soon as I started to thank the Lord for these angels, I began to have a prophetic experience.

Now, think about the supernatural realm for a minute—thunder and lightning and the four living creatures around the throne with the faces of a man, ox, lion, and eagle. Because this description of the throne room sounds like fantasy, it may be difficult for you to grasp what I'm talking about. It seems out of this world—it seems so Star Trek. Often we can't experience this supernatural world because we spend most of our life focused on the natural world. Until we hear more messages about the invisible realm in the church today, the eyes of our hearts will remain closed to the wonderful reality of heavenly places. You see, faith comes by hearing God's Word (see Rom. 10:17); everything we receive from God, we receive by faith and without faith it's impossible to please God (see Heb. 11:6). As we hear more about the invisible realm from Scripture, our faith will grow and we will increasingly experience this realm.

I've made a practice of reading, hearing, and meditating on Scriptures about the heavenly realms. Never more than a few days go by that I don't encounter some kind of prophetic experience or the third Heaven. We need to have the eyes of our heart opened. Many Christians today approach worship as singing a few songs or as something to get through to get to the preaching, or so they can get their healing and go home. They forget to take time to ask themselves, *What's going on in Heaven right now as I worship? I wonder what it looks like. Who is in the room with me right now? If my eyes were open in the spirit, what would I see in the service?*

HONORING THE ANGELIC REALM

In the Western world, we've been too distracted by the natural realm to spend time focusing on what we don't see. But the more we acknowledge the spiritual realm, the more we become aware of it. When you honor healing and preach healing, you get healing! When you honor salvation and preach salvation, you get salvations. Did you know that? When you honor and talk about the supernatural and angels, guess what happens? Angels start showing up. The Holy Spirit confirms the word with signs following.

Many of us don't live in the supernatural because we don't have an understanding, openness, or grid for it. We don't expect God to show up today. We have erected mental barriers or created limits to God's work in our lives. Some people believe this realm of experience is only for biblical characters or the prophets. However, God really does want us to enjoy this supernatural realm. If Elisha could pray that the eyes of his servant would be opened to see the angels, I believe that I can pray that God would open up your eyes so that you can see what the prophets see. It's biblical. We can live in that supernatural place.

ANGELIC JOB DESCRIPTION

Let me show you several things that angels do. The following Scripture gives us a list of some of the tasks that angels carry out:

> *The Lord has established His throne in heaven, and His kingdom rules over all. Bless the Lord, you His angels, who excel in strength, who do His word, heeding the voice of His word. Bless the Lord, all you His hosts, you ministers of His, who do His pleasure. Bless the Lord, all His works, in all places of His dominion. Bless the Lord, O my soul!* (Psalm 103:19-22)

Now let's examine each of the jobs listed in these verses.

Angels Bless the Lord

"Bless the Lord, you His angels...." Note that the first thing that angels do is bless the Lord. They are involved in worship and they praise the Lord. Some are assigned permanently to earth, but others

216

get a command from the Father, go and do it, and then return to bless the Lord again.

Angels Are Obedient

"…who do His pleasure." They are obedient servants. Angels are the ones who do God's work on the earth for Him. They carry out many of the tasks that need to be done in the world. They minister to people, to His children, and to those who are not yet saved. Whatever the Father purposes, the angels do.

When the soldiers came to arrest Jesus, He said that He could pray to His Father to mobilize angels on His behalf: "Or do you think that I cannot now pray to My Father, and He will provide Me with more than twelve legions of angels?" (Matt. 26:53). Jesus knew that the angels were available to Him.

Angels Do His Word

"…heeding the voice of His word." The most important thing angels do is they heed the voice of God's word. I believe this job also includes the word spoken by His saints on the earth. The angels heed His voice as it comes through His saints who declare His word on the earth. I don't speak to the angels directly; I ask the Father to send them and bring me victory, or, I'll release a decree and say, "You angels do His decree." They come to administrate the activities of Heaven. They want to bring forth the manifestation of God's will.

As the rhema word of God goes forth, it has the Father's breath on it. The angels recognize the spiritual scent of God's spoken word and they work to bring it to pass. When I begin to proclaim to people on earth (and to demonic powers and principalities in the unseen realm) what

God shows me in the spirit realm, a powerful spiritual dynamic takes place. As I declare that which already exists in the heavenly realm, the angels give heed to the voice of His word on my lips; they hear me decree God's will and so they go establish God's Kingdom on earth.

According to Jesus' words, what you do and don't do can bind and release Heaven. "And I will give you the keys of the kingdom of heaven, and whatever you bind on earth will be bound in heaven, and whatever you loose on earth will be loosed in heaven" (Matt. 16:19). This verse is clear—whatever you loose (permit) on earth is loosed (permitted) in Heaven, and whatever you bind (forbid) on earth is bound (forbidden) in the heavens. Angels carry out those words that we speak as we proclaim, decree, and prophesy God's will in a church or region.

Angels Protect Believers

Let's see what the Book of Psalms tells us about angels and believers:

For He shall give His angels charge over you, to keep you in all your ways. In their hands they shall bear you up, lest you dash your foot against a stone. You shall tread upon the lion and the cobra, the young lion and the serpent you shall trample underfoot (Psalm 91:11-13).

According to this passage, angels are released into your life to protect you. Scripture suggests that every believer has a guardian angel (see Matt. 18:2-3,10). Angels help to protect us in all our ways. They also help us "overcome the lion and the cobra." The Bible also says, "The angel of the Lord encamps all around those who fear Him, and delivers them" (Ps. 34:7).

So, how can you access their service in intercession and release them in your life, church, region, and ministry? The key is not by directly inviting angels but by praying to the Father. It's OK to ask the Father to bring angels into your life or your church, and to tell others when angels manifest in your meetings.

I believe that because Jesus could call for the angels, as sons and daughters, we also have legions of angels at our disposal. Like Jesus, we can pray to our Father:

> *Father, I thank You for the angels. I thank You that the Angel of the Lord encamps around those who fear Him. I thank You for the reality of angels from the beginning of the Bible to the end. I thank You for the angels that carry out Your purposes, for the angels that protect me and are involved in the harvest. I also thank You for the angels that are involved in the glory realm. Lord, let those angels come right now.*

Angels Partner With Us in Warfare

The Bible shows us that you and I are partners with the angels. What goes on in Heaven in the invisible, whether we are overcoming the works of darkness or whether we are being overcome, has something to do with our partnership with angels. It is so important that we release angels to work on our behalf—we do so as we become involved in intercession and spiritual warfare. Let me give you one example:

> *War broke out in heaven: Michael and his angels fought with the dragon; and the dragon and his angels fought, but they did not prevail, nor was a place found for them in heaven any*

longer. So the great dragon was cast out, that serpent of old, called the devil and satan, who deceives the whole world; he was cast to the earth, and his angels were cast out with him. Then I heard a loud voice saying in heaven, "Now salvation, and strength, and the kingdom of our God, and the power of His Christ have come, for the accuser of our brethren, who accused them before our God day and night, has been cast down. And they overcame him by the blood of the Lamb and by the word of their testimony, and they did not love their lives to the death" (Revelation 12:7-11).

The fact that the demonic forces didn't prevail means that it was possible that they could have. Not only did the angels prevail against the dragon, the believers overcame him too. This Scripture illustrates a partnership in the warfare going on in Heaven. Victory came by the blood of the Lamb and the word of the saints' testimony. They didn't love their lives even unto death. Through laying our lives down, appropriating the blood of Christ, and declaring the word of our testimony, we overcome. These acts have prophetic power that gives strength to the heavenly battle against the devil and his angels. The word that comes out of our mouth actually gives strength to the battle that is going on in Heaven and destroys the enemy's works.

God is looking for partners who will proclaim, prophesy, and pray for the release of angels to overcome the warfare. In prayer, we have authority to release angels to work on our behalf. It's important that we learn to pray for the angels to come: "In my city, oh God, we are in a battle against demonic hosts. Father, I ask You for the angels right now. I ask that they would come fight with us now, and that they would prevail in this city."

Every day war rages in the second heaven—war for your soul, war for your house, war for your body, and war for your money. We don't wrestle against flesh and blood but we constantly battle against powers and principalities. We need to be sober and alert, understanding the reality of the demonic and the angelic realm. We release His word into the spirit realm when we make prophetic decrees of God's known will, including what He is doing and about to do.

Angels Are Commissioned for Soul Winning

Angels minister to those who will inherit salvation. In other words, angels are involved in winning souls. "Are they not all ministering spirits sent forth to minister for those who will inherit salvation?" (Heb. 1:14). Thus, we can be more successful in soul winning if we simply say, "Father, I ask for angels right now to come into this region to help gather the harvest. Let angels come right now to minister to lost souls in the north, south, east, and west of my city. Father, I release the angels."

It is important that we release the angels because if we don't release them, angels can be kept out of the battle. The devil can prevail in a region until we begin to release, bind, and loose in Heaven, and ask the Father to release the angelic hosts as reinforcements. Scripture tells us that the god of this age is blinding hearts and minds, so there are times where souls can't be saved because of the deep darkness that covers the earth. However, as we begin to prophesy, we can command the captive to come out of his prison and we can prophesy salvation into our city and region saying, "Father, give us the reinforcements, give us the angels that we need. We release them right now. We acknowledge them in the region so they can come and help us get victory in warfare and so we can have the harvest."

The apostle John saw these harvesting angels in action. "And another angel came out of the temple, crying with a loud voice to Him who sat on the cloud, 'Thrust in Your sickle and reap, for the time has come for You to reap, for the harvest of the earth is ripe'" (Rev. 14:15). God has assigned specific angels to world evangelism. As we pray to the Father, we can have an increase of harvest in our lives. As we've now seen, Jesus talked about angels coming to gather the wheat and reap the harvest: "...the harvest is the end of the age, and the reapers are the angels" (Matt. 13:39b).

Angels Minister Divine Strength

Another aspect of the angelic job description is that of ministering divine strength. When you are in a place of hardship, trial, warfare, and suffering, or you're burned out and beaten down, it is scriptural for angels to come and minister to you. An angel ministered to Jesus in the Garden of Gethsemane and at the end of His 40-day fast in the wilderness, after He had resisted the devil's temptations: "Then the devil left Him and behold, angels came and ministered to Him" (Matt. 4:11). The angel imparted divine strength and life to Him. For those of you who have been in the desert or under attack from the enemy, I pray that the angels will come and minister to you as well.

An angel also ministered to Elijah after he fled from Jezebel:

> But he himself went a day's journey into the wilderness, and came and sat down under a juniper tree; and he requested for himself that he might die, and said, "It is enough; now, O Lord, take my life, for I am not better than my fathers." He lay down and slept under a juniper tree; and behold, there was an angel

touching him, and he said to him, "Arise, eat." Then he looked and behold, there was at his head a bread cake baked on hot stones, and a jar of water. So he ate and drank and lay down again (1 Kings 19:4-6 NASB).

Angels Deliver Messages

Angels are also messengers. An angel came to Zacharias to announce the birth of John the Baptist:

Then an angel of the Lord appeared to him, standing on the right side of the altar of incense. And when Zacharias saw him, he was troubled, and fear fell upon him. But the angel said to him, "Do not be afraid, Zacharias, for your prayer is heard; and your wife Elizabeth will bear you a son, and you shall call his name John" (Luke 1:11-13).

Often angels come in our dreams. An angel came and brought Joseph directions:

But while he thought about these things, behold, an angel of the Lord appeared to him in a dream, saying, "Joseph, son of David, do not be afraid to take to you Mary your wife, for that which is conceived in her is of the Holy Spirit" (Matthew 1:20).

Angels Are Active in Healing

God also sends angels to operate in the area of healing. The angel who was active in the Voice of Healing revival, named Healing Revival, has been showing up more in recent years. This is not the first time that this kind of angel has ministered to people. Scripture also gives us an example of a healing angel. Often people think they've never heard of angels of healing until I point them to this passage in John 5:

> *After this there was a feast of the Jews, and Jesus went up to Jerusalem. Now there is in Jerusalem by the Sheep Gate a pool, which is called in Hebrew, Bethesda, having five porches. In these lay a great multitude of sick people, blind, lame, paralyzed, waiting for the moving of the water. For an angel went down at a certain time into the pool and stirred up the water; then whoever stepped in first, after the stirring of the water, was made well of whatever disease he had* (John 5:1-4).

The angels don't do the healing, but they are involved in bringing healing. You'll see more miracles and healings in your life and ministry when you include angels. We need angels in healing because demons cause many sicknesses and diseases today. We need angels to war and take authority over the demonic realm.

Angels Take Souls Into God's Presence

According to Scripture, the angels take us into the presence of the Lord when we die. "So it was that the beggar died, and was carried by the angels to Abraham's bosom. The rich man also died and was buried" (Luke 16:22). Won't it be awesome when you take your last breath on earth and an angel comes to lead you into God's glorious presence?

Angels Release Finances

According to Psalm 103:20, the angels "do His bidding." When the Father wants to command blessings, often the angelic messengers are sent to help us get our inheritance. In Philippians 4:19, the Bible assures us that God will *supply all our needs* "according to His riches in glory by Christ Jesus." When I need a financial breakthrough I don't only pray and ask God for it, I intercede and partner with the angels by petitioning the Father to release the angels that are assigned to finances. "Father, give me the angels that are assigned to get me money," I'll say. "Let those angels be released on my behalf. Send them into the four corners of the earth to gather money."

Do you know why it's important to pray like this? Because the devil wants to cut off our cash flow and block our finances. He wants to do whatever he can to hinder the blessing and provision that God has for us. Sometimes praying about it isn't good enough, because we need to overcome in Heaven where the angels and demons are actually fighting. We want to push back the demonic forces, so sometimes we need to say, "Father, let those legions of angels assigned to release financial breakthrough come to the earth right now and loose the devil from the money assigned to me. I call in that money in the name of Jesus!"

Sometimes when I pray this way, *bam!* I'll have the money I need within a few days. Yes, I get financial breakthrough because God is my source. If man doesn't have it for me, God does. Yet the devil is trying to keep it from me. Even though God heard me on the first day, the devil wants to delay it as long as he can. But I've got to get the angels involved through prayer: "C'mon, God, let those angels come and help fulfill Your word—You promised me the blessing of the Lord that makes one rich and You add no sorrow with it" (see Prov. 10:22).

CONTEMPORARY ANGELIC ENCOUNTERS

A while ago, for a number of weeks, I had daily visitations of angels and an increase of the presence of angels in our meetings. Many have told me about increases of spiritual activity in their own lives too. We're in need of reinforcements in the Western church to neutralize the demonic assignments and backlash that have caused pastors and leaders to burn out. This message will prophetically call forth reinforcements in the angelic realm and bring healing to many who are under attack.

I have asked God to send angels to work in my life and ministry: "God, I love to feel the presence of the angels that minister around Your throne. Your Word says that angels encamp around those who fear You. I would like to know that angels are encamping around me. It would be great to *experience* what the Bible says I have. It would be awesome to feel the angelic presence in my house and meetings and to have others in meetings say, 'Man, there were angels in that service.'"

Angels of Financial Breakthrough

I was at a meeting in Atlanta when my wife, Shonnah, saw two angels walk into the service and pour oil on the pastor. Shonnah saw gold in the oil and knew there was financial breakthrough coming. That night two people wrote the pastor checks for $16,000 and $17,000. Others also wrote checks of thousands of dollars to Fresh Fire for our missions work.

Gold appeared on hands and faces. In addition, many experienced great financial blessing within 24 hours. The day after this angelic visitation, one gentleman had millions of dollars released to him—he'd waited almost ten years for this breakthrough.

I also once had a personal visitation of a financial angel in my hotel room in Albany, Oregon. It looked like the living creatures described in Ezekiel chapter 1, with four sets of hands and eagles wings. Out of its feathers grew jewels—topaz, rubies, diamonds, emeralds, and pearls. At that moment, I knew that this was an angel of finance with stewardship of finances in Heaven. God began speaking to me about financial breakthrough for the Body of Christ. Within the next two years, the finances of Fresh Fire increased by about 50 percent.

The financial breakthroughs in the church and in our ministry came because financial angels visited. Can you imagine? The angels increased financial blessing in our ministry and broke the spirit of poverty over the church. Often the churches that I visit will see a doubling of their income within 12 months. With this angelic assistance, as God's people, we will prevail and overcome the warfare trying to hold back our financial breakthrough.

An Angel Called Healing Revival

I first saw the angel called Healing Revival on December 5, 2000, in Grants Pass, Oregon. That was the 50-year anniversary of the day William Branham and Paul Cain brought the healing revival to the Pacific Northwest. The conference was all about re-digging the ancient wells. The moment I received that angelic visitation my gift of revelation came and my prophet's mantle accelerated tenfold.

The angel came to me again in Albany, Oregon, the next February. He stood in the church service and then his body passed through the ceiling of the church. The Lord told me the angel's name and that he was the same angel I saw in Grants Pass. God also revealed to me that this angel was involved in the ministry of John G. Lake, William Branham, and John Knox. The Lord said this angel was from the Northwest healing revival and is manifesting again as a sign that God is restoring the Voice of Healing revival and opening up the ancient wells.

Over the last year, the angel called Healing Revival has come to my meetings on many different occasions. When he comes I get a gift: the ability to diagnose people's sicknesses. If I touch someone with my left hand, I immediately know his or her condition.

At times, this angel brings very accurate words of knowledge including people's names, nicknames, the year they were injured, and where they're from. Many people have also seen or had contact with this angel in the meetings. Whenever he shows up the miracles go off the charts. Instead of a few healings, we'll get three blind eyes healed in one night or even see someone walk out of a wheelchair.

The angel showed up in Albany in February 2001 as a sign that God was endorsing what was taking place and opening up a healing well. Everywhere I have seen this angel, the miracles continue after I leave and a healing well is established—that place becomes like the pool of Bethesda, in John 5, where the healing angel used to visit.

Years ago, I was taken to Heaven and deposited on the playing field of a stadium with several other Christians. We were in the game and had the ball. The seats were filled with tens of thousands of angels cheering, "Go Church go! Go Church go!" The Lord showed me they were healing angels like the angel in John 5. He said they were ready to be assigned to churches, regions, and nations, which would become resident healing wells. He said it would be like the Voice of Healing revival. Ever since that vision in Heaven, those angels visit me.

An Angel Named Promise

I had an angel come to me in Kansas City, Missouri. He said, "Todd, my name is Promise and I've come to bring the fulfillment of God's promises and the prophetic words spoken to intercessors. I have come for those who have been like Hannah—they have prayed, waited, and carried a promise in their hearts. There will come a time when God has heard and I will release the answer."

Be encouraged. There is an angel called Promise involved in bringing your intercessory breakthrough. When this angel attends my meetings, people receive breakthroughs and answered prayers. The Lord showed me the description of this type of angel in Revelation 8:1-6:

> When He opened the seventh seal, there was silence in heaven for about half an hour. And, I saw the seven angels who stand before God, and to them were given seven trumpets. Then another angel, having a golden censer, came and stood at the altar. He was given much incense, that he should offer it with the prayers of all the saints upon the golden altar which was before the throne. And the smoke of the incense, with the prayers of the saints, ascended before God from the angel's hand. Then the angel took the censer, filled it with fire from the altar, and threw it to the earth. And there were noises, thunderings, lightnings, and an earthquake. So the seven angels who had the seven trumpets prepared themselves to sound.

Please pay attention here. There is a devil in the invisible realm who wants to keep us from receiving the manifestation of God's presence. In the same way that Daniel's answer was delayed 21 days, at times, our answers are delayed in the heavenly places by a demon keeping us from receiving our spiritual breakthrough. Our prayers go up before God's throne as incense and they go into a bowl. When it fills up the angel comes and releases the answer and the fulfillment of that promise.

In several meetings where I've spoken on the topic of receiving answers to delayed prayers, the angel of Promise has appeared. In some instances, people who have prayed for breakthrough for years receive it the very next day. Others are healed, come into financial breakthrough, or receive miracles.

I'm asking right now for God to allow the angel "Promise" to gather the incense that has gone up before His throne through the lives of every reader. "Oh God, take the prayers of every intercessor and let an angel begin to release those prayers into the earth. Push back the darkness, resistance, and warfare that keep us from spiritual breakthrough. Father, I thank You for the angel called Promise."

An Angel of the Prophetic

A while ago, Bob Jones told me about an angel that helped birth the entire prophetic movement in Kansas City in the 1980s. The Lord had sent this angel to help nurture the prophetic ministry (and gift), at a time when it was being re-established in the modern-day church in North America.

A few weeks after our conversation, I attended a service in Beulah, North Dakota. In the middle of the meeting, an angel glided in. As I stared wide-eyed at the angel, I heard the Lord tell me that this was the same angel that was involved with the prophetic movement in Kansas City. The angel floated a couple of inches off the floor emitting brilliant light and colors. He appeared young—about 22 years old—but old at the same time. It was as though he carried the wisdom, virtue, and grace of Proverbs 31.

He carried bags and pulled gold out of them. Then as he walked up and down the aisles, he put gold dust on people. "God, what is happening?" The Lord answered that the angel was releasing gold, which represents both the revelation and the financial breakthrough that He was bringing into that church. At the Lord's direction, I announced that the same angel that appeared in Kansas City had showed up in the meeting as a sign that the Lord was endorsing and releasing a prophetic spirit in the church.

When angels come, they always come for a reason. We need to ask God what the purpose is. When the angel of the prophetic came, it mentored, nurtured, and opened up a prophetic well that allowed God's people to receive fresh waters of revelation from God. Following that visitation, the congregation of 150 saw greater financial breakthrough than they had ever seen. The pastor testified that within weeks, the church offerings had doubled. Later, the church sent me the biggest offering I had received up to that point in my ministry—thousands of dollars!

The angel not only released a financial anointing but a prophetic anointing as well. The people in the church had trances and visions, and the pastor received words of knowledge and moved in healing. During this visitation, the Holy Spirit literally blasted the pastor's wife, and she received such a powerful prophetic anointing that she called complete strangers on the telephone and prophesied over them!

The Scribe Angel

Sometimes when I prophesy over people, a scribe angel appears behind them. He kind of looks like Abraham Lincoln and has the presence of a historian. He has a scroll and one of those old-fashioned quill pens. As I prophesy, he listens to what I say, watches the person's reaction,

231

and writes things down in gold ink. I asked the Lord about it and He said the angel records history, destiny, and legacy. At times God releases a grace to choose to do great things. The scribe angel waits for the person to make a decision. He also gives people the ability to understand visions, dreams, and teaching.

The Scroll Angel

The scroll angel comes with the little honey scrolls for us to eat (see Ezek. 3:3; Rev. 10:9). They are impartations of our destiny and inheritance, and as we eat them, we'll understand about the next season in our lives. We'll examine these scrolls more in a later chapter.

Counsel and Might

The angel of counsel and might's job is to bring us counsel so we can demonstrate God's might. You'll learn more about this in the *Seven Spirits of God* chapter.

ANGELIC AWARENESS BRINGS BREAKTHROUGH

If you could live in the reality of this message and see what is going on in Heaven when you pray and worship, you would see far greater supernatural manifestations in your life. We are called to a life of signs and wonders. As we set our mind on things above rather than on the temporal, God will open the eyes of our heart to the invisible realm. We need to be ruthless in ridding ourselves of all the distractions of everyday life that keep us from real supernatural Christianity. Meditating on the unseen realm and hearing about the supernatural lifts us into a place of walking in the spirit realm.

I live in a place of breakthrough because I am so aware of the angels that I can say, "Lord, I'm going to Uganda. Let worldwide evangelistic angels come with me now. There are people who are going to inherit salvation. I don't want the devil to prevail over the crusade, so I release the angels. I loose them in Heaven now in Jesus' name."

Then in Uganda, they'll give me a press conference and access to every television station and all the major newspapers in the whole country. I'll preach and have an incredible revival because God releases the angels.

The Bible is full of angels from the beginning to the end. We need to pray, "God, let us see the angels. Let them come into the church, the city, and the region." The Lord wants us to hunger to live in His presence and in the supernatural realm. Let's continue to ask Him to open the eyes of our hearts to the invisible, to the cherubim, the seraphim, the guardian angels, and the angelic hosts. He wants to make us aware of angels involved in healing and intercession, as well as those angels around His throne that radiate His glory.

As God's children, we have a right to ask for angelic ministry in our lives, in our children's lives, and in our church. Ask the Lord to make you aware of angels who come with direction and warnings, or angels who come to strengthen you with new life wherever suffering and warfare has brought discouragement and death. He wants to make our lives and churches modern-day pools of Bethesda where His healing angels come to bring wholeness.

As you allow God to make you more aware of the angelic hosts, you may even begin to feel the wind of angels' wings as they minister the life of God to you. He will commission angels of promise to release breakthroughs and long-awaited promises into your life. They will cause your winter to turn into spring. As you trust God to mobilize angelic forces on your behalf, you will arise and walk triumphantly out of the wilderness into new life—the victorious life that the Bible calls *walking in the Spirit* (see Gal. 5:16,25).

Chapter Nine

THE SEVEN SPIRITS OF GOD

Would you like to know the deep things of God? If your heart is loyal to Him, the Holy Spirit invites you to know those deep things through revelation and wisdom, counsel and knowledge. God's eyes search to and fro for believers who desire the flowing river of His abiding presence. He wants to abide in you constantly and give you greater revelation of His supernatural world—this teaching on the manifestation of the seven Spirits of God will help that happen.

The teaching is deep, and may have you puzzling over it at first, but as you continue to read, I believe you'll receive a greater revelation and understanding of the riches hidden in God. We'll begin by examining several references to the seven Spirits of God and His different manifestations; then we'll cover each Spirit in depth. The prophet Isaiah speaks about the Spirit of the Lord resting on Jesus, saying:

> *The Spirit of the Lord shall rest upon Him, the Spirit of wisdom and understanding, the Spirit of counsel and might, the Spirit of knowledge and of the fear of the Lord* (Isaiah 11:2).

Throughout this chapter, I have capitalized the word *Spirit* (for seven Spirits) in every case, just as the Bible does in Isaiah 11:2 (even though Spirit is not always capitalized in Scripture). This verse lists the seven Spirits of God as:

1. The Spirit of the Lord
2. The Spirit of wisdom
3. The Spirit of revelation (understanding)
4. The Spirit of counsel
5. The Spirit of might (signs and wonders)
6. The Spirit of knowledge
7. The Spirit of the fear of the Lord

The seven Spirits of God are seven expressions, each one an aspect of the Holy Spirit. The Amplified Bible actually speaks of "the sevenfold Holy Spirit" (Rev. 1:4). The Holy Spirit isn't split; it's just that sometimes He manifests Himself in different ways. He manifests as the Spirit of wisdom when we need wisdom, as the Spirit of counsel when we need guidance, and so on. The mystery of the seven Spirits of God is the same as the mystery of the Trinity—separate but One.

SEVEN EXPRESSIONS OF THE HOLY SPIRIT

The seven Spirits of God are seven functions, manifestations, or expressions of the Holy Spirit, but they're more than that. Look at Revelation 1:4: "John, to the seven churches which are in Asia: Grace to you and peace from Him who is and who was and who is to come, and from the seven Spirits who are before His throne." The seven Spirits of God deliver the message, and the letters to the churches are addressed to the angels (messengers) of each church (see Rev. 2:1). In turn, these messengers seem to have the task of taking the message to the churches.

So, in the first chapters of Revelation, we see seven Spirits of God and seven angels (or messengers) and the seven churches. Scholars hold different views about who the angels (or messengers) are. Some believe that they are the pastors of each of the churches. You see, in Scripture, three types of messengers appear to be called angels—angelic beings, human beings, and the divine being, Jesus Himself. First, angelic beings visit people with messages throughout Scripture (see Chapter Eight). Also, in Scripture, a human being (the prophet Haggai) is called God's "messenger" or "angel" (Hag. 1:13). The Hebrew word *malak* used in this verse means "angel" or "messenger." Finally, theologians also say that God, the Son, appears as an angel in the Old Testament when the phrase "Angel of the Lord" is used (Gen. 16:7-13; Judg. 2:1).

So, now that we understand the different angelic beings in the Bible, who or what else could the seven angels in Revelation be? In the first chapter of this book we're told that the revelation is sent (or from) both "His angel" and "the seven Spirits" (Rev. 1:1,4). Is it possible, throughout John's Revelation, that actual angelic messengers are fulfilling each of the seven functions of the Holy Spirit? Could it be that in this book one Holy Spirit is revealed in seven expressions of the Spirit, but that each expression reveals itself as an angelic messenger?

I want to ensure that I explain this well before we move on. Please don't get confused and think that I'm saying the Holy Spirit is an angel. The Holy Spirit expresses Himself through seven different manifestations of His person—each appears to function as a messenger, not necessarily an angelic being. The seven Spirits of God are a part of the Holy Spirit and the Trinity, so they are not angelic beings. The messengers are not part of the Trinity; they are messengers on behalf of the seven Spirits.

EACH SPIRIT HAS A FUNCTION

The personality of each Spirit is in its function. The Spirit of knowledge is the Holy Spirit, but there's a personality of this Spirit that we don't find in the Spirit of the fear of the Lord, but it's still the Holy Spirit. For instance, in the Book of Proverbs, wisdom is portrayed as "she"—that's a personality. She is lifting up her voice (see Prov. 1:20). God even said that wisdom was with Him when He formed the earth. You may want to re-read these last few paragraphs again just to make sure that you understand this concept. We're done with the theology for a while, so you can relax now.

I've had four of the seven Spirits visit me in the form of angels. Several years ago in Kelowna, British Columbia, the Spirit of revelation came to me looking like an angel. He held a lantern in his hand and He guided me into a room of hidden treasures and revelation. He said, "Come with Me into the deep things of God."

Wisdom visited me, and she also had the form of an angel. Now when you think about the Spirit of wisdom or the Spirit of revelation, do you think about a person? "Hi, I'm the Spirit of wisdom!" "Hi, I'm the Spirit of revelation." They can come personified. I also saw the angel representing the Spirits of counsel and might. The Spirit of the fear of the Lord also visited me, but this Spirit didn't appear as an angel.

The Bible says the Holy Spirit doesn't have form. The Father does, Jesus does, but not the Holy Spirit—He is without form. However, could it not be that He reveals aspects of His nature by manifesting in the forms of angels or messengers?

I heard about an encounter that one young man had with the seven Spirits of God. He was taken up into a classroom as a pupil, and each one of the Spirits was personified as a schoolteacher with a personality and a message. There was a chalkboard in the back where each of the seven Spirits would teach and then write His message. If you want an increase of the sevenfold Spirit of God in your life, you have to go through their schools where you will grow in the Lord, in wisdom, revelation, counsel, might, knowledge, and the fear of the Lord.

LAMPSTANDS AND EYES

Now that you're familiar with the seven Spirits of God, you'll begin to notice many Scriptures in God's Word that refer to them. Sometimes the seven Spirits of God are represented by symbols, or possibly, by seven angelic forms.

Lampstands are one depiction of the seven Spirits of God: "And from the throne proceeded lightnings, thunderings, and voices. Seven lamps of fire were burning before the throne, which are the seven Spirits of God" (Rev. 4:5). The lampstands burn before the throne in Heaven; the throne is the presence and glory of God. The menorah (lampstand) in Moses' tabernacle is a prophetic representation of the seven Spirits. It burned before the Ark of the Covenant, which also represented the glory and presence of God.

GOD'S GOT HIS EYE ON YOU!

Eyes are another symbol: "And I looked, and behold, in the midst of the throne and of the four living creatures, and in the midst of the elders, stood a Lamb as though it had been slain, having seven horns and seven eyes, which are the seven Spirits of God sent out into all the earth" (Rev. 5:6).

The four living creatures before the throne have eyes under their wings: "The four living creatures, each having six wings, were full of eyes around and within…" (Rev. 4:8). Almost every reference to the *eyes of God* in the Bible refers to the seven Spirits of God. They represent the all-knowing, all-seeing, omniscient nature of God and His Spirits.

"For the eyes of the Lord run to and fro throughout the whole earth, to show Himself strong on behalf of those whose heart is loyal to Him…" (2 Chron. 16:9). The seven Spirits of God look for people to manifest through. Are you available?

Here's a prophecy from Zechariah about Jesus that refers to the seven Spirits of God: "Hear, O Joshua, the high priest, you and your companions who sit before you, for they are a wondrous sign; for behold, I am bringing forth My servant the Branch. For behold, the stone that I have laid before Joshua: upon the stone are seven eyes…" (Zech. 3:8-9).

Jesus is also referred to as the *Branch* in Isaiah 11:1: "There shall come forth a Rod from the stem of Jesse, and a Branch shall grow out of his roots." So upon Jesus are seven eyes, and the seven eyes are the seven Spirits of God.

Zechariah is trying to explain to us that it's not by might or power, but by the Spirit. Again, Scripture references the seven in Zechariah, this time in chapter 4:10: "For who has despised the day of small things? For these seven rejoice to see the plumb line in the hand of Zerubbabel…." *These seven* are the eyes of the Lord that run *to and fro* throughout the whole earth.

Do you know how God leads us? He says, "I will instruct you and teach you in the way you should go; I will guide you with My eye" (Ps. 32:8). What does that tell you? God has His eye on us. When God's eye is on us, we see things the way He sees them, and we receive counsel and direction. When I look through His eye, not only do I see two feet in front of me, but also I see the next season, the next ten years of my life. I see over the mountains and through the hills. He's the all-seeing, all-knowing One. Have you ever looked through His eyes and viewed your life from His perspective? God looks at you and then He looks at where He wants you to go—in an instant, you're in His vision and His eyes begin to lead you.

However, many of us stumble around in darkness; we can't see two feet ahead of us, and we can't get a sense of who we are and where we are going. God's eyes will lead us.

So that's a little background on lampstands and eyes representing the seven Spirits of God. Let me highlight this again: The seven Spirits of God are different manifestations of the Holy Spirit that can and may appear as angelic messengers. The lampstands and eyes in Scripture symbolize the seven Spirits of God. That's not so confusing is it? Now let's talk about mantles of anointing that God wants to place on our lives.

THE ABIDING ANOINTING

There is a difference between the nine *gifts* of the Spirit in First Corinthians 12:7-10 (word of wisdom, word of knowledge, faith, gifts of healings, working of miracles, prophecy, discerning of spirits, different kinds of tongues, interpretation of tongues); and the seven *mantles* of the Spirit in Isaiah 11 (Spirit of the Lord, Spirits of wisdom, of understanding, of counsel, of might, of knowledge, and of fear of the Lord). These mantles are the seven Spirits of God that rest on Jesus.

In His ministry, Jesus didn't operate in the word of wisdom, one of the *gifts* of the Spirit; He operated in the *Spirit of wisdom*. He didn't operate in the *gift* of healing. The Spirit of the Lord anointed Him with the Holy Ghost and power and it remained *on* Him. This was a mantle that didn't lift. The Spirit distributes the gifts of the Spirit evenly to each one, as He wills. What does that imply? They come and go. The seven Spirits didn't come and go on Jesus. They were always there abiding with Him.

MORE THAN A WORD OF KNOWLEDGE

The Spirit of wisdom is a lot different than a word of wisdom. The Spirit of wisdom is a constant river of wisdom and revelation as opposed to one word. Picture all of God's wisdom represented as an endless ocean of marbles. If He gives you one, that's a word of wisdom, but the Spirit of wisdom is the ever-increasing flowing river of wisdom from the One who possesses all wisdom. That's what rested on Jesus.

Do you remember the story of Nathaniel and the fig tree? Imagine Nathaniel's delight when he finally realized just how open Heaven was to him—this when Jesus proved it to him by giving him a word of knowledge about where he'd been earlier. In effect, He said, "Yo, Bro! Remember when you thought you were alone the other morning? I saw you studying and heard you praying under the fig tree over back there yonder." It amazed Nathaniel that Jesus knew, and Nathaniel's faith took a huge leap:

Nathaniel answered and said to Him, "Rabbi, You are the Son of God! You are the King of Israel!" Jesus answered and said to him, "Because I said to you, 'I saw you under the fig tree,' do you believe? You will see greater things than these." And He said to

242

him, "Most assuredly, I say to you, hereafter you shall see heaven open, and the angels of God ascending and descending upon the Son of Man" (John 1:49-51).

Jesus basically said: "This isn't about a word of knowledge. You will see Heaven open and the angels of God ascending and descending upon Me. I am not just getting a gift of the Spirit; I am an open Heaven. I am a portal; Heaven is ascending and descending to Me. Twenty-four hours a day I am a gate of Heaven with wisdom and revelation. I am the open Heaven of Genesis 28:12-16! I am Jacob's Ladder set up on the earth to Heaven. There is free access between Heaven and earth with Me. That is who I am."

The Spirit of God dwells in us, but He also comes on us from time to time. There is a day coming when we are going to operate in these mantles. The Spirit of the Lord will rest upon us, and abide in us, and it won't be fleeting or temporary. Instead of, "Wow, I had one word of knowledge this week," it's going to be a flowing river of wisdom in every circumstance. It's gonna be there all of the time! The Spirit of the Lord shall rest, remain, and abide on you:

The Lord God has given Me the tongue of the learned, that I should know how to speak a word in season to him who is weary. He awakens Me morning by morning, He awakens My ear to hear as the learned (Isaiah 50:4).

EXPECT REVELATION ALL THE TIME

I expect revelation every morning and every night. I don't know why we believe that we can't hear from the Lord each day. Look again at this verse: "…He awakens Me morning by morning, He awakens My ear to hear…" (Isa. 50:4). I expect to hear from the Lord daily.

Even as we sleep, the Lord teaches us: "I will bless the Lord who has given me counsel; my heart also instructs me in the night seasons" (Ps. 16:7)—and when we awaken, wisdom is there (the word for *heart* is also *mind*). Doesn't that rock? I mean, there we are in la-la land, fast asleep, snoring loud enough to set off a tsunami, and all the while our mind instructs us, thanks to the Spirit of wisdom. The best part of waking up is not Folgers coffee in our cups, but the Spirit of wisdom in our hearts, for wisdom is there when we awaken too.

So let's review this once more. We don't want merely to function in the word of wisdom, but rather in the Spirit of wisdom. The Spirit of wisdom is an ever-increasing, abiding river of wisdom that we can dive right into and pull out thoughts from. Need a towel?

OPERATING IN THE ANOINTING

When the Spirit rests on our lives, we're operating in the anointing of First Corinthians 2:9-16. God has prepared some things that eye has not seen. They are the hidden mysteries of God:

> …*"Eye has not seen, nor ear heard, nor have entered into the heart of man the things which God has prepared for those who love Him." But God has revealed them to us through His Spirit. For the Spirit searches all things, yes, the deep things of God. For what man knows the things of a man except the spirit of the man which is in him? Even so no one knows the things of God except the Spirit of God. Now we have received,*

not the spirit of the world, but the Spirit who is from God,
that we might know the things that have been freely given to
us by God. These things we also speak, not in words which
man's wisdom teaches but which the Holy Spirit teaches,
comparing spiritual things with spiritual. But the natural
man does not receive the things of the Spirit of God, for they
are foolishness to him; nor can he know them, because they
are spiritually discerned. But he who is spiritual judges all
things, yet he himself is rightly judged by no one. For "who
has known the mind of the Lord that he may instruct Him?"
But we have the mind of Christ.

God wants to reveal the deep things by His Spirit. No one knows the deep things of God but His Spirit, which is in Him. We have received this Spirit! We have the ability continually to be in the mind of Christ. Isn't this revelation awesome? This is the realm of ministry God wants to open to believers today.

While the gifts of the Spirit are wonderful, the flowing river of the Lord's abiding presence is even more so, and that's what we should desire and seek with all of our hearts. Why settle for one word, one revelation, one pearl of wisdom, when God offers you an endless ocean of them?

THE SEVEN SPIRITS: WHO ARE THEY?

Before I describe each Spirit, I want to point out that certain ones partner together in ministry. "The Spirit of the Lord shall rest upon Him, the Spirit of wisdom and understanding, the Spirit of counsel and might, the Spirit of knowledge and of the fear of the Lord" (Isa. 11:2). Notice the three partnerships. I'll discuss this idea in more detail later in the chapter; however, let's first examine each of the Spirits one by one.

1. The Spirit of the Lord

This first one is quick and simple: The Spirit of the Lord is the Holy Ghost.

> *Behold! My Servant whom I uphold, My Elect One in whom My soul delights! I have put My Spirit upon Him…* (Isaiah 42:1).

> *The Spirit of the Lord God is upon Me…* (Isaiah 61:1).

John preached:

> *How God anointed Jesus of Nazareth with the Holy Spirit and with power, who went about doing good and healing all who were oppressed by the devil, for God was with Him* (Acts 10:38).

The Spirit of the Lord enables you to do things that you can't or are unable to do in your flesh, such as when you minister healing or deliverance to someone. Do you remember what a great orator Moses was, even though he stuttered?

What the Spirit of the Lord Demands

Earlier I talked about the seven Spirits as being teachers, each of whom requires something of the students. What does the Spirit of the Lord demand? Yieldedness. In effect, He says, "I want you to be yielded. I want you to surrender. I want you to be an empty vessel. I want you to be like the apostle Paul, 'I die daily to my own way, to my own will, to my own self, to my own flesh.'"

2. The Spirit of Wisdom

Wisdom gives us counsel in every situation to know what to do, when to do it, and how to do it. Wisdom teaches us how to rightly apply revelation. Without wisdom, revelation is no good. The Spirit of wisdom gives us a wise and discerning heart.

When Jesus was 12 years old and teaching in the synagogues, everyone marveled at what He said (see Luke 4:22). That was the Spirit of wisdom. He can even give us a language, or the right words to help us communicate.

Remember that the Spirit of wisdom is the abiding anointing, not a momentary gift: "Now Joshua the son of Nun was full of the spirit of wisdom, for Moses had laid his hands on him; so the children of Israel heeded him, and did as the Lord had commanded Moses" (Deut. 34:9). Joshua was able to receive the Spirit of wisdom by having Moses lay hands on him. He went on to lead the children of Israel into the Promised Land.

The Benefits of Wisdom

Solomon had his first of two visitations of the Lord in Second Chronicles 1:7,10-12:

> On that night God appeared to Solomon, and said to him, "Ask! What shall I give you?"… "Now give me wisdom and knowledge, that I may go out and come in before this people; for who can judge this great people of Yours?" Then God said to Solomon: "Because this was in your heart, and you have not asked riches or wealth or honor or the life of your enemies, nor have you asked long life—but

have asked wisdom and knowledge for yourself, that you may judge My people over whom I have made you king—wisdom and knowledge are granted to you; and I will give you riches and wealth and honor, such as none of the kings have had who were before you, nor shall any after you have the like."

Wisdom Brings Wealth and Honor

Solomon said he needed wisdom to rule well. God was pleased with his request. He not only granted wisdom and knowledge to this King but also riches, wealth, and honor.

Wisdom Instructs

"To know wisdom and instruction, to perceive the words of understanding, to receive the instruction of wisdom" (Prov. 1:2-3a). Wisdom teaches us how to apply biblical knowledge and truths to our circumstances. We know what the Bible instructs, but we need to know what to do, when to do it, and how to do it so we can apply its truths to *our* lives.

Wisdom Pours Out Her Spirit

Wisdom cries aloud in the street; in the markets she raises her voice; on the top of the walls she cries out; at the entrance of the city gates she speaks: "How long, O simple ones, will you love being simple? How long will scoffers delight in their scoffing and fools hate knowledge? Give heed to my reproof; behold, I will pour out my thoughts to you; I will make my words known to you" (Proverbs 1:20-23, RSV).

What an invitation wisdom has extended to us! She (personified as a female messenger) says she is looking for *simple ones* on whom to pour out her thoughts. Ask God to pour out the Spirit of wisdom on you. Apostle Paul prayed for this same outpouring on his spiritual children (see Eph. 1:17). That's a great prayer to pray every day for yourself and your family.

Wisdom Protects

Say what? How can wisdom protect us? See if you can figure that out in the following verses:

> *Whoever listens to me will dwell safely, and will be secure, without fear of evil* (Proverbs 1:33).

> *When wisdom enters your heart, and knowledge is pleasant to your soul, discretion will preserve you; understanding will keep you, to deliver you from the way of evil, from the man who speaks perverse things* (Proverbs 2:10-12).

What will wisdom do? She will deliver you from the way of the evil. Wisdom protects those who love and pursue her. What a blessing!

Wisdom Brings Long Life

> *For her proceeds are better than the profits of silver, and her gain than fine gold. She is more precious than rubies, and all the things you may desire cannot compare with her. Length of days is in her right hand...* (Proverbs 3:14-16).

> *Exalt her, and she will promote you; she will bring you honor, when you embrace her. She will place on your head an ornament of grace; a crown of glory she will deliver to you. Hear, my*

son, and receive my sayings, and the years of your life will be many (Proverbs 4:8-10).

Nothing you desire can compare with her. She even brings long life. Now, if all these benefits weren't enough, let me conclude this section with a few more verses for you to ponder. Meditate on what these verses promise. If someone could bottle wisdom and sell her, people would kill for these benefits:

> *... In her left hand [there is] riches and honor. Her ways are the ways of pleasantness, and all her paths are peace. She is a tree of life to those who take hold of her, and happy are all who retain her. The Lord by wisdom founded the earth; by understanding He established the heavens* (Proverbs 3:16-19).

> *Listen, for I will speak of excellent things, and from the opening of my lips will come right things ... by me kings reign, and rulers decree justice* (Proverbs 8:6,15).

> *Get wisdom! Get understanding! Do not forget, nor turn away from the words of my mouth* (Proverbs 4:5).

We'll discuss the demands of the Spirit of wisdom a little later in this chapter. Now, let's learn how to receive more divine revelation in our lives.

3. *The Spirit of Revelation (Understanding)*

Revelation means to bring light and unveil hidden things, to take the cover off or to disclose. A disclosure of what? The answer may surprise you—a disclosure of the Lord's secrets. These hidden treasures become known to you. You will receive insight into how God works and how the anointing works. The Spirit of revelation takes the veil off and the Bible verses jump off the page. You'll think, *I've read this chapter a dozen times before and I've never seen that; where did that come from?*

Two Types of Revelation

When somebody says "the Spirit of revelation," you probably think of understanding the Bible, but let's examine two other kinds of revelation: revelation that comes by prophetic experiences—dreams, visions, or encounters—and divine revelation.

1. Prophetic Revelation

But God came to Abimelech in a dream by night… (Genesis 20:3).

For God may speak in one way, or in another, yet man does not perceive it. In a dream, in a vision of the night, when deep sleep falls upon men, while slumbering on their beds, then He opens the ears of men, and seals their instruction (Job 33:14-16).

Today, just as in Scripture, these prophetic experiences happen in a variety of ways. You may be caught up in a place, have a conversation with the Lord, or an angel may explain something to you. Perhaps you're translated somewhere, or learn from God through a dream or vision. The Bible is full of such experiences!

2. Divine Revelation

Divine revelation is a second way to gain revelation. It's a piece of knowledge imparted to your spirit about something that you didn't know before. You didn't get it by listening to a speaker. You didn't get it because you had a dream, a vision, or an angelic visitation. When somebody asks how you got it, you can't explain it, you just say, "by revelation."

Have you ever awakened and had a three-hour sermon on a subject that you had never preached and you knew all the Greek words? That is the Spirit of revelation. It is coming on the Church today.

A dyslexic child came to my meeting. He'd never been able to read. I rebuked the deaf and dumb spirit and he was healed. He went home that night, picked up a book, and read the whole thing to his dad. When divine revelation hits, you gain wisdom beyond your years.

Paul's Divine Revelation

Paul didn't get discipled by Jesus or the apostles. He didn't even go to Bible school after he got saved. He received his revelation in the desert: "But I make known to you, brethren, that the gospel which was preached by me is not according to man. For I neither received it from man, nor was I taught it, but it came through the revelation of Jesus Christ" (Gal. 1:11-12).

I want you to see it again. Look at Ephesians 3:3-4: "…how that by revelation He made known to me the mystery…when you read, you may understand my knowledge in the mystery of Christ."

Paul wrote more books in the New Testament than anyone else did and he said (paraphrased), "What I have I received by the Spirit of revelation—it just came to me by a divine impartation of the Holy Ghost." You can't really know Jesus without the Spirit of wisdom and revelation.

Revelation Partnered With Wisdom

Wisdom helps you apply what revelation shows you, so you can teach it to others or apply it yourself. Without wisdom, you won't know what to do with the divine revelation. Revelation really is composed of four parts: interpretation, delivery, timing, and application. When you receive revelation, you need insight in each of these four areas. That is what the Spirit of wisdom does.

Now here's what the Spirits of wisdom and revelation do together:

> [I pray] *that the God of our Lord Jesus Christ, the Father of glory, may give to you the spirit of wisdom and revelation in the knowledge of Him, the eyes of your understanding being enlightened; that you may know what is the hope of His calling, what are the riches of the glory of His inheritance in the saints, and what is the exceeding greatness of His power toward us who believe, according to the working of His mighty power* (Ephesians 1:17-19).

God's provision comes through the Spirits of wisdom and revelation. His provision is according to *His* riches in glory. The Spirit of wisdom and revelation will bring you knowledge of how to get supernatural provision, because He will supply all your needs according to His riches in glory. You can't know that without the Spirit of wisdom and revelation—nor can you know who you are in Him and the glorious inheritance that is yours.

You could spend months studying these heavenly blessings that the Spirit of wisdom and revelation bring into our lives.

What Wisdom Demands

The first few chapters of Proverbs give us an understanding of the value of wisdom. But guess what wisdom demands in exchange?

> *Now therefore, listen to me, my children, for blessed are those who keep my ways. Hear instruction and be wise, and do not disdain*

it. Blessed is the man who listens to me, watching daily at my gates, waiting at the posts of my doors (Proverbs 8:32-34).

She is saying, "I love those who love Me and those who seek Me diligently will find Me. I want you to seek Me. I want you to lift up your voice and cry out for understanding and for discernment." She says this in every situation and circumstance that you seek Her, when you cry out, "Spirit of wisdom come help me." Chase after wisdom—when you catch Her you will experience incredible rewards. Don't do anything without Her; wait for Her instructions.

Here are some Scriptures to study about the benefits of wisdom: Proverbs 2:10-13; 3:13-18; 3:21-24; 4:5-9; 7:4-5; and 24:3-6.

What Revelation Demands

We are quick to pray, "God, I want visions and revelations," but the Spirit of revelation demands that you go through His school first. He is a tough teacher. He goes to the Father and essentially says: "They want revelation so I am going to have to bring humility and brokenness before I can give more. I want yieldedness and I want them to trust Me."

Let's look at Paul's life to see what he endured to partner with the Spirit of revelation:

And lest I should be exalted above measure by the abundance of the revelations, a thorn in the flesh was given to me, a messenger of satan to buffet me, lest I be exalted above measure (2 Corinthians 12:7).

Because of the abundance of revelation, Paul could have easily become proud, so God gave him a thorn in the flesh (a messenger from

254

satan, not a disease). The messenger's assignment was to bring blow after blow, pressure, and death to self, for the purpose of humility and brokenness. Here are some of Paul's external pressures: trials, shipwreck, beatings, prison, stoning(s), criticism, judgments, and hardships.

Paul must have successfully completed Revelation's school because we can see his humility in this verse: "I know a man in Christ who fourteen years ago…was caught up to the third heaven" (2 Cor. 12:2). Paul is talking about himself but he didn't even say, "I was caught up." He didn't want people to think of him more highly than they ought. The more humble you can be, the more God can trust you with revelation: "Therefore I take pleasure in infirmities, in reproaches, in needs, in persecutions, in distresses, for Christ's sake. For when I am weak, then I am strong" (2 Cor. 12:10).

Revelation demands character, intimacy, humility, brokenness, and death to self. Paul learned these lessons well, completed his school, and went on to be a history maker.

4. The Spirit of Counsel

The Spirit of counsel is simply taking God's advice and listening for His plan of action. When Jesus went up on the mountain of transfiguration, He took James, Peter, and John. I am sure all the other guys said, "I want to go. I'm an intern. Don't forget me." But Jesus had the counsel of God, and heeded God's counsel.

In the realm of healing and miracles, God does everything according to His plan and strategy. The Lord told Joshua (paraphrased), "Walk around Jericho for six days. The priests will carry trumpets in front of the Ark. On the seventh day, march around seven times and the priests will make a loud blast and the people will shout and then the walls will come down" (see Josh. 6:3-5). Joshua must have been thinking, *Why can't the walls come down after we just do it once?*

When Jesus healed the blind men, He used different methods. He spat on one man, rubbed mud into another's eyes, and spoke healing to the other. It was the same disease, so why the varied approaches? I'll bet that second guy was really surprised to find mud in his eyes!

We can't help heal someone who is blind without the counsel of God. Every case is different. If we pray for someone and they receive healing, but another person with the same condition doesn't receive healing after prayer, it may be because we failed to listen for counsel the second time. Perhaps we used the model that worked for the first healing and didn't consider that God may prefer to heal the next person in another way. God may choose a different healing method in each circumstance. If you're praying and it's not happening, stop and ask the Lord for counsel:

> *In Him also we have obtained an inheritance, being predestined according to the purpose of Him who works all things according to the counsel of His will* (Ephesians 1:11).

The Pattern of Heaven

How important is the pattern of Heaven? In every meeting, God has a strategy to release power and healing. It is critical that we wait for the counsel of God, because if we are even an inch off, the Kingdom won't come. I recall one meeting when the Holy Spirit said, "Todd, I want to heal that man who has cancer, and I'm going to give you the method. Tell him to stand up and move over two feet." I replied, "God, what does it matter if he stands there or moves over two feet?" and the Lord said, "Because that is where the angel is."

I've actually had to reposition the pulpit because that was the way that I saw it in Heaven before I got to the meeting. I call these "healing scenes," and they come from the Spirit of counsel.

Think of the story of Jesus' first miracle—changing water into wine. I can imagine Mary glancing at Jesus and giving Him a smile and a wink before telling the servants: "Whatever He says to you, do it" (John 2:5). She understood.

Jesus did all His miracles in the Spirit of counsel. He was on the mountain all night in prayer and the Spirit of counsel said, "Go to the pool of Bethesda and heal the crippled man who has been there for 38 years" (see John 5:2-8). How could Jesus walk away from so many other sick people? John 5:19-20 is the key:

> ...the Son can do nothing of Himself, but what He sees the Father do; for whatever He does, the Son also does in like manner. For the Father loves the Son, and shows Him all things that He Himself does....

The Father loves His sons and daughters in the Church today. He wants to show you all of the things that He Himself does. It may require you to be all night on the mountain or to withdraw into the wilderness and pray in solitude in a place of waiting.

Counsel Partnered With Might

I was in my hotel room in Kansas City, and in my mind, I saw myself on my hands and knees bowing before Jesus. In this vision, He placed a purple-red healing mantle over my shoulders. Then the Lord told me to act out the vision, and when I did so, Heaven unlocked and opened. I went from having a vision in my mind to acting it out. When I synchronized Heaven and earth, it opened the way for a visitation.

Immediately, an angel descended and stood over me. One of his legs bore the word "counsel," and the other was inscribed with the word "might." He carried a sword of power and authority. The angel said, "Take this sword." It had Hebrews 4:12 written on the blade:

> For the word of God is living and powerful, and sharper than any two-edged sword, piercing even to the division of soul and spirit, and of joints and marrow, and is a discerner of the thoughts and intents of the heart. And there is no creature hidden from His sight, but all things are naked and open to the eyes of Him to whom we must give account (Hebrews 4:12-14).

The angel said that this was the anointing he was releasing today, and that I should ask Paul Keith Davis, the prophet and teacher, what it meant. Paul Keith told me that the anointing of counsel and might rested consistently on the life of William Branham. He was able to discern thoughts, secrets of the heart, and names and addresses. William Branham called it "pushing back the curtain." He started out with partial knowledge, and then the Spirit of counsel revealed the hidden things to him. Then God's power was released. Jesus operated in this. He had the living Word and He knew people's thoughts.

I went to church that night in Kansas City and found out that four others had experienced the same visitation at the same time, including Jill Austin who had her visitation at the meeting. God said, "Tell the church I'm about ready to trust them with Hebrews 4:12, the living Word."

We get pieces, glimpses, a word of knowledge here and there, but an anointing is coming that pulls the curtain back to reveal every detail of the secret things. The Lord said He was bringing this fullness of His heart and mind to the Church. Imagine the day when the prophets come into this place where all the fullness of God and the hidden things are opened up to them. (We'll discuss the demands of the Spirit of counsel a little later in this chapter.)

5. *The Spirit of Might (Signs and Wonders)*

When the Spirit of might comes on me, I can go for weeks on the run, ministering and preaching. When it lifts, I'm dead on my feet! The Spirit of might brings the mighty acts of power, strength, miracles, signs, and wonders. The Spirit of might takes us through the hardest school of all. You have to go through discipline, fasting, prayer, character improvements, and death to self. That's the price that you have to pay before you can have God's power. It's costly.

The Mighty Acts of God

These mighty acts went past physical healings and miracles to signs in the heavens above and to wonders in the earth beneath.

Elijah

I love the story in First Kings 18:20-40 where Elijah confronts the 450 prophets of baal and the whole nation turns to God. That was revival. Elijah waited for God's counsel. Before he even got to Mount Carmel, he asked, "How, how, how, how?" God told him to drench the sacrifice. Elijah said, "I am Your servant, and I have done all these things at Your word" (1 Kings 18:36). Later the Spirit of might came on him and he outran the chariots.

Moses

> *Then the Lord spoke to Moses and Aaron, saying, "When Pharaoh speaks to you, saying, 'Show a miracle for yourselves,' then you shall say to Aaron, 'Take your rod and cast it before Pharaoh,' and let it become a serpent"* (Exodus 7:8-9).

God gave Moses the counsel he needed before his meeting with Pharaoh. When the world demands a miracle, we need God to tell us what we are to say and do.

Every day I take my journal and lie in the Lord's presence. I say, "God, tell me how I can open the Red Sea. Tell me how I am going to heal blind eyes." Waiting for the counsel of Heaven brings the Spirit of might. Here are a few examples of how the counsel of God has manifested in my own life and resulted in a mighty demonstration of God's power.

The Miraculous in Mexico

I was in Mexico, and the counsel of God said, "I will heal every deaf person in this service. The key to releasing the healing anointing is for you to tell the people before you pray that *every* deaf person will be healed." I could have kept it safe and said, "There is an anointing here for the deaf." I probably would have seen a few healed, but God said the Kingdom wasn't going to come unless I told the people that every deaf person was going to be healed before it happened. Twelve people who had arrived deaf that evening all left hearing!

Tumors Dissolve in Malawi

I was in Malawi for the first time. People came out and their attitude was, *We know Bonnke, but who is this white guy from Canada?* They came skeptical. I usually like to first build a little relationship with the audience and let the people get to know me. However, before I even got up to introduce myself, God said to me: "Just call everyone who has a visible tumor on his or her body. We want the tumors that even a skeptic can't deny." It was like, "Hi, I'm Todd Bentley from Fresh Fire Ministries. If you have a visible tumor come on down!" We prayed and the Holy Spirit moved, and instantly seven people had their tumors disappear.

Four Kinds of Power

I am going to share the four different New Testament Greek words for God's power. The Bible says in Ephesians 6:10: "Finally, my brethren, be strong in the Lord and in the power of His might."

1. Dunamis Power

But you shall receive power [dunamis] *when the Holy Spirit has come upon you; and you shall be witnesses to Me in Jerusalem, and in all Judea and Samaria, and to the end of the earth* (Acts 1:8).

Dunamis power is the Holy Ghost coming in Acts 1:8, "And you shall receive power…." Dunamis power is healing power, dynamo, dynamite, explosive power. How are you going to receive it? Jesus said to "wait for the Promise of the Father…" (Acts 1:4b). Wait until you have an encounter. The Spirit of might demands these things.

2. Ischus Power

Therefore confess your sins to one another, and pray for one another, that you may be healed. The prayer of a righteous man has great power [ischus] *in its effects* (James 5:16 RSV).

Do you know what *ischus* means? It means, "energizing power."
Ischus power will give you dunamis because the Spirit energizes the faith
that you already have. Ischus is the prayer of faith that will save the sick.
See, dunamis power is like a battery in your inner man. To charge the
dunamis power you need the ischus power, which is like the current that
charges the battery.

3. *Kratos Power*

> *So the word of the Lord grew mightily* [with kratos power]
> *and prevailed* (Acts 19:20).

Kratos power is a completely different dimension of God's power.
Kratos takes what you do, multiplies it, and makes it prevail. It's like a
nuclear explosion. It's God's Kingdom and dominion coming upon an
entire city. Acts 19:20 is kratos power.

The kratos of God comes through meditating on Scripture and
the authority and the proclamation of the spoken word. Kratos power
is the manifestation of the sovereign rule and dominion of God. It's
literally the manifested majesty and splendor of God, the works of
God through the will of God, which comes through the Word of God.
It means the rule of the King. It speaks of God's government geographically.

4. *Exousia*

> *And when He had called His twelve disciples to Him, He gave*
> *them power* [exousia] *over unclean spirits, to cast them out,*
> *and to heal all kinds of sickness and all kinds of disease*
> (Matthew 10:1).

Exousia is delegated authority. It is stepping out in faith because of what God said (paraphrased), "Believe you are who I said you are and you can do what I said you can do. Do it because it is written in the Word." Do it regardless of what you see or feel. It is healing that comes by the faith principle. It's not an anointing; it's an authority. When you speak the Word, there's authority. Smith Wigglesworth, a well-known faith healer during the early part of the 20th century, operated in this kind of authority—exousia power.

When you want to see an increase of might, the risks increase. When I was in Africa I asked, "God, the anointing is here; people are being healed, but why aren't the cripples being healed?" He said, "I want you to take that cripple's leg and bang it up and down on the platform like a baseball bat." So, I grabbed his leg and, in front of 50,000 people, I just started going boom, boom, boom, boom, banging it up and down. The man was totally healed! Gloriously healed! And right after that one of my team members prayed for another cripple and banged *his* legs and he was also healed. Please notice that I was operating under the Spirit of counsel in order to activate the Spirit of might.

In Malawi, one of the team members received the counsel of God to pray for the blind under a tree. Then members of the team began announcing in a village, "There are going to be some white guys under the tree. Bring anyone who is blind." People gathered under the tree, they prayed for them, and 42 blind were healed. These were ordinary believers on a mission trip doing the works of Jesus.

Spirit of Might Partnered With Counsel

As I mentioned earlier, the Spirit of counsel and the Spirit of might are partners. Might is the strength of God, the power of God, and the mighty acts of God. Many of us are going after God's power without

God's counsel. You need counsel to guide you into might. You will notice that it is the Spirit of counsel *and* might. Isaiah 9:6 says, "…His name will be called Wonderful, Counselor, Mighty God…." You see the connection again? His mighty acts are connected with His counsel.

The word *counsel* means "advice" and "plan" or "to guide." God's counsel is simply God's advice—the plans and the methods of God. Counsel guides you into the manifestation of might. Might is simply acts of power and strength from the Holy Spirit. The Spirit of counsel tells us how to work miracles. He gives us advice and methods and guides us into every circumstance and in every situation. Counsel comes before acts of power. If we don't have the Spirit's counsel, we risk operating on assumption or hope.

Job remembered the anointing upon his life and referred to "God's counsel":

> *Job further continued his discourse, and said: "Oh, that I were as in months past, as in the days when God watched over me; when His lamp shone upon my head, and when by His light I walked through darkness; just as I was in the days of my prime, when the friendly counsel of God was over my tent; when the Almighty was yet with me, when my children were around me…"* (Job 29:1-5).

Do you know what "the friendly counsel of God" means? It means the inward secret of the Lord. It means that Heaven comes and lets you in on secrets. It's the same as when Moses spoke to God face-to-face as a friend speaks to a friend.

Can you imagine waking up and the Spirit of counsel is there, "Hello.

How would you like Me to lead you today?" You're a friend of God, and friends share secrets: "No longer do I call you servants, for a servant does not know what his master is doing; but I have called you friends, for all things that I heard from My Father I have made known to you" (John 15:15). I'm talking about revelation being right there waiting for you. Don't settle for the *gift* of counsel, get the abiding anointing which comes through friendship and intimacy with the Lord.

What the Spirit of Counsel Demands

The Spirit of counsel demands friendship with you before He gives access to the secrets of the Lord. Counsel demands listening prayer, waiting, and obedience. People want the power of God, but the works of God are connected to waiting. Wait for God's counsel.

One thing about the counsel of God is that you need to obey if you want more. Counsel will leave you when you disobey:

> *But My people would not heed My voice, and Israel would have none of Me. So I gave them over to their own stubborn heart, to walk in their own counsels. Oh, that My people would listen to Me, that Israel would walk in My ways! I would soon subdue their enemies, and turn My hand against their adversaries. The haters of the Lord would pretend submission to Him, but their fate would endure forever. He would have fed them also with the finest of wheat; and with honey from the rock I would have satisfied you* (Psalm 81:11-16).

Why should God give you another prophetic word if you haven't done anything with the first one? Counsel demands obedience. You need to obey the counsels, the ideas, and the pictures of Heaven that come.

What God gives us on the earth is a shadow of Heaven above. It's important that when God speaks, we follow exactly. If we aren't operating in the Spirit of counsel, we can get into presumption. What if Naaman had only dipped six times in the river Jordan (see 2 Kings 5:14)? He would have gone home with leprosy. Remember when David was instructed to move the Ark of the Covenant? Instead of carrying it on poles as God had instructed, they opted to move the Ark on a cart. Uzza died (see 1 Chron. 13:7-10).

Sometimes I wait for hours for counsel. "Father, what do You want to do tonight and how do You want to do it?" It may be the same disease God healed last night, but a different method tonight. If we don't get the counsel of Heaven, we can pray for those with cancer but they won't be healed. God wants them healed, but we need to get fresh advice from Him.

I want you to begin to pray right now and invite the Spirit of counsel. And I want you to repent for not taking the time to position yourself like Samuel to wait. Practice waiting for the Spirit of counsel; get the plans and advice and follow it through, and it will lead you to might and victory. Before you preach and teach, spend 30 minutes listening for counsel.

What the Spirit of Might Demands

The Spirit of might demands fasting, discipline, and the energizing power that comes by prayer. The Spirit of might demands meditation in the Word as well as tarrying and waiting in your Jerusalem until you have an encounter with the Holy Spirit and His power. It demands authority. It demands the power that comes through the inerrant, infallible Word. It demands the power that comes by ischus. It demands the energizing power that comes by prayer as you charge the battery of dunamis—the battery of explosive power within your spirit, which becomes a nuclear blast.

6. *The Spirit of Knowledge*

The Spirit of knowledge allows us to see God as He really is. It also means, "to be intimately acquainted with." You don't become intimately acquainted through knowledge of Church history, or by being a biblical scholar who preaches eloquently; that's not what the Spirit of knowledge is. Look at First John 2:20: "You have an anointing from the Holy One, and you know all things." This is the knowing in the inner man that comes from the Spirit within you. The Spirit of knowledge brings us into knowledge of Him through an encounter. It's divine knowledge, a supernatural knowing as the Lord teaches you.

The Spirit of knowledge can also anoint you to bring people into the experience of God rather than just the head knowledge of God. People will actually come into encounters when you teach.

There will come a time when your young children will come to you with revelation and you'll ask, "Where did you get that? You can't even read yet." Isaiah 54:13 says, "All your children shall be taught by the Lord…."

One night, as I was putting my four-year-old daughter, Esther, to bed I said, "Let's say your prayers." I was expecting "God bless Mom and Dad, etc." Without pausing and in one long sentence, she prayed, "God, I thank You now that Your presence will come into Lauralee's room and that the angels would come and we invite and pray for Your presence and angels to come into Elijah's room and let Your presence and angels come into my room and into Mommy and Daddy's room." Then she looked at me and said, "Jesus taught me and I pray the way He tells me." I got goose bumps.

My oldest daughter, Lauralee, who was six, went out for 20 minutes under the power (slain in the Spirit) at one of our conferences. I actually thought she was bored and fell asleep. When she awoke, she told me, "I went to the Easter story. I saw the cross on the hill. I was there." I also heard her speaking in tongues once. Shonnah and I hadn't talked to her about tongues yet, because we wanted her to be old enough to "understand." When I asked, "What are you doing?" she responded, "It's called tongues, Daddy. I started in the bathtub." There is an acceleration coming when the Lord, through the Spirit of knowledge, will teach all of our kids: "No more shall every man teach his neighbor, and every man his brother, saying, 'Know the Lord,' for they all shall know Me, from the least of them to the greatest of them, says the Lord..." (Jer. 31:34).

The Spirit of knowledge goes beyond teaching and preaching. The knowledge of the Lord will come like the waters of the sea cover the earth. That knowledge will come through an experiential presence.

What the Spirit of Knowledge Demands

The Spirit of knowledge demands that you be acquainted with Him in intimacy. Hosea 6:3 says, "Let us pursue the knowledge of the Lord." What does that look like? The ways of God are waiting for you. It's as sure as the morning sun every day. Let us pursue not information, but intimacy with Him, as defined by the Bible. Let's pray: *Father, I ask You to help me meet the requirements to have the seven Spirits of God abide with me. I pray that Your Spirit would come and open and enlighten the eyes of my understanding and take me deeper into encounters with You.*

If the Bible says He's good, then I should be able to lie on the floor and *feel* His goodness. If it tells me that He's loving, then I should be able to feel His love. When the Bible speaks about God as healer, I should be able to experience that during intimate time with Him.

When that happens, the knowledge "God is a healer" becomes a revelation to me.

In fact, I should pursue every spiritual experience, Scripture, dream, vision, and promise that I read about, so it will become, not just what God gave to a prophet of old, but an opportunity to receive revelation as a prophet today.

If the prophets of old were caught up in the heavens, then I believe the Spirit of knowledge wants to take me into those experiences, because it's promised to me in the Bible. If I read about an angelic visitation and I have an experience with an angel, then those Scriptures about angels take on completely new meaning to me.

Psalm 46:10 says, "Be still, and know that I am God...." The word *still* means "alone, idle, quiet." The Spirit of knowledge lives in and manifests in the contemplative lifestyle. You must get away from distractions and focus your mind on Jesus. He will cause you to know Him. It's as if He grabs you and brings you an encounter rather than you just asking, "Where are You? Where are You?" God can visit you in any kind of prayer, but this type God especially honors. I receive more from one hour of soaking than I do reading 50 Bible chapters, because God instructs me in stillness.

7.   *The Spirit of the Fear of the Lord*

If you don't have the Spirit of the fear of the Lord, you can't have any of the other Spirits. This is the only thing that will guard you in a holy fear of God, so that He can trust you with heavy-duty wisdom, revelation, counsel, knowledge, and might. That's why this Spirit is the most important one, because you'd be dangerous without it. "His delight is in the fear of the Lord..." (Isa. 11:3).

The fear of the Lord is to depart from evil. It's the guard that keeps you. When you start moving in might, you need to be kept in fear, so you don't get flippant or compromise your holiness.

The fear of the Lord was the angel that went before Israel's tiny army and caused the larger enemy armies to tremble and kill each other, or to turn and flee. When this angel walks with me, no gang or devil can get to me. There's authority and power when this angel comes. He'll go before you.

The *fear of the Lord* means "dread, awe," or "to revere." My definition would be, "Wow, wow, wow!" over God's majesty, holiness, and strength. Think of this Spirit as an angel called "the Spirit of holiness." He ministers to you and enables you to be holy. You can't produce it yourself. It's grace from Heaven.

There are times when God comes in His presence or Spirit to impart supernatural grace and power so that we can be free of sin. This can only come out of His glory and presence, and fear, dread, or terror sometimes accompanies this presence.

> Now all the people witnessed the thunderings, the lightning flashes, the sound of the trumpet, and the mountain smoking; and when the people saw it, they trembled and stood afar off. …And Moses said to the people, "Do not fear; for God has come to test you, and that His fear may be before you, so that you may not sin" (Exodus 20:18-20).

Years ago, the Spirit of the fear of the Lord visited me. As I relaxed and enjoyed a peaceful and joyous fellowship with the Lord, the atmosphere suddenly changed. *What's happening? I don't know this,*

God. I haven't experienced this manifestation before. I paced the room and started to weep. I felt fear well up—and it turned to terror. I flew down the hallway to my bedroom yelling, "Get away from me. Get away!" I slammed the door behind me. I shook and trembled. I just wanted to crawl under my bed and hide. I felt like one foul thought would do me in.

A few minutes earlier, I had been praising and fellowshipping, and now everything I'd ever said felt like it was bouncing back at me from the ceiling. I couldn't find words to communicate with a God who was so holy. I couldn't say, "God, You are holy," because there would be no meaning in it. I felt that I would be judged and surely die. I didn't understand at that time that He was offering me His grace to make me holy. He wanted to bring a power upon my life so that I wouldn't sin.

Hebrews 4:16 says to approach the throne to obtain mercy and grace in time of need. Mercy is for the sins we've committed (we don't get what we deserve). However, God also gives us grace, which is an enduement of power to help us overcome sin. It even keeps us from the desire to sin. It's as if we're in a protective cocoon. The battle tips in our favor. So, when we sin, we don't just ask for forgiveness but for grace so we won't fall again.

The fear of the Lord brings us into His presence. When we're in God's presence, we don't want to sin. When we're not in His presence, we sin and then feel so guilty we don't want to get back into His presence. It's a Catch 22. Guilt keeps us from the glory pillar—the refiner's fire that can burn that sin tendency out of us. You can't be holy without being in the glory and being in front of the throne of grace. Without holiness, we won't enter in, and it's by entering in that we receive the enduement of power.

What the Spirit of the Fear of the Lord Demands

The fear of the Lord keeps you in check so the rest of the Spirits can work through you. What does He demand in exchange? Consecration, holiness, and separation from sin. Simple to say; harder to do. Pray for that grace from the Lord to remove your desire to sin and give you power over it.

REMINDERS: WALKING OUT THESE TRUTHS

I hope this chapter has enlightened you. I know I've given you lots to chew on. If you don't have the full understanding of these truths, don't worry—you will, as you seek the abiding anointing of the Spirit upon your life. Here are a few reminders that will help you walk out the truths in this chapter:

- Seek God's abiding presence. Ask the Lord to help you meet the requirements to have the seven Spirits of God abide with you.

- Pray that His Spirit would come, open the eyes of your understanding, and take you deeper into encounters with Him.

- Seek forgiveness for those times when you've not given heed to the seven Spirits, whether they were nudges, unctions, visions, the still, small voice of His presence, or even His audible voice.

- Repent for not obeying His counsel.

- Desire the friendly counsel of God in your life. Ask Him to send you the Spirit of might—the mighty acts and works of the Holy Spirit.

- Thank Him right now for the Spirits of wisdom and revelation.

- In prayer, start to release the methods God wants to use to get things done in your life—the who, what, when, where, and how.

- Finally, ask Him for a river of revelation to flow through your life. Desire that the abiding anointing of all of the mantles of the Holy Spirit would rest on your life.

Chapter Ten

THRONE ROOM
ENCOUNTERS

I t's a real place, where real angels, real people, real wonder, real glory, and the real and living God dwell in eternity. The glory and wonder of Heaven is far beyond anything we've ever conceived. The first and most important feature is that Jesus will be there. His presence there is what makes Heaven, Heaven.

The throne room of God, or third Heaven, is in another dimension (see 2 Cor. 12:2). We can't see it by peering through the clouds; we can't see it through a telescope. To see it, God has to pull back the spiritual veil between Heaven and earth as He did for Ezekiel: "…as I was among the captives by the river Chebar…the heavens were opened and I saw visions of God" (Ezek. 1:1). As Ezekiel stood on the earth, earth's atmosphere was removed for a moment, and he saw Heaven and visions of God.

Apostle John also had third Heaven experiences. The first thing he saw in his Revelation 4 vision of Heaven was an open door:

After these things I looked, and behold, a door standing open in heaven. And the first voice which I heard was like a trumpet speaking with me, saying, "Come up here, and I will show you things which must take place after this" (Revelation 4:1).

OPEN DOOR POLICY

The entrance to the throne room of God is an open door! He is told to "come up here"—come hither! Whenever we need to enter God's presence, we have an invitation. We are *invited* to come. Think on that a moment!

The Bible talks about streets of gold as clear as crystal and walls of precious stones (see Rev. 21:18-21). Someday when I die, I'll walk on those streets and talk with the apostle Paul. I'll see the four living creatures and the fiery beings of Heaven. I'll join the hosts of angels as the 24 elders bow before God's throne, and it will be awesome. I will meet with the great cloud of witnesses and see Heaven's glory. As an inhabitant of Heaven, I'll have the freedom to visit with the saints, to mingle, chat, and learn from them, rather than through indirect sources. How amazing is that?

So many images come to mind when I think of Heaven. Oh, what a day that will be—I can't wait until I'm there eternally (forever), but until then, I'd like to visit from time to time.

For me, the realm of Heaven is as real as the natural realm. I am grateful for throne room encounters. They take me into God's presence and show me open heavens. But, I want to re-emphasize their purpose. A throne room encounter *is all about Jesus* and about knowing Him more and loving Him more. It's also about being changed by His glory and being equipped for the things He has called us to.

Many in the church today have no idea what Heaven is like—the throne, the glory, the angels, the anointing, the function of miracles, or other heavenly things. They're not acquainted with the realm of "as it is in heaven." That's because their spiritual eyes are closed. How about you? Grab the eye drops and prepare for some wonderful spiritual sights, as we study some of the scenes going on in the only real, lasting realm—the spiritual one.

A PROPHETIC DECREE TO PRINCIPALITIES AND POWERS

Who created all things through Jesus Christ; to the intent that now the manifold wisdom of God might be made known by the church to the principalities and powers in the heavenly places, according to the eternal purpose which He accomplished in Christ Jesus our Lord, in whom we have boldness and access with confidence through faith in Him (Ephesians 3:9b-12).

As we speak forth the reality of a heavenly realm on the earth by making prophetic decrees or declarations, we prophesy to a realm called the second heaven. We actually declare to that realm the manifold wisdom of God. And why do we make declarations to that realm? We want to make known to demonic powers and principalities in the heavenly places the manifold wisdom of God.

As I see into Heaven by vision and revelation, I begin to do on earth what I see the Father doing. Job 22:28 says, "...declare a thing, and it will be established...." It's like calling forth those things that are not as though they were (see Rom. 4:17). I'll say it again—it's not that they're not; it's that they're not in *our* experience. Currently, they're not in our realm, but they have always been in God's eternal realm. As we make proclamations of what it's like around the throne or in the invisible, those things in the eternal realm become a reality. Our prophetic declarations in prayer commission angels into action to overcome the demonic principalities and powers that resist the will of God. That's the purpose of communicating any kind of prophetic revelation, not just throne room revelation. When we make the proclamation of what we have heard or seen, we usher in the anointing that came with it. Often when I share in a meeting about the heavenly realms, people actually have supernatural experiences. Why? Because the testimony of Jesus is the spirit of prophecy (see Rev. 19:10). There is anointing that comes in when we testify of what we see and hear.

HEAVENLY ACCESS

I've said it before, but I want to emphasize it again—the door in Revelation 4:1 is still standing open in Heaven today. We have an invitation to come boldly before God's throne of grace (see Heb. 4:16). And just like everything else in the Scripture, we have access by faith.

I believe that every prophetic encounter creates a gate or a door that remains open in Heaven. When Jacob said, "This is none other than the house of God, and this is the gate of heaven!" (Gen. 28:17b), it wasn't just for his time. Forever, this geographic place would be a gateway.

If the house of God is the gate to Heaven, when we gather as His Church, and God inhabits our praises, that place and that attitude of heart becomes a potential gateway. Every encounter we have is an access point to get back into Heaven. If I'm sharing about an experience I had with angels two weeks ago, then the same anointing revisits when I talk about it now. That is why we can re-visit a previous experience when we return to the same geographic place or the same place of attitude and focus. God's door is always open, but we have to learn how to open our door by faith. In Revelation 3:20, Jesus stands at the door and knocks. The door is our heart.

TEMPLE/TABERNACLE THEOLOGY

Before we get into the specific elements of the throne room, I need to define a term—*temple/tabernacle theology*. It sounds complicated, but all it means is that the tabernacle of Moses and David and the temple of Solomon are prophetic pictures of the throne room in Heaven. God gave Moses very specific instructions for building the tabernacle (see Exod. 25) because He was going to dwell there.

The Book of Hebrews, which speaks of the superiority of Christ, refers several times to "copies" or "shadows" as opposed to the heavenly original. Hebrews 9:24 says that Christ didn't enter the man-made tabernacle which was patterned after the one in Heaven, but that He entered Heaven and He dwells in the presence of God, in the throne room that the earthly temples were patterned after. The writer of Hebrews also speaks of Moses' tabernacle being a shadow of the heavenly original:

> *For if He were on earth, He would not be a priest, since there are priests who offer the gifts according to the law; who serve the copy and shadow of the heavenly things, as Moses was divinely instructed when he was about to make the tabernacle. For He said, "See that you make all things according to the pattern shown you on the mountain" (Hebrews 8:4-5).*

In temple/tabernacle theology, our physical body is also portrayed as a temple, just like the temple in the Old Testament, with an outer court, an inner court, and the Holy of Holies. When people receive Jesus into their lives as Savior, they become a temple of the Holy Spirit (see 1 Cor. 6:19). As believers, our body is the outer court; our soul, mind, will, and emotions are the inner court; and where the Holy Spirit dwells is the Holy of Holies. We have to learn to quiet our mind and emotions so we can get into the Holy of Holies.

To summarize, if you can understand the earthly tabernacle, you can get a better understanding of the throne room. We'll see that many of the elements in the earthly tabernacle are representations or symbols of what is in the heavenly throne room. This is really a whole study in itself, and I recommend three books by Kevin Conner on this topic: *The Tabernacle of Moses*, *The Tabernacle of David* and *The Temple of Solomon* (City Christian Publishing).

ELEMENTS OF THE THRONE ROOM

There's one thing I can tell you about the throne room—it's not boring. It's full of activities, singing, noises, colors, the glory, fire, the throne, the Trinity—I could go on and on. There are many Scriptures describing it. Let's look at some of the things you'll see when you get to the throne room of worship:

Immediately I was in the Spirit; and behold, a throne set in heaven, and One sat on the throne. And He who sat there was like a jasper and a sardius stone in appearance; and there was a rainbow around the throne, in appearance like an emerald. Around the throne were twenty-four thrones, and on the thrones I saw twenty-four elders sitting, clothed in white robes; and they had crowns of gold on their heads. And from the throne proceeded lightnings, thunderings, and voices. Seven lamps of fire were burning before the throne, which are the seven Spirits of God. Before the throne there was a sea of glass, like crystal. And in the midst of the throne, and around the throne, were four living creatures full of eyes in front and in back. The first living creature was like a lion, the second living creature like a calf, the third living creature had a face like a man, and the fourth living creature was like a flying eagle. The four living creatures, each having six wings, were full of eyes around and within. And they do not rest day or night, saying: "Holy, holy, holy, Lord God Almighty, who was and is and is to come!" Whenever the living creatures give glory and honor and thanks to Him who sits on the throne, who lives forever and ever, the twenty-four elders fall down before Him who sits on the throne and worship Him who lives forever and ever, and cast their crowns before the throne, saying: "You are worthy, O Lord, to receive glory and honor and power; for You created all things, and by Your will they exist and were created" (Revelation 4:2-11).

Revelation 4:2-11 describes the throne, the imagery of the throne, and the different things that are taking place in God's presence. Often we stop reading at the end of Revelation chapter 4. However, we need to continue reading chapter 10 to get more revelation of the throne.

THE THRONE ROOM

Did you know that in the Bible, God's throne is closely associated with Zion, Jerusalem, the temple, and the Ark of His Covenant? At times, it seems that these places are interchangeable with the idea of God's throne. Within the temple, God's throne is the place where God and His presence dwell: "Then I heard Him speaking to me from the temple, while a man stood beside me. And He said to me, 'Son of man, this is the place of My throne and the place of the soles of My feet, where I will dwell in the midst of the children of Israel forever'" (Ezek. 43:6-7a).

Revelation 11:19 also tells us that the Ark of God (symbolic in Scripture of God's presence) resides within God's temple: "Then the temple of God was opened in heaven, and the ark of His covenant was seen in His temple. And there were lightnings, noises, thunderings, an earthquake, and great hail" (Rev. 11:19). So, we can think of every reference to the throne of God as a reference to the Ark of God as well because both symbolize God's presence. We know that God's temple is within the heavenly Zion or the New Jerusalem, just as His presence rested in the temple within Jerusalem (Zion) on earth in the Old Testament. Also, the throne of God was thought of as the place of covenant and where covenants were honored (see Ps. 132:12; Jer. 14:21). The written tablets of the Old Covenant were actually kept within the Ark (of the Covenant) in the temple. So, we can speak of Zion, Jerusalem, the temple, and the Ark of His Covenant as the place of God's throne—they are almost synonymous in Scripture.

The throne room in Revelation 4 is the true heavenly sanctuary. The tabernacle of Moses became a shadow (a representation) of the throne room (temple) in Heaven. The tabernacle of Moses in Exodus chapters 35–38 and Solomon's temple in First Kings chapters 6–8 are also prophetic pictures of the throne in Heaven. Whenever we talk about the throne room, we should picture all the tabernacle imagery, including the furniture, precious stones and metals, and the different parts of the building layout. Each of these aspects of the natural temple represents something in the heavenly sanctuary.

Ezekiel had a vision of the glory of the Lord filling the temple, and God said, "This is the place of My throne…where I will dwell" (Ezek. 43:7). Did you know the word for *dwell* means "sit enthroned"? Anywhere the presence of God dwells, God sits enthroned. If God dwells in your heart, God sits enthroned in your heart.

THE TRINITY

The first thing that I want you to see in the throne room is the representation of the Trinity. Can you see it? The Father presides on the throne: "Immediately I was in the Spirit; and behold, a throne set in Heaven, and One sat on the throne. And He who sat there was like a jasper and a sardius stone in appearance" (Rev. 4:2-3a). Next, we have the seven lamps burning before the throne, which are the Holy Ghost: "And from the throne proceeded lightnings, thunderings, and voices. Seven lamps of fire were burning before the throne, which are the seven Spirits of God" (Rev. 4:5). And, in the midst of the elders in chapter 5, we have Jesus, the Lamb with the seven horns:

And I looked, and behold, in the midst of the throne and of the four living creatures, and in the midst of the elders, stood a Lamb as though it had been slain, having seven horns and seven eyes, which are the seven Spirits of God sent out into all the earth (Revelation 5:6).

So we have the Father on the throne, the Spirit as seven lamps burning, and the Lamb of God.

In the Ark of God, we have two different revelations of the Trinity. The mercy seat represents Jesus who is the atonement for our sins. The mercy seat dwells between the two cherubs, which in this instance represent the Father and the Holy Spirit.

We also see the Trinity represented in God's pattern to Moses for making the Ark (see Exod. 37:1-3). It was to be gold on the outside, wood in the center, and gold within. The gold on the outside represents the Father. The wood in the center represented Jesus in His humanity as the suffering servant. The gold within represented the Holy Ghost.

THE GLORY OF THE LORD

"I saw the Lord sitting on a throne, high and lifted up, and the train of His robe filled the temple" (Isa. 6:1b). When you read that the glory of the Lord filled the temple, what do you think of? The presence of God, right? Let me show you what the glory of the Lord is:

And the glory of the Lord came into the temple by way of the gate which faces toward the east. The Spirit lifted me up and brought me into the inner court; and behold, the glory of the Lord filled the temple.... And He said to me, "Son of man, this is the place of My throne and the place of the soles of My feet, where I will dwell in the midst of the children of Israel forever (Ezekiel 43:4-5,7a).

The glory of God (the Kabod glory, the Shekinah glory, the *weighty glory*) is actually the manifestation of God's Kingdom and God's throne in your midst. One emphasis on the message of the throne in the Church today is God saying, "I am coming in My Kingdom, in My glory."

TWENTY-FOUR ELDERS AROUND THE THRONE

Around the throne were twenty-four thrones, and on the thrones I saw twenty-four elders sitting, clothed in white robes; and they had crowns of gold on their heads (Revelation 4:4).

The twenty-four elders fall down before Him who sits on the throne and worship Him who lives forever and ever, and cast their crowns before the throne, saying: "You are worthy, O Lord, to receive glory and honor and power; for You created all things, and by Your will they exist and were created" (Revelation 4:10-11).

These Scriptures provide for us a symbolic and prophetic picture of Old and New Testament believers worshiping together before the throne. This vision illustrates the significance of worship and salvation (royal priesthood).

Here, John sees God Himself seated upon His throne and 24 thrones and 24 elders (as he calls them) who sit on those thrones. He must have thought the elders significant to describe them so well. He gives us three aspects to help identify them. (These three aspects also appear in the letters to the seven churches—they are things that Jesus promises to those who overcome.)

He tells us they were clothed in white, that they had crowns of gold on their heads, and that they sat on thrones. Although there are different trains of thought as to whom these elders were, some believe that the 24 represented the 12 sons of Jacob plus the 12 tribes of the nation of Israel (named after the sons).

Now, here's another explanation of who the 24 are. Scripture tells us that at Jesus' death, many saints rose from the dead.

> *Then, behold, the veil of the temple was torn in two from top to bottom; and the earth quaked, and the rocks were split, and the graves were opened; and many bodies of the saints who had fallen asleep were raised; and coming out of the graves after His resurrection, they went into the holy city and appeared to many* (Matthew 27:51-53).

When He ascended to Heaven, Jesus took these saints with Him, as the first fruits of His risen people: "When He ascended on high, He led captives in His train and gave gifts to men" (Eph. 4:8 NIV). Thus, 12 of the elders can represent God's people (divided into 12 tribes) under the Old Covenant; the other 12 can represent the 12 apostles, judging Israel (see Luke 22:28-30; Matt. 19:28). As those who helped form the foundation of the Christian church, these apostles represent God's people under the New Covenant.

The *Strong's Concordance* defines the crown of gold as a "badge of royalty"—a "symbol of honor," and more "elaborate" than an earthly crown. It's the same term used by James when he described the crown of life that we'll receive when we accept Jesus. Jesus too, used the same word in Revelation 2:10 when He told us to be faithful unto death—that He would give us the crown of life. The Greek word used here for crowns is *stephanous,* which indicates a victor's crown—the kind awarded to athletes. Thus, it appears that these elders are the ones given crowns because they have overcome. The 24—symbolizing all believers from the Old and New Testaments before the throne—wear these promised crowns. The elders' golden crowns and thrones also suggest their kingly role, as ones who rule over and judge nations. According to Dean Davis in his book, *The Heavenly Court Judgment of Revelation 4–5:*

> Traditionally, the elders, or heads of families, were the leading citizens who dealt with community affairs in council sessions and served as judges for the people. In Jehoshaphat's reform of 2 Chron. 19:4-11, there was appointed at Jerusalem "a court of priests, Levites, and the heads of Israelite families, who were to act as a court of first instance for the inhabitants of Jerusalem (according to the Greek) and as a court of appeal for cases referred to them from other towns…In 2 Chron. 19, as well as other passages in the Old Testament, priestly and civil functions are often performed by the same individual. This doubling of roles accounts for the fact that in Rev. 4–5 the elders fulfill both priestly and judicial functions.[21]

The elders' white robes suggest that they also serve as priests. They are dressed in white for priestly service, a role calling for purity, holiness, and righteousness. Isaiah 1:18 tells us that even though "your sins are like scarlet, they shall be as white as snow." Matthew 5:8 tells us, "Blessed are the pure in heart for they shall see God." The 24 elders and their robes, as we've discussed, give us a vision of a Church, forgiven and reigning with Christ, the Savior. As priests, the elders represent 24-hour-a-day, non-stop prayer and worship. They are a prophetic picture of the constant prayer and worship God has called His Church to.

This entire scene portrays an important theme—salvation. It's a simplified picture of God and us. The elders understand that Jesus alone is responsible for their salvation, and they honor Him by casting their crowns at His feet and worshiping Him without ceasing.

THUNDERS AND LIGHTNINGS

"And from the throne proceeded lightnings, thunderings, and voices. Seven lamps of fire were burning before the throne, which are the seven Spirits of God" (Rev. 4:5). Have you ever wondered why there are lightnings, thunderings, and voices before God's throne? I am going to share a few reasons that came out of a visitation I had. We find the first reason in Revelation 8:3-5:

> Then another angel, having a golden censer, came and stood at the altar. He was given much incense, that he should offer it with the prayers of all the saints upon the golden altar which was before the throne. And the smoke of the incense, with the prayers of the saints, ascended before God from the angel's hand. Then the angel took the censer, filled it with fire from the altar, and threw it to the earth. And there were noises, thunderings, lightnings, and an earthquake.

Why all the commotion? Answered prayer. The Lord said, "Todd, the angel comes before My presence and says, 'Here is so and so's prayer.'" Every time the Father says, "Yes, let it be done!" thunder, lightning, and voices resonate around Heaven. God takes the golden censer, speaks, and thunder follows. "Yes," boom! "Yes," boom! "Yes," boom! The voices before the throne are the cloud of witnesses interceding and agreeing with the prayers of God's people. They are shouting, "Yes and amen!" And the golden censor is thrown to the earth, followed by noises and thunders and lightnings and, I believe, *answered prayers.*

Voices, noises, lightning, earthquakes, and thunderstorm-like conditions accompany God's glory. Let's look at two more references. Remember how the glory of God came down on the mountain and Moses' face shone as bright as the sun? Put a veil on, Moses!

> *Then it came to pass on the third day, in the morning, that there were thunderings and lightnings, and a thick cloud on the mountain; and the sound of the trumpet was very loud, so that all the people who were in the camp trembled. And Moses brought the people out of the camp to meet with God, and they stood at the foot of the mountain. Now Mount Sinai was completely in smoke, because the Lord descended upon it in fire. Its smoke ascended like the smoke of a furnace, and the whole mountain quaked greatly* (Exodus 19:16-18).

The Lord came with a dark canopy. What an entrance! God's presence was like a thunderstorm, hurricane, wildfire, and earthquake all at once. No wonder the people were afraid they'd die. God's appearance is like every weather/natural calamity known to man. Now go over to Exodus 20. Here is the glory of God again. Look at how God comes.

> *Now all the people witnessed the thunderings, the lightning flashes, the sound of the trumpet, and the mountain smoking; and when the people saw it, they trembled and stood afar off. Then they said to Moses, "You speak with us, and we will hear; but let not God speak with us, lest we die"* (Exodus 20:18-19).

Why these stormy conditions? There is so much energy at the throne; there is so much intensity that Heaven is like an electrical storm system. It's the fire of His presence. There are sparks, there are thunderings, and there are flashes of lightning.

Know what swirling wind sounds like? Think tornado. That's the kind of noise I heard around the throne. Imagine a tropical storm birthing and building up over the sea. Think category 5 hurricane. That is one aspect of God's glory. The four living creatures also cause a commotion.

THE FOUR LIVING CREATURES

The four living creatures seem like something right out of a book by Dr. Seuss. In addition to looking unique, these creatures are very noisy. The four living creatures are another reason why there are thunderings and lightnings, noises and voices, proceeding from the throne of God. These living creatures are also called cherubim in Scripture (read Ezek. 10:2-22). The description of these creatures is slightly different in different passages of Scripture. Just as the Gospel accounts are different as each one is told from a unique perspective, so it is likely that the descriptions of these creatures are told from different perspectives. In addition, even though the prophet may only have seen four of them, it doesn't mean that there aren't many others in Heaven who may look different or be of different ranks. However, each of their roles is the same. They are personal attendants and guardians of God's glory—wherever you have the glory of God, you have the cherubim:

> *Before the throne there was a sea of glass, like crystal. And in the midst of the throne, and around the throne, were four living creatures full of eyes in front and in back. The first living creature was like a lion, the second living creature like a calf, the third living creature had a face like a man, and the fourth living creature was like a flying eagle. The four living creatures, each having six wings, were full of eyes around and within. And they do not rest day or night, saying: "Holy, holy, holy, Lord God Almighty, who was and is and is to come"* (Revelation 4:6-8).

One day as I lay on my carpet waiting on the Lord, I woke lying on the sea of glass like crystal. I felt hot breath on my neck, turned, and looked into the face of a lion. His breath was like fire on my neck. At first, I thought it was the Lion of the tribe of Judah, but then I understood it was one of the four living creatures.

It had a face on both sides of its head—on the front and on the back. Although its head was round, it rotated like a Rubik's Cube—do you remember those? The creature's head revolved sideways so fast, I couldn't see anything but swirling, rapidly moving faces. It was a blur. Every time the creature moved, its face would change to that of an ox, lion, man, or eagle.

The body had small stubby legs, which reminded me of the haunches of a pit bull dog, but it was about the size of a hippo. It didn't have hair. It had what looked like rhino skin. Two wings protruded straight out from its side and two wings from under its belly, and they were covered with eyes. Underneath its belly were many sets of human hands. I am talking about a winged creature that walked up to me on all fours, stood over the top of me and breathed in my face. Ezekiel records the same description:

> *Each one had four faces, and each one had four wings. Their legs were straight, and the soles of their feet were like the soles of calves' feet. They sparkled like the color of burnished bronze. The hands of a man were under their wings on their four sides; and each of the four had faces and wings. Their wings touched one another. The creatures did not turn when they went, but each one went straight forward. As for the likeness of their faces, each had the face of a man; each of the four had the face of a lion on the right side, each of the four had the face of an ox on the left side, and each of the four had the face of an eagle* (Ezekiel 1:6-10).

FAST AS LIGHTNING

No wonder there's lightning in Heaven! In my vision, these creatures zipped from place to place like a flash of lightning. I didn't even see them move—they just appeared here and there and their faces changed every time. Their flapping wings made sounds like thunder. As you'll soon see, the thunder was also the sound of the Almighty, or the voice upon the waters.

I know this is a wild vision. However, Ezekiel saw these creatures long before I did. Then the Lord actually allowed me to live the prophet's encounter before I read the following Bible account:

> *As for the likeness of the living creatures, their appearance was like burning coals of fire, like the appearance of torches going back and forth among the living creatures. The fire was bright, and out of the fire went lightning. And the living creatures ran back and forth, in appearance like a flash of lightning* (Ezekiel 1:13-14).

They ran back and forth, and when they moved I didn't see the creatures, I saw lightning. Then they would appear somewhere else. When they moved their wings, I heard thunder. Let's look at verse 24 of the same chapter: "When they went, I heard the noise of their wings, like the noise of many waters, like the voice of the Almighty, a tumult like the noise of an army; and when they stood still, they let down their wings." What does the voice of the Almighty sound like? It sounds like thunder. And guess what? "The God of glory thunders" (Ps. 29:3)!

Part of the reason we have thunders and lightnings before the throne is because the four living creatures create it when they move. Other things that create the thunder and lightning are: the Ancient of Days' judgment, and answered prayer. The very atmosphere of the glory before God's throne creates thunder and lightning. Heaven is a very noisy place!

THE LIVING CREATURES TRANSPORT THE THRONE

Beneath the sea of glass are the living creatures that provide a chariot for God's throne to move from city to city, from room to room, from nation to nation. These living creatures are also called cherubim (the plural of cherub), and God doesn't move without them.

Ezekiel 1 describes the moving throne carried on its celestial chariot, the cherub. If you read Ezekiel chapters 1 through 10, the throne is moving from north to south, and God is moving throughout the land of Judah to judge His people. The cherubim carry the throne in and out of the temple. In fact, the glory of God was only in the temple for 14 months, and then it departed by way of the east gate. It went from the north to the south, and God on His throne, on His chariot, was carried throughout the land of Judah in an investigative judgment to look at the sins of the people:

> *Then I looked, and behold, a whirlwind was coming out of the north, a great cloud with raging fire engulfing itself; and brightness was all around it and radiating out of its midst like the color of amber, out of the midst of the fire. Also from within it came the likeness of four living creatures…* (Ezekiel 1:4-5a).

> *Now as I looked at the living creatures, behold, a wheel was on the earth beside each living creature with its four faces. The appearance of the wheels and their workings was like the color of beryl, and all four had the same likeness. The appearance of their workings was, as it were, a wheel in the middle of a wheel. When they moved, they went toward any one of four directions; they did not*

turn aside when they went. As for their rims, they were so high they were awesome; and their rims were full of eyes, all around the four of them. When the living creatures went, the wheels went beside them; and when the living creatures were lifted up from the earth, the wheels were lifted up. Wherever the spirit wanted to go, they went, because there the spirit went; and the wheels were lifted together with them, for the spirit of the living creatures was in the wheels. When those went, these went; when those stood, these stood; and when those were lifted up from the earth, the wheels were lifted up together with them, for the spirit of the living creatures was in the wheels (Ezekiel 1:15-21).

When the throne goes up and moves, the wheels go up and move. These are massive wheels set up on earth with rims reaching "so high they were awesome" (Ezek. 1:18). The wheels are constructed as a wheel within a wheel and eyeballs cover the rims. Wherever the living creatures went, so did the wheels. When they lifted up from the earth, the wheels accompanied them.

We can see the throne moving in these verses too: "He rode upon a cherub, and flew; and He was seen upon the wings of the wind" (2 Sam. 22:11). Look at Psalm 68:17: "The chariots of God are twenty thousand, even thousands of thousands; the Lord is among them as in Sinai, in the Holy Place." The Lord is among the chariots. The Lord is among the celestial cherubim, which provide a chariot for the throne of God that moves in Heaven.

This is also a prophetic picture of the Levitical priests who carried the Ark of the Covenant, which was a sign of God's presence (see 1 Chron. 15:2). Where the Ark went, so did God's presence.

SINGING "HOLY, HOLY, HOLY"

The four living creatures, each having six wings, were full of eyes around and within. And they do not rest day or night, saying: "Holy, holy, holy, Lord God Almighty, who was and is and is to come!" Whenever the living creatures give glory and honor and thanks to Him who sits on the throne, who lives forever and ever, the twenty-four elders fall down before Him who sits on the throne and worship Him who lives forever and ever, and cast their crowns before the throne, saying: "You are worthy, O Lord, to receive glory and honor and power; for You created all things, and by Your will they exist and were created" (Revelation 4:8-11).

The living creatures sing around the throne day and night, "Holy, holy, holy, Lord God Almighty, who was and who is and who is to come." Now think about that for a minute. Day and night, 24 hours a day, 7 days a week, they sing the same song. How do you sing the same song over and over? My friend Don said, "Todd, they sing the same song until we get there and then the song changes." In Heaven we will sing the song of Moses and the Song of the Lamb (see Rev. 15:3-4).

IN SPIRIT AND TRUTH

God wants worship in spirit and in truth, with all that is in us, and we will fully enter into the joy of that kind of worship in Heaven. Those in the throne room today are worshiping in spirit and truth continuously. How can they keep the intensity going? How can they sing "holy" and mean it just as much as when they sang it a thousand years before? Here's the answer. I believe that every time the 24 elders and the four living creatures sing, "Holy, Holy, Holy, Lord God Almighty, who was and is and is to come," God just reveals more of His holiness. The new revelation overwhelms them, and with renewed wonder, adoration, passion, and fervor, they worship with even more intensity and conviction: "Oh! Holy, Holy, Holy." Then God rips off another veil covering His nature, and they are amazed at His holiness all over again.

In Heaven, we're also going to see continual fresh revelations of God's holiness—then it will be as if we've never seen that attribute in Him before. It's going to be an ongoing revelation, and it's going to be happening all the time as we go from glory to glory. He's going to go "wham!" and you are going to say, "WOW!" and the revelation of His holiness (and other aspects of His nature) will be alive and fresh. You'll just keep falling deeper and deeper in love. The throne room is eyes and wings, unceasing watchfulness, living creatures and glory, noises of the swirling wind, voices, thunder, and lightning. It's awesome!

You are going to go there and bow down and say, "You are worthy, O Lord, to receive glory and honor and power, for You created all things, and by Your will they exist and were created. You are worthy Lord! You are worthy! You are Holy! O, the glorious throne of Your Kingdom, God," and it's never going to lose its intensity.

EYES AND WINGS

The four living creatures, each having six wings, were full of eyes around and within. And they do not rest day or night, saying: "Holy, holy, holy, Lord God Almighty, who was and is and is to come" (Revelation 4:8).

We have the four living creatures full of eyes. The wheels, wings, hands, and back are all covered with eyes. What is it with all the eyes? I like what a good friend of mine, Stacey Campbell, says, "Eyes to see and wings to get there." The eyes represent the all-seeing, all-knowing, unceasing watchfulness of God.

The life and personality of just one of the eyes pierces you and looks through your entire soul. The eyes of the Lord run to and fro throughout the whole earth because God is looking to show Himself strong on behalf of someone (see 2 Chron. 16:9). Day and night the eyes of the Lord run to and fro. *Who am I going to anoint? Who am I going to choose? Who am I going to call?* It's the all-seeing, all-knowing knowledge of God. You need a whole lot of eyes to do that.

"I will guide you with my eye" (Ps. 32:8b). I talked about this a little in *The Seven Spirits of God* chapter: One look from one eye and not only does it see and know you, but it provides direction for you. All He needs to do is look at you and He can move you where you need to be.

MORE SYMBOLISM IN THE FOUR LIVING CREATURES

There's a lot to be said about the four living creatures, besides the fact that they are very unique. The four living creatures also symbolize or represent several different things:

The Four Faces of God

The four faces of God are expressions of the character of God revealed through Christ in the four Gospels. Matthew focuses on Jesus the King of the Jews, which is the lion. Mark proclaims Him as the Son of Suffering, which is the servant—the ox. Luke presents Him as the Son of Man in His humanity. He is presented in His divinity, as an eagle, in the Gospel of John.

Each face of the living creatures portrays aspects of God's character. This is not the full revelation of God, but one aspect. These heavenly creatures have been in His glory for so long that they have taken on His nature and character in their faces. I think that the attribute God is showing at the time determines which face they show. If God was showing His kingliness, you may see the lion's face, or if He's showing the suffering servant then you may see the ox.

The Cross and the 12 Tribes

Do you know what else the four living creatures speak of? Whenever the 12 tribes of Israel camped in the wilderness, it was a symbolic depiction of the four living creatures (which speak of the throne). The Bible continually points to the King on His throne and His eternal Kingdom.

When the children of Israel set up the tabernacle in the wilderness, they followed a pattern that God had given them. God instructed them to commission 40,000 Levites into priestly service in and around the tabernacle. The Levites and their wives would set up their tents around the tabernacle of His presence. The Levites were personal attendants of the Lord's presence.

Then the rest of the camps set up—to the north, south, east, and west—according to their population and their tribe's color. Each tribe camped under one of four banners, chosen to represent it—each banner had a symbol and a specific color (see Num. 2:1-30; Exod. 28:17-21; Ps. 60:4). The colors used on the banners are also the colors around the throne. The lion acted as Judah's emblem; the eagle represented Dan; the ox was on Ephraim's banner; and the man represented the tribe of Reuben. Here we see the four faces of the living creatures revealed in the 12 tribes of Israel.

The tribes camped under the faces of the eagle, ox, lion, and man, depicted on the banners of the four lead tribes mentioned—Reuben, Ephraim, Dan, and Judah. The 12 tribes were divided into four groups of three tribes—each group of three tribes camped under one of the four banners held by the lead tribe. When God looked down from Heaven, through the sea of glass like crystal, He saw a formation of the cross around the tabernacle. The encampment of the 12 tribes of Israel, under the four banners, gives us a prophetic picture of the four living creatures, or the four faces of God.

THE HEAVENLY REPRESENTED THE EARTHLY

If you want an idea of what goes on in Heaven, study the building plans of the earthly temple God gave to Moses and then to Solomon. The plans were incredibly accurate templates of God's heavenly tabernacle. Solomon's temple was an accurate depiction of chapter 4 of Revelation. Cherubim were carved in its walls and were placed almost everywhere:

> *Inside the inner sanctuary he made two cherubim of olive wood, each ten cubits high. One wing of the cherub was five cubits, and the other wing of the cherub five cubits: ten cubits from the tip of one wing to the tip of the other. And the other cherub was ten cubits; both cherubim were of the same size and shape. The height of one cherub was ten cubits, and so was the other cherub.*

Then he set the cherubim inside the inner room; and they stretched out the wings of the cherubim so that the wing of the one touched one wall, and the wing of the other cherub touched the other wall. And their wings touched each other in the middle of the room. Also he overlaid the cherubim with gold. Then he carved all the walls of the temple all around, both the inner and outer sanctuaries, with carved figures of cherubim, palm trees, and open flowers.... Then he carved cherubim, palm trees, and open flowers on them, and overlaid them with gold applied evenly on the carved work (1 Kings 6:23-35).

How did they know about the cherubim? There weren't Old Testament Scriptures that described them yet. When God gave the plans for the temple, he told them to make cherubim, but didn't tell them what these creatures looked like. Either they had Holy Ghost insight or someone had an unrecorded vision back then. Later, Ezekiel and John saw the true throne room that the earthly temples are patterned after.

Now we can all experience the real, heavenly throne room because Jesus came to tear down the veil. Now we have access to the holy place. We don't have figurative artwork; we have literal experiences. We have now become the temple. First Kings 6:23-35 describes the shadow of the true throne room that we can all experience in Christ.

COLORS AROUND THE THRONE

In the Old Testament, colorful stones on the priest's breastplate, called the ephod, were a symbolic picture of the colors around God's throne (see Exod. 28:15-21).

They not only represent the colors of the 12 tribes of Israel, they also point to Jesus. Sardius is a deep blood-red or yellow-red color, like a ruby. It speaks of the justice and judgments of God. The sardius stone represents the tribe of Benjamin. *Benjamin* means "son of my right hand." Jesus is also the Son at the right hand of the Father.

The jasper stone is opaque quartz, and it represents the purity and holiness of God. This stone represented the tribe of Reuben, which was the first tribe. Jesus Christ is the representation of Reuben in that He was the first-born, only begotten, and first from the dead. The rest of the many-colored stones all represent a tribe, as well as an aspect of God's nature.

A predominantly emerald-colored rainbow is around the throne (see Rev. 4:3). The color green speaks of God's goodness. The rainbow serves as a reminder of all God's promises to Abraham, Isaac, and Jacob. God also promised Noah that He'd never flood the earth again. Then He reached above His throne, grabbed the rainbow, and threw it down to earth as a symbol of that promise.

The only time that you can see the rainbow is when the rain and the sun appear together. God wants you to remember your prophetic words in the midst of life's storms. When it's dark and dreary, He comes through with His rainbow of hope and promise. Whenever you see a rainbow, let it be a reminder to you of God's goodness and that He is always faithful to fulfill His promises.

THE SEA OF GLASS LIKE CRYSTAL

Remember Revelation 4:6? "Before the throne there was a sea of glass, like crystal." The sea of glass like crystal is a transparent sea. In a vision, I was standing in it chest deep. Its waves went over me.

Do you know why it's before His throne? Because the entire world is before that throne and nothing is hidden from His sight under that glass sea. Have you ever been at the top of a tall building in a glass observatory and you could see far and wide? That is what the sea of glass is like. Every nation, every man, every thought of every man, all at once are beneath the transparent sea. God can see everything from His throne.

Remember that the things on the earth are a shadow of the heavenly original (see Heb. 8:5). (Did God look out from His throne and say, "Look at My sea of glass like crystal; we've got to put *that* in the tabernacle!"?) He instructed Solomon to create what was called the bronze sea or the molten sea for the temple: "And he made the Sea of cast bronze, ten cubits from one brim to the other; it was completely round. Its height was five cubits, and a line of thirty cubits measured its circumference" (1 Kings 7:23).

In the tabernacle of Moses, this was called the "bronze laver," a wash pan filled with saltwater. The salt was for purification. The bronze laver represented the "washing of water by the word" (Eph. 5:26)—a necessity before entering into the most holy place.

In Heaven, it's not bronze because it is glorified. It's crystal because there is no sin. Because of Jesus' sacrifice on the cross, we are without spot or blemish and we are washed in the blood of the Lamb. There is no more need to go through the ritual washing of our bodies or the traditions of the old tabernacle. Hallelujah!

Let me tell you something else about the sea of glass like crystal. It speaks of the sanctifying power of the Word of God and the washing of the water by the Word. It's as a mirror that you look into. It's a reflection of who Christ is, who you are, what you look like, and the conviction of your sin. It's transparent; you see yourself, your true image. It gets rid of your mask. There are actually shafts of light that bounce off the sea of glass like crystal. It's reflection and it's illumination.

JOIN THE CELEBRATION AROUND THE THRONE!

I teach about the throne and angels and prophetic encounters so you can begin to exercise your spiritual senses, according to Hebrews 5:14, so that you can begin to prophesy as it is in Heaven and declare the manifold wisdom of God. Then the angels heed the voice of His word in the mouth of His servants and the Kingdom comes.

I've said it before, but let me emphasize it again—if you don't have your own prophetic visions, revelations, and experiences, then listen to everybody else's and it will rub off on you. Get a vision in your spirit of what it is like in Heaven. Fill yourself with the images of what Heaven looks like. Use your spiritual inner eyes and gaze on the throne and the One who sits upon the throne who is like jasper and a sardius stone. Picture the rainbow around the throne like an emerald. Imagine the 24 elders bowing down; see the Ancient of Days and hear the thunder, voices, and noise of Heaven.

We are spiritual creations, saints—citizens of Heaven. We don't have to wait until we're absent from the body and present with the Lord to enter in. Whatever we consider a joy here on earth is heightened zillions of times beyond anything we can conceive in Heaven.

Be thankful for throne room encounters. They give us the opportunity to worship the King on His throne in His glory. We can approach that throne by grace, because the Bible says we can, and we can do it boldly! Join with the angels now, and declare the Lord God Almighty "Holy! Holy! Holy!"

The apostle Paul put it this way: "Eye has not seen, nor ear heard, nor have entered into the heart of man the things which God has prepared for those who love Him" (1 Cor. 2:9). Come here! Come on up! Come up here!

Chapter Eleven

ACTIVATING PROPHETIC DESTINY

> *I watched till thrones were put in place, and the Ancient of Days was seated.... The court was seated, and the books were opened* (Daniel 7:9-10).

Almost every politician and Hollywood celebrity eventually writes, or has someone else write, his or her memoirs. Although you may not be famous, in God's eyes, you're important, and He cares enough about you to record the story of your life. He has a library overflowing with books written about you. In this chapter, we'll examine through Scripture, the book of remembrance and the book of the future. I pray that God uses this study to remind you of your unfulfilled dreams, and to give you a new realization of how right you are to dream them. Have you put your dreams on a shelf, or set them aside as unattainable? God hasn't.

The contents of both books give us powerful insight into how to activate our full God-ordained prophetic destiny. They don't just record our good and bad deeds! Angelic hosts continuously record the details of your life—the legacy you leave and the destiny you discover.

During the time of the Jewish festival of Rosh Hashanah, my wife, Shonnah, received a vision of a heavenly library. It was like a museum, with endlessly high wall-to-wall bookshelves. There was a ladder that two angels used to retrieve books and to restock the shelves. The angels removed two books titled "Destiny" and "Future," and as they opened them, Shonnah saw her life presented before God in a type of examination, not unlike the Jewish people's life-examination, customary during this festival period. Israelites (past and present) metaphorically examine the book of remembrance in an evaluation of their lives (past, present, and future) including areas of sin they must make atonement and restitution for.

Earlier I shared with you about the scribe angel who sometimes appears in my meetings. As I prophesy, he listens and watches the person's reaction, and then with an old-fashioned quill pen and gold ink, he records the prophecies on parchment paper. The Lord told me the angel's function was to record our history, our legacy.

THE BOOK OF REMEMBRANCE

The Old Testament Book of Daniel mentions a book that holds the names and actions of the righteous: "…And at that time your people shall be delivered, every one who is found written in the book" (Dan. 12:1b). Malachi specifically refers to the book of remembrance: "Then those who feared the Lord spoke to one another, and the Lord listened and heard them; *so a book of remembrance* was written before Him for those who fear the Lord and who meditate on His name" (Mal. 3:16).

Many know about the book of life and the fact that it contains records of our actions; however, few are aware of the book of remembrance. Note that God has this book constantly in front of Him as a reminder of the life and works of those who love Him. He listens, hears, and writes everything in it.

God hears all of our conversations and is not as far away as some believe. He remembers His promises and our own as well. He records our words in this book of remembrance, even those known only to us personally. When you said, "Here I am, Lord, send me…I want to lay hands on the sick and see them recover," He noted your burning desire and recorded it.

You may have forgotten what God promised 20 years ago, or the pledge you made to God at a youth conference, but He remembers. From the moment of your conception, He recorded every desire, dream, passion, prophetic word, revelation, and vision, and He wants you to remember them, to stir them up—especially if you've buried them under the weight and burdens of trials, heartache, and sickness. He wants to reignite the passionate fire that once burned in your heart to serve Him, and so He reveals that which He's recorded within the book to re-stoke the desire.

Remembering Stirs Up

In Second Timothy, Paul reminds Timothy to stir up the gifts God had put in him: "…that I may be filled with joy, when I call to remembrance the genuine faith that is in you…Therefore I remind you to stir up the gift of God which is in you through the laying on of my hands" (2 Tim. 1:4-6).

Paul was saying, "Timothy, I'm encouraging you to remember, to think about the gifts of God that He put into your life. You haven't remembered; you haven't dreamed. You haven't imagined walking in the anointing that the prophets imparted into your life when they laid their hands on you. What did the prophets say about you? Remember it, Timothy."

I encourage you to remember not only what God has told you prophetically, but also to recall how you desired Him to use you. People often ask me how they can know what God has put in their spirit regarding their destiny. My first question in response is, "What moves you—what do you speak of most often?" This gives us insight into determining our gifting, which usually has something to do with our destiny. However, often these gifts lie dormant. Some don't understand or aren't even aware what God has already placed in their hearts, and so they continue to wait for a prophetic word, while all the time God just wants them to move forward with the desire in their heart.

God wants us to understand the power of those Holy Ghost dreams and desires. Remembering allows God to release forgiveness, healing, and restoration into our hearts. He wants us to remember because doing so activates old gifts in our lives. The burning desire you already carry may be your destiny. It could be a women's ministry, a prison ministry, street evangelism, music, dancing, or writing. Whatever your passion is, move out in it! Use it! Your destiny usually lies in areas where you are gifted or talented.

It's important for you to remember the days when your heart was full of passion for Jesus, those days when you had visions and dreams. Maybe you once experienced that fervor, but now after years of spiritual abuse, control, and poor leadership, you have shut down. How can you stir up that prophetic song when your heart is dull? How do you rouse your musical gifting or special anointing for deliverance?

David experienced a time when he realized he needed to move forward: "You hold my eyelids open; I am so troubled that I cannot speak. I have considered the days of old, the years of ancient times. I call to remembrance my song in the night; I meditate within my heart, and my spirit makes diligent search" (Ps. 77:4-6). In that place of trouble, David says, "I can't sleep. I need a breakthrough." He remembers every time the Lord has rescued him, instead of worrying or tossing and turning:

> *When I remember You on my bed, I meditate on You in the night watches. Because You have been my help, therefore in the shadow of Your wings I will rejoice* (Psalm 63:6-7).

Remembering builds faith and allows us to rejoice in dry times and trials. We need to make sure we don't become like the children of Israel. God brought them out of Egypt, and almost instantly, they forgot His miracles. We need to purpose in our hearts to remember, to contemplate, and to ponder those past times of breakthrough, especially in times of lack, adversity, or spiritual dryness. If you keep a journal, read it and celebrate God for those times He intervened. Remembering stirs up faith.

How Do We Remember?

I love to remember! It's one of my favorite things to do. At night in bed, I think of all the times the Lord moved; I recall tough situations when He came to my aid and those wonderful moments when He supernaturally intervened. My spirit quickens, and I feel joy and excitement— so much so, I can hardly sleep. Those memories of Him as He moved in

311

my life rekindle my passion and my motivation to serve Him. I have a hard time falling asleep and have to ask God to close His book and let me rest.

Quietness is necessary for remembering. There is something powerful about pondering and speaking prophetic words, destinies, and dreams in a quiet place. The Bible often uses the word *meditation*. King David was big on meditating, and he encourages us to "Meditate within your heart on your bed, and be still. Selah" (Ps. 4:4b). David is saying, "I am going to remember how You have been my help in the past because it builds my faith for the future." He understood that the quiet place of remembering is important to increasing faith. The word "selah" means a pause or rest. Modern-day Christians need a little more *selah*-time because God brings visions and dreams and births prophetic words in those times of rest.

So, go lie on your bed and let the Holy Spirit sanctify your imagination as you remember the anointing on your life years ago. Remember a season of harvest, or a time when the Word leapt off the Bible pages and influenced you. Remember prophetic words and dreams. Think about every miracle, every vision, every salvation, every prophetic word, and every dream.

Remembering stirs up your heart and your spirit, so get into those Holy Ghost memories. Soon you'll say, "I'm tired of remembering, Lord. I want to step out and see You do new things!" When you step out, the anointing of God will flow again.

Remembering Brings Anointing

This is the word of the Lord to Zerubbabel: "Not by might nor by power, but by My Spirit," says the Lord of hosts. "Who are

312

you, O great mountain? Before Zerubbabel you shall become a plain! And he shall bring forth the capstone with shouts of 'Grace, grace to it!'" Moreover the word of the Lord came to me, saying: "The hands of Zerubbabel have laid the foundation of this temple; his hands shall also finish it. Then you will know that the Lord of hosts has sent Me to you. For who has despised the day of small things?..." (Zechariah 4:6-10a).

Zechariah means "the God who remembers" or "the God who calls to remembrance." Here the prophet Zechariah urges King Zerubbabel to remember his prophetic commission of rebuilding Solomon's temple. What a huge task! However, if God gives you a vision that seems bigger than you, don't throw it out, or toss it aside as impossible, just because you don't or can't understand how it is going to happen.

Zerubbabel started thinking about what he didn't have in the natural and why he could never complete the vision God had given him. He cried out, "God, how am I ever going to do it? How is it ever going to happen?" The Lord said, "Of course you can't do it! It's not by might; it's not by power; it's all done by My Spirit! You need the anointing. You need My power on your flesh to enable you to do what you can't naturally do."

The key to your breakthrough is the anointing. Don't take your eyes off the anointing, the vision, the Word, and the heavenly resources that God has given you or given you access to. Do not let your eyes settle on what you can't do or what the situation looks like in the natural. Everything you have need of will come with the anointing. It's not in your mind, it's not in your strength, it's not in your gift, it's not in your talent, it's not in your past, and it's not in your circumstances. It's only by His Spirit!

The devil wants to discourage you by the enormity of God's vision, but God wants dreamers. He wants people who declare, "Who are you, O mountain, mountain of hindrance, of opposition, of impossibility? Who are you, O mountain? You shall become a plain because the key is in the anointing." God can and will get it done! With God, anything is possible. That means that God is going to do something so supernatural in your life through the anointing that it will cause people to declare, "Grace—that was truly the grace of God!"

Zechariah declared this when he said, "And he shall bring forth the capstone with shouts of 'Grace, grace to it!'" (Zech. 4:7b). From a young age, I filled my life with drugs, illegal activities, prison, and other dark sins. My story is full of *Grace, grace*. God called me to full-time ministry four years after touching my life—Grace, grace. Now the ministry has about 100 staff and I preach all over the world—Grace, grace. If I think I am special in some way and I am responsible for my own success, I would not be bringing this message to you. I want every man and woman to come into the reality of the supernatural. I want to see you lift your standard of expectation. What God can do for one, He can do for all. Don't stop dreaming—and dream big!

Tears in a Bottle

Some give up on ever seeing their destinies, prophetic words, or desires fulfilled because of circumstances (family, work loads, marital status, financial burdens); feelings of unworthiness (thinking God couldn't possibly want to use them now); fear (afraid He'll give them something too big, or that they'll fail); disappointments (from past failures); or feelings of insignificance ("I'm too small to be used of God").

Well, think about this: God knew every bad choice and sinful act that you were going to commit before the foundation of the world, and He chose you as His child anyway. The sin may have surprised you, but the sin didn't sneak up on God. He knew about it all along, and He still calls you His own. Don't let the enemy run you away from God in shame—run to God and receive forgiveness.

It is never too late to step out into what God has for you. Smith Wigglesworth gave his life to Jesus Christ when he was 48, and we are still experiencing the impact of his ministry on our world. God isn't just moving on people in my generation, but those of every age and generation. Every single saint needs to dream, to remember, to allow the Holy Spirit to open the book of remembrance and revive memories and old dreams.

Read what God says about you in the Word, ponder His promises, find those old, transcribed prophetic words you wrote down long ago, and proclaim over them, "God, I believe You for what You said 5 years, 20 years, or 25 years ago." He knows the abuse, the hurt, the pain, and its effect on you. You have made some bad decisions, so you say, "God, this must be Your discipline; I wish I had done what You said I should do." No more shoulda's, woulda's, or coulda's. Let go of those. God has numbered every tear and wandering and has recorded them: "You number my wanderings; put my tears into Your bottle; are they not in Your book?" (Ps. 56:8).

God has numbered your wanderings and God knows where you've been! He knows about your divorce and why you think you're disqualified, and He has put all those shed tears into a bottle. It doesn't matter what you have walked through. You need to forget about yesterday. It doesn't matter where you were; it's where you are now and where you're going tomorrow that's important. You can make a decision to serve God now, to have the anointing, to press on to the mark of the high calling, no matter the cost. It may cost you your land, your house, your job, or it could mean sacrifices in other areas of your life. God may ask, "How hungry are you for the anointing I've had ready and waiting for you?"

I believe there will be acceleration, a special grace to see those delayed prophetic promises fulfilled. There are times in Heaven when God speaks with creative power into the spirit realm and, suddenly, it's breakthrough-breakthrough-breakthrough! This is what I sense now. I want you to take that as a word from God. For those of you who are looking for direction in your life right now, go back and remember what God spoke to you about seven or eight years ago. Get out those tapes or journals. You will find many of the prophecies you received seven or eight years ago are just now coming to pass. Isn't that amazing? God wants you to remember because those words are relevant again.

A Martyr's Seed

Words can still be relevant and possible even after a person has passed away. My mother was deaf, and even though I had prayed for her healing, at the time of her death she still was unable to hear. She passed away because of complications from a stroke while I was at a healing revival, praying for the deaf. It shook me, and I had to make a decision—was I going to press in further, or was I going to quit? I recalled every miracle that I'd seen. I proclaimed that her death would be my martyr's seed and that it would release a mighty anointing on my life so tens of thousands of people who suffered from a stroke or deafness would be healed.

If you open the book and you can't claim a particular promise, if the seed has truly died, then let it be a martyr's seed, a promise that will fall into the ground, die, and lie waiting for a new generation. Then let it come to life and reproduce in your children and grandchildren. Don't let that vision fade away. If you don't have grandchildren, then claim it for a young person in your church. We can also claim the fulfillment of others' promises in our lives. I regularly pray, "God, I'll take the anointing that was never fulfilled in the lives of men of God who have died prematurely. I'll take up their unfinished mandates." You can pray that way, too.

THE BOOK OF THE FUTURE
(THE BOOK OF DESTINY)

The second book, the book of the future, is also called the book of destiny. God has thoughts, God has a plan, and God has a purpose that will give you a hope and a future: "For I know the thoughts that I think toward you, says the Lord, thoughts of peace and not of evil, to give you a future and a hope" (Jer. 29:11).

God wants to encourage our hearts with prophetic destiny and visions. He's given many in our meetings trances and visions in which they've seen the heavenly library. The Father takes a book off a shelf and opens it, and these people see themselves healing the sick or preaching in the mission field. God reveals their destiny—their future—from the pages of this book.

Daniel calls this book the Scripture of Truth: "I will tell you what is noted in the Scripture of Truth..." (Dan. 10:21). Daniel knew that the generation Jeremiah prophesied would come out of Babylonian captivity was actually his generation. Daniel set his heart to understand, and tried to look into the future. The book of destiny records your future. If you can tap into what God has planned, no evil spirit of hell can stop or hinder your destiny—but you need to know what it is.

317

God writes and stores chapters of destiny in Heaven, and when Jesus came to earth, He fulfilled His own prophetic destiny: "Then I said, 'Behold I have come—in the volume of the book it is written of Me—to do Your will, O God!'" (Heb. 10:7).

God has a future for you and your children. Remember God's past deeds, but also dream and look into your book of the future. Maybe you are turning a new page or a new chapter. Sometimes we need to say, "Father, give me a glimpse into the Scripture of Truth. I can't see tomorrow. Holy Spirit, come and show me, because people who have no vision, perish." Forget about your yesterdays and say, "I'm starting a new chapter, God. Where do You want to take me tomorrow?"

Edible Books

Let me share another part of the prophetic encounter that I had in Seattle with the angels while Bill Johnson spoke. I was suddenly taken up through the ceiling and found myself on an operating table. In this spiritual experience, four angels appeared and stood there, two on either side of me. My heart pounded as I saw them approach me with a circular saw. They put the saw on my chest and cut me open. All my insides spilled out. Then they placed little boxes inside of me. They explained that these were impartations of truth in my inward parts. It was like getting implants of the Holy Ghost! They told me that the time is short; the harvest is coming. There is still so much to be done that sometimes 20 years of knowledge needs to be implanted in one single impartation. The harvest is very near.

Then the Lord told me He would visit me in power at the hotel. Just as He said, an angel appeared, and came with fire and smoke. As I described earlier, the next day the two rooms above mine caught fire and burned! Revelation talks about His mighty angel:

*I still saw another mighty angel coming down from heaven...
his face was like the sun, and his feet like pillars of fire....
Then the voice which I heard from heaven spoke to me again
and said, "Go, take the little book which is open in the hand
of the angel who stands on the sea and on the earth." So I went
to the angel and said to him, "Give me the little book." And he
said to me, "Take and eat it; and it will make your stomach
bitter, but it will be as sweet as honey in your mouth." Then I
took the little book out of the angel's hand and ate it, and it
was as sweet as honey in my mouth. But when I had eaten it,
my stomach became bitter. And he said to me, "You must
prophesy again about many peoples, nations, tongues, and
kings"* (Revelation 10:1,8-11).

Notice that the Lord tells John to prophesy again—that means he wasn't prophesying at that time! God imparted the next chapter, the next pages of the book of the future, so John could prophesy. The moment he ate those pages, he received every prophetic word he would ever give to peoples, nations, and kings. It was an impartation to his spirit-man that would manifest in prophesies for years to come. John couldn't even read what was written on the pages. That means that in the natural he couldn't understand it, because it was only something his spirit could comprehend. As his spirit needed it, it would manifest.

Some angels have just one job—they take books of your destiny and impart pages or chapters of them to your spirit-man. Honey represents revelation. See, it's sweet initially, but with persecution, hardship, trials, testing, rejection, pain, and death, it can turn bitter. In 1998, I had a similar experience to John's experience. An angel appeared carrying a jar filled with honey. In the jar were many little scrolls that were about the size of lipstick tubes. He pulled one out and had me eat it, and many things I'm teaching now came from that. Ezekiel had a similar experience:

> *"You shall speak My words to them, whether they hear or whether they refuse, for they are rebellious.... Open your mouth and eat what I give you." Now when I looked, there was a hand stretched out to me; and behold, a scroll of a book was in it. Then He spread it before me; and there was writing on the inside and on the outside, and written on it were lamentations and mourning and woe. Moreover He said to me, "Son of man, eat what you find; eat this scroll, and go, speak to the house of Israel." So I opened my mouth, and He caused me to eat that scroll. And He said to me, "Son of man, feed your belly, and fill your stomach with this scroll that I give you." So I ate, and it was in my mouth like honey in sweetness. Then He said to me: "Son of man, go to the house of Israel and speak with My words to them"* (Ezekiel 2:7–3:4).

The day God called Ezekiel, he had no revelation. God sent an angel with a revelatory scroll and Ezekiel ate it. Notice that God told him to eat the scroll and then go prophesy. Ezekiel received his prophetic commissioning and every prophecy that he would give from that day forward. I believe the Book of Ezekiel was written on that scroll.

The little book the angel gave to John in Revelation 10:2,8 is the same book that is in Ezekiel 2. In Ezekiel's case, it was a scroll he was told to eat which would be as sweet as honey in his mouth and bitter in his stomach. Then the Lord told him to speak to his people, and Ezekiel was released into his mandate. As he digested that scroll, I believe it became an impartation in his spirit-man of the ministry he was being launched into.

Your Scroll of Impartation

You need a scroll of impartation for your life, and you need to eat that book and get it down into your spirit, so it can commission you into what God is about to do tomorrow. Are you going into the next chapter of your life and in need of a commissioning? There's an angel that wants to come and put something in your spirit.

We need a divine encounter. God still does everything He did in the Bible. This stuff is real. Even if you can't understand it with your mind, let your spirit-man eat the scroll in faith. Regularly ask the Lord to show you what He's written in your book; stir up the giftings within you; and prayerfully venture further into your destiny.

The good news is we're co-writers and co-workers with God (see 1 Cor. 3:9). I believe He allows us to write our own destinies into the book, just as He gives us permission to do great things by exercising the spiritual authority God has delegated to us. We partner with God to do great exploits through His power, and He records everything as it happens. God, however, doesn't write anything in the book of destiny that we don't choose to have there. He gives us free will to choose our future destiny because He loves us and made us creative beings. Yet, He recorded our future in the book of destiny even before the foundation of the world. He also records our deeds each day. Think of Him as a parent, proudly and lovingly recording a child's accomplishments in a journal or scrapbook.

I believe God wants to let you catch a glimpse into the book of the future so you can partner with Him in living out the great exploits He has for you. He wants to give you one of those scrolls to eat. "I know the thoughts that I think toward you, says the Lord" (Jer. 29:11). Sometimes His destiny for you is so great that you can't even understand it. But when you get the impartation inside, it becomes a part of you and it will come forth when you need it. He wants to give you prophetic impartation now, because if you don't get it today you can't release it tomorrow!

Are you ready to ask the Lord for a honey scroll and a glimpse into your book?

Pray with me:

> *Father, I want to eat the scroll. I want to eat pages from my book of the future that will become knowledge—the when, where, and how of my destiny. Show me the title of my book. Is my destiny apostolic, or is it prophetic, or does it involve a specific country? What page and chapter am I in? How many books are written about me? Show me what's coming in my ministry. Show it to me like You unrolled the scroll for Ezekiel. I want to eat the book, and I want an impartation that becomes knowledge. Let me see around the corner and over the hill. Lord, I'm waiting for commissioning and new mantles. Let the scrolls come now. I thank You for the books of remembrance and of the future. I commit myself to both, Lord, and I place myself in Your arms to read them with You. Allow me to see what You have written about me. Sanctify my imagination so that I can see and then meet the expectations You have for me. What a joy to think You have plans for me. I long to fulfill them, Lord Jesus. Amen.*

Chapter Twelve

THE TRANSFER OF REVELATORY ANOINTING

The Lord is about to reveal mysteries that have been hidden since the beginning of time. God is inviting His people, in a greater way, to have revelatory understanding of things that are only going to be revealed in this generation. He wants to reveal those treasures that are hidden in Christ, but He will only disclose them to those who seek His face. The Lord has shown me that He is unveiling His hidden mysteries and secrets to those who fear Him.

I believe that God wants to bring *you* into heavenly experiences with Him. I want to activate something for you in this dimension, because touching this realm with someone who knows how to go there releases a type of spiritual explosion of supernatural experiences. Do you believe that the anointing is transferable? Do you believe that, like Saul, when you come under the prophetic anointing of others you can begin to have prophetic experiences you've never had before?

Remember, Jesus said, "…all things are possible to him who believes" (Mark 9:23b). The centurion knew the power of the prophetic words of God. He said to Jesus, "But only speak a word, and my servant will be healed" (Matt. 8:8b). Let's believe together that as we call on the Lord, He will speak and His presence will rest powerfully on your life, with the anointing of revelation, deliverance, and healing.

I believe that God is releasing the supernatural upon the Church today so we can step into the marketplace carrying such a level of God's manifest presence that everyone around us receives words from Heaven and is saved and healed. I believe that in this next season, there's going to be a great release of signs, wonders, and revelation in your life as you walk by faith into the supernatural dimension and allow the Holy Spirit to hover over your life.

When we have a biblical foundation for our lives and we see how naturally God's people have lived in the realm of revelation from the beginning to the end of the Bible, we can rest in the knowledge that such prophetic experiences are good gifts from the Father.

Do you want an increase of the prophetic in your life so you can hear God's voice more clearly and experience an increase in wonderful Holy Spirit encounters? If so, then today is your day for flying higher in the supernatural realms of Heaven.

Expectation and Faith

My desire is to raise the level of your expectation that God will speak to you and that He will give you supernatural revelation if you open your spirit to Him by faith. The first thing you need to understand is that true divine revelation is available in abundance and it's available to you! You can truly trust Him to bless you with revelation because Scripture tells you that if you ask for a good gift He won't give you something harmful—God is in the business of giving good things to those who ask Him (see Matt. 7:10-11).

What I'm speaking of is more than an occasional prophecy, word of knowledge, or leading of the Holy Spirit. It's about the extreme level of the prophetic—visitations by angels, trances, visions, and visits to the third Heaven. I believe God wants to speak in these "extreme" ways as well as through promptings and the still small voice.

Zechariah speaks of the access we have to the courts of God:

> *Thus says the Lord of hosts: "If you will walk in My ways, and if you will keep My command, then you shall also judge My house, and likewise have charge of My courts; I will give you places to walk among these who stand here"* (Zechariah 3:7).

"Have charge of My courts" means free access to His courts. Expectation and faith are key. Expect more than the still small voice, or divine thoughts. Instead, believe in the "seer" anointing like Elisha had. Realize that you too can experience trances like Peter, or visit Paradise like Paul, or be taken by the Spirit into visions of God like Elisha. Let's examine what triggers these extreme prophetic experiences for us:

> *After these things I looked, and behold, a door standing open in heaven. And the first voice which I heard was like a trumpet speaking with me, saying, "Come up here, and I will show you things which must take place after this"* (Revelation 4:1).

If Heaven is going to touch earth with miracles, healings, signs, wonders, visions, and revelation, it must open, and that's what we need to pray for. It was when Heaven opened that John began to receive revelation, as you learned in Chapter Seven (*Ministering Under an Open Heaven*). You can also find open heavens over actual geographic places on earth today, for instance in the place that Jacob had a vision of angels. I've been to Moravian Falls, North Carolina, several times, where there is a revelatory open Heaven. This is the same location where the Moravians settled years ago after leaving Germany, where they had been part of a 100-year prayer meeting. It is believed that they carried an open Heaven and saturated this area of America with prayer too.

This is the place where Rick Joyner received revelation for his book *The Final Quest*. The first time I was there, I could hardly sleep or shut the revelation off for three days and nights. When I did sleep, I'd have prophetic dreams. When I awoke, I had angelic visitations. So much revelation came at once, it was as if I was a radio with a big antenna and tuning into different stations. While I was there, someone took me down a trail toward "the rock." The closer I got to this place, the more I was overcome with God's presence. When we got closer, I saw three angels that glowed with the glory. I learned from others that these angels were just yards from the worship center and that they were worship angels.

The angelic and the prophetic are normal manifestations of an open Heaven. Yes, we can go to certain places like Moravian Falls to get an open Heaven, but how much better to press in to God for a constant open Heaven over our own lives. As you begin to see Heaven open over your life, you will start receiving revelation that will supernaturally transform your imagination and understanding. I believe that being in the anointing and being exposed to the Spirit of wisdom and revelation quickens your understanding. Revelation actually does something to your physical body and mind. Perhaps you're saying today, "That is what I need! Give me a taste of the Spirit of wisdom and revelation."

REVELATION SPARKS PASSION

Apostle Paul petitioned the Lord on your behalf:

That the God of our Lord Jesus Christ, the Father of glory, may give to you the spirit of wisdom and revelation in the knowledge of Him, the eyes of your understanding being enlightened; that you may know what is the hope of His calling, what are the riches of the glory of His inheritance in the saints (Ephesians 1:17-18).

Notice that in this Scripture Paul refers to a singular spirit of wisdom and revelation. I believe that because the word "spirit" is not capitalized in this case, he is not referring to the Holy Spirit or the seven Spirits, but rather, to an anointing of the Holy Spirit for wisdom and revelation. In this chapter I will speak of wisdom and revelation, like Paul, as an anointing from the Holy Spirit.

We must have wisdom and revelation in our lives because only then will we have the rest of what Paul talks about in verse 18 where he prays that "the eyes of your understanding [would be]…enlightened; that you may know what is the hope of His calling…."

That is what revelation does—it brings an understanding of God's call and a sense of His purpose and destiny for your life. Without revelation, we don't have that desire, that love of Christ, or that fire in our spirit that motivates, moves, and compels us. We need that passion inside us that says, "This is who I am, and this is what I am going to do." This passion comes out of revelation.

God also wants the eyes of our heart opened so we can understand how much He has to give:

... The riches of the glory of His inheritance in the saints, and what is the exceeding greatness of His power toward us who believe, according to the working of His mighty power which He worked in Christ when He raised Him from the dead... (Ephesians 1:18b-20).

The spirit (or anointing) of wisdom and revelation also brings us into the manifestation of God's power. Without revelation, we won't have a manifestation of God's power because revelation is connected to miracles, signs, and wonders. Revelation is always connected to raising the dead.

Is this power in your life? Where is the manifestation of the exceeding greatness of His power? We really haven't had revelation; we've only had knowledge. However, when the revelation happens, the manifestation happens, and then the demonstration happens. That is how Elijah operated. Think about the great things that happened when he overcame the 450 prophets of baal on Mount Carmel, and the whole nation turned back to God. They had revival and reformation on that mountain. Fire came down from Heaven; God displayed signs and wonders. And how did all this happen? After this mighty manifestation, Elijah said, "Lord...I have done all these things at Your word" (1 Kings 18:36b).

That is the secret to God's power—doing everything according to God's word. If we have eyes to see and ears to hear the Spirit of wisdom and revelation, we will operate in the exceeding greatness of His power because the Spirit of counsel always works with the Spirit of might. As we ascend into Heaven and receive revelation, we bring the manifestation back to earth.

SPIRITS OF WISDOM AND REVELATION

Wisdom means to "rightly divide knowledge." It involves correct delivery of revelation. When we receive God's wisdom, we know when and how to present our revelation to others. As the Lord discloses the secrets of His heart, our faith increases to see these spiritual things become a natural reality. If we don't have a revelation of the exceeding greatness of His power, we won't ever see the *manifestation* of the exceeding greatness of His power.

Revelation comes from the Holy Ghost. Remember Jesus' words to Peter after he said that Jesus was the Son of God: "Flesh and blood has not revealed this to you, but My Father who is in heaven" (Matt. 16:17b). Yes, the Father has sent the Holy Spirit to give us revelation—He lives inside each born-again believer. Second Peter 1:1-4 is my favorite passage about revelation, and I encourage you to study it. I have found several keys to increase the Spirit of wisdom and revelation in our lives.

INTIMACY

Revelation is always connected to intimate knowledge of Him. According to Second Peter 1:3, God has given us His divine power to activate the provision of everything that we need to live a life of godliness—it's all connected to the intimate knowledge of Him. All these treasures come from acquaintance with Him through prayer, intimacy, and worship, sitting at His feet, and being in His presence. As a result, the manifestation of His divine power comes automatically to give us everything we need to be godly. God has already made the provision; we just receive it through growing in intimate knowledge of Him.

Paul prayed: "Grace and peace be multiplied to you…" (2 Pet. 1:2). How would you like the multiplication of grace and peace? Again, we see these blessings automatically poured into our lives in intimacy with Jesus. This grace is the divine influence or the evidence of God on the heart, as well as the gift, favor, and benefits of God. Wouldn't you like more of the favor of God, His divine benefits, and His supernatural influence in your life? God's power manifests on your life when that grace multiplies. It automatically takes place in intimacy. Isn't that awesome? The knowledge of Him releases grace and peace. You can't have this knowledge without the Spirit of wisdom and revelation.

As we grow in revelation of the exceeding great and precious promises of God's Word, an impartation of the divine nature of God comes automatically. When we flow in the prophetic anointing, the very divine nature, character, Spirit, and personality of Christ imparts to us in intimacy through revelation. We will find people saying to us, "Why are you so blessed? You have more wholeness, prosperity, shalom, quietness, and rest in your life than most people." Then we can tell them that it all comes from our intimate connection with Him. We become more like Him just because we are having revelation of the exceeding great and precious promises of God's Word!

Rhema Promises Through Scripture Meditation

Rhema is a Greek word that means "that which is or has been uttered by the living voice."[22] Receiving the rhema promise of God through meditation also stirs up wisdom and revelation in our life. When I want revelation, I live meditation. King David understood this: "My mouth shall speak wisdom, and the meditation of my heart shall give understanding" (Ps. 49:3).

Meditation and revelation are interconnected—meditation brings revelation and revelation brings the manifestation of what has been revealed. When we first see or hear the Word, it's not fully revealed. However, when we meditate on it and when we pray it, revelation comes and begins working to bring the manifestation. Often we don't have the manifestation of what we know because we haven't meditated until we received that blazing revelation inside our spirit that releases the manifestation of the promise.

Once a verse becomes revelation to you, the devil can never take it from you. If you are not partaking of God's Word, you won't receive revelation or partake of that divine nature.

GODLY CHARACTER

This passage in Second Peter provides a blueprint for godly character:

> *But also for this very reason, giving all diligence, add to your faith virtue, to virtue knowledge, to knowledge self-control, to self-control perseverance, to perseverance godliness, to godliness brotherly kindness, and to brotherly kindness love. For if these things are yours and abound, you will be neither barren nor unfruitful in the knowledge of our Lord Jesus Christ. For he who lacks these things is shortsighted, even to blindness, and has forgotten that he was cleansed from his old sins* (2 Peter 1:5-9).

Some saints are barren and unfruitful in revelation because of character issues. There is a connection. We need to long to be more like Jesus. We have to cry out for the Spirit of God to change us: "Lord, I want to be like You. Let me behold You, for I can only become like the one I see. Holy Spirit, help me." When our heart cries out like that, the Spirit brings us into an increase of the Spirit of wisdom and revelation, because the Bible says that if these things are ours and abound in us, we will not be barren or unfruitful.

As we begin to behold the glory of the only begotten Son, and spend time in His presence, His character and very nature is forged in us. Transference takes place by the Spirit of God to transform us from glory to glory. Godly character continues to grow as we yield ourselves to the Holy Spirit's cleansing process and as we submit to the discipline of the Father.

We can't become who God wants us to be without partaking of Him, without His grace and without His divine influence. This is crucial because through divine influence comes everything pertaining to life. God's blessings pour out on our finances, family, business, and physical health—all things. The whole process weaves together. God has put His divine nature in the prophetic word. In that word comes character growth. A passion to grow in Christ-like character is vitally connected to growing in wisdom and revelation. However, this divine influence doesn't happen if we are not in the knowledge of Him or if we are not intimately connected to Him. If we aren't doing these things, there isn't the multiplication of grace, peace, and divine influence to become who He wants us to be.

Take time to meditate on Second Peter 1:1-8 until you receive the wonderful revelation of the message.

WAITING FOR GOD'S COUNSEL

Psalm 106:13,15 shows us that receiving revelation is closely connected to waiting for counsel: "They soon forgot His works; they did not wait for His counsel....And He gave them their request, but sent leanness into their soul." Verse 15 shows us the consequences of their neglect: He put a disease in their soul. This spiritual condition is like First Samuel 3:1 when the word of the Lord became rare and visions were infrequent.

Are you in a place where the word of the Lord is rare, visions are infrequent, or you lack prophetic vision? The increase of revelation comes as we wait for His counsel. Revelation was rare to the people of Israel because they weren't waiting in His presence or expecting to hear from Him. We need to come to Him saying, "Here I am, Lord, an hour before the service tonight, to receive Your counsel." Jesus wants us only to do those things that we see the Father doing—He doesn't want us doing things because of tradition or because of man's ideas.

In His place of waiting, Jesus saw what the Father was doing—He awoke long before daybreak, or He waited on the mountain all night in prayer. Jesus received counsel and revelation because He often withdrew into the wilderness and prayed. And it wasn't just about praying. I believe He had times when He sat at the Father's feet, like Mary sat at His feet, and He didn't say anything. He just looked up at the face of God waiting, waiting, and waiting.

This is not about being in the Word or being in prayer—it's about being in God's presence where you don't do anything but wait. As we learn to wait on the Lord, revelation, fruitfulness, favor, and financial prosperity overcome the wasting disease and leanness of soul. As we spend time waiting before the Lord, He opens up the television screen in Heaven for us to see what the Father is doing.

The longer I wait, the more revelation God gives me about people's afflictions or needs. I take time daily with Him.

SANCTIFIED IMAGINATION

You have to be free to dream—a big God means big dreams and big visions. I want you to have Holy Ghost fantasies. Holy Ghost fantasies helped birth my ministry and fulfill the prophetic words over my life.

Ministry begins in the imagination. It begins in your dreams. It begins in Holy Ghost fantasies. It begins in seeing yourself be who God has called you to be. Sanctified imagination is a powerful tool to get you over barriers of fear, unworthiness, rejection, and insecurity. I kept pressing in and something actually birthed that brought forth my destiny. Now I do all those things I used to dream about.

Many of you have lost your vision because the devil told you it was pride. He has robbed the power from your goals and dreams. There are things that God has placed in you that make you tick and make you weep. Something resonates within you. My heart burns with evangelism—the masses, the crusades, the multitudes, and cities—that's what motivates me. What motivates you?

SEEK WISDOM

As you've learned in Chapter Nine, God talks about wisdom using the personal pronoun "her." To get wisdom, you have to seek, love, honor, desire, promote, and make yourself available to her.

When I was saved, I prayed every day for the Spirit of wisdom and spent hours seeking revelation. It became a part of me because it is a part of Jesus. King Solomon, a man known for his wisdom, encouraged the seeking out of understanding: "My son, if you receive my words, and treasure my commands within you, so that you incline your ear to wisdom, and apply your heart to understanding; Yes, if you cry out for discernment, and lift up your voice for understanding…" (Prov. 2:1-3).

The Lord wants us to lift our voice and cry out for understanding. He wants us to "seek her as silver, and search for her as for hidden treasures," then we will "understand the fear of the Lord, and find the knowledge of God" (Prov. 2:4-5). The Lord gives wisdom, knowledge, and understanding to the upright. Listen to Solomon's counsel about wisdom:

> *Get wisdom! Get understanding! Do not forget, nor turn away from the words of my mouth. Do not forsake her, and she will preserve you; love her, and she will keep you. Wisdom is the principal thing; therefore get wisdom. And in all your getting, get understanding. Exalt her, and she will promote you; she will bring you honor, when you embrace her. She will place on your head an ornament of grace; a crown of glory she will deliver to you* (Proverbs 4:5-9).

Ask for the anointing of the Spirit of wisdom and revelation in your life. Also, ask the Lord to send the fullness of the Holy Spirit to you, with the manifestation of each of the seven Spirits of God. Cry out for wisdom and understanding; pray for counsel and might; petition God for knowledge and greater fear of the Lord. Wait on God until He rests on you, as He rested upon Jesus, with a powerful manifestation of the Spirit of the Lord.

RECEIVE THE TRANSFERABLE SUPERNATURAL ANOINTING

It's time to receive that transferable anointing for new adventures in the supernatural realm. Confess your sin and ask for a new washing—

appropriate the cleansing power of the blood of Jesus. Then ask for a safe place to hide in Him. Now with your heart, begin to touch the Lord through worship. Submit yourself to the Lord and ask for the Spirit of truth. The Father so wants to give you good gifts—just rest in His goodness. Just as the apostle Paul petitioned the Lord on your behalf (see Eph. 1:17-18), I want you to align yourself in simple faith with this prayer that I've prayed for you. Then I will include a simple prayer of faith for you to pray wherever you are.

> *Father, I ask You, in the name of Jesus, to begin to release Your transferable supernatural anointing for those asking right now for more of the supernatural realm. I release it now in Jesus' name! I pray that today they will walk into a greater level of the reality of the supernatural—dreams, trances, prophecy, and visions. I pray for an open heaven and an increased ability to hear Your voice. I also ask that the Holy Spirit will descend on their life and release scrolls containing their commissions and destiny in the spirit. Now, God, I ask You to pour out Your power and grace, that those agreeing with this prayer will receive an open Heaven and be led by You into the spiritual realm.*

Now, by faith, receive supernatural experiences and encounters with God! Let an explosion of miracles and healing come into your ministry now. I want you to pray this prayer aloud now:

> *Father, activate me in the supernatural. Open my spiritual senses; let me see into the true, lasting realm, the realm You*

336

live in. Help me to keep my eyes on the supernatural and not be distracted by the temptations of this world that are corrupt and fading away. I want this anointing transferred onto my life. I want to walk in my heavenly inheritance now. I don't want to wait until I die to see Your lovely face. I believe that You are no respecter of persons and if You performed miracles and sent angels and transported people in times past, You also want to do that with me for the purpose of knowing You better, loving You more, and serving the lost with a loving heart. Make me useful for Your Kingdom. I pray that the gifts of the Spirit and the seven Spirits of God would fill me and abide with me. Give me a greater release of miracles, prophecy, signs, and wonders. Holy Spirit, I receive—come now. I put my faith out for an increase in the supernatural. Thank You, Lord. I ask in Jesus' name.

Now I want you to pray this prayer regularly from this day forward, and believe that God is opening your spiritual eyes and taking you deeper into the supernatural realm. Live more in the invisible realm and learn how to walk daily in that place. Focus on the higher things of God that transcend the daily distractions in the natural realm. Then watch God take you on an incredible journey with Him as He lifts you higher in His spirit realm and carries you further into your destiny. You'll find the treasures of Heaven as you fix your eyes on the reality of the eternal, supernatural world of God.

Set your mind on things above, not on things on the earth (Colossians 3:2).

We do not look at the things which are seen, but at the things which are not seen. For the things which are seen are temporary, but the things which are not seen are eternal (2 Corinthians 4:18).

Chapter Thirteen

SUPERNATURAL ENCOUNTERS

As you've read so far, a great host of men and women in the Bible, from Genesis through to Revelation, experienced trances, visions, dreams, angelic visitations, prophecy, visitations of God, and even the audible voice of the Lord. The good news is, it happens to saints today, and as God's children, we should all experience genuine encounters with the Spirit of truth for He is the One who inspires all true supernatural encounters.

In this chapter, you will read some inspiring testimonies of ordinary people who have experienced powerful spiritual encounters. Every single one of these encounters is a result of a passion to know, experience, and see the Master. They've sought the "spirit of wisdom and revelation in the knowledge of Him" (Eph. 1:17).

You are destined to be a sign and a wonder, and it's my hope that you, too, will reach out into the spiritual realm and live and walk in God's power. God wants to bring you into a heavenly experience with Him. I pray that these accounts will ignite a fire of desire in your heart that moves, motivates, and compels you to open your spiritual eyes to all that God wants to give you and work through you. It is possible for ordinary saints today to experience His presence, incredible intimacy, and friendship, as testified here.

God will work through our testimonies when we lift Him up from the earth. He promises to draw all men unto Himself (see John 12:32). The word *draw* in the Greek translation means "to drag." It is my prayer that through the witnesses below, Jesus will drag you unto Himself, and that these testimonies will be an inspiration for your own open heavens.

I'm so thankful for those who have shared their stories here, and I rejoice for what God has done in their lives and through our ministry. We thank them for "saying so," for declaring His works, and making known to our readers that the Kingdom of Heaven is now.

VISION TRANSFORMS LIFE

I went to the "Secret Place" conference [January 2008] by faith and I knew that God was going to do something big in me, but I didn't know what.

It seemed like every time Jason Upton sang, I would cry. The first three days, I was crying a lot. On the third day, the guest speaker gave an altar call. I went as close to the front as I could and he said, "You have to love yourself before you can love others." And I thought to myself, "No! How can I love myself when I don't even like myself?" The speaker kept saying this: "Love yourself." And I kept saying, "No." I decided to close my eyes, and try to block out what was being said. When I closed my eyes, I had a vision: I was in a field and in the field, waiting for me, was Jesus. So I went up to Him and I asked

Him, "How can You love me? I've messed up and fallen short so many times. How can You love me?"

Jesus ran up to me, and gave me a big hug. He said, "My son, I love you, your sins are covered by the blood, and My Father loves you...." Right then and there, I accepted myself. For the first time, I can say, "I do love myself, like Jesus loves me." I couldn't help but cry...Praise God! Thank God for His love and grace. *I have come so that you may have life, and have it to the fullest* (see John 10:10).

ROGER SMITH

Kitimat, British Columbia

GLORY VIA E-MAIL

At about 6 P.M. on Wednesday, February 7, 2007, I opened the e-mail from Todd about his encounter with "The Greater Glory." As I read the message, the Glory of God broke through and touched me! There was an incredible power that came off the very words of that message and jolted my spirit! I was in the fourth day of a fast and crying out to God for MORE of Him. Somewhere in my prayers earlier that evening, I had spoken to the Lord about the story of "Balaam's Donkey." I was asking Him to again move that "spirit" that was involved in that biblical encounter. I wasn't even sure what exactly I was asking. I just knew in my spirit there was a key there. I remember asking Father to raise up another "Balaam's Donkey" to speak truth.

Today, I just now listened to Todd's full description of his supernatural encounter (that he wrote about) in the Podcast. I nearly fell down as he taught on the "Spirit of the Fear of the Lord" that was present in that story of Balaam's Donkey! I love the Holy Spirit and how He moves within the Body simultaneously. Also, today, I received a prophetic email message prophesying for all of us to "leave the past behind… deliberately break yourself free from rejection and regret so you can pursue your spiritual path in PURITY and liberty." This is in total agreement with the Angel ("being") in Todd's vision, breaking off the shackles of the past that keep us from our future.

I stand in the prayer of agreement with Todd and Fresh Fire Ministries in seeking the Lord to release greater glory and for our hearts to be changed in holiness for greater capacity to bear this glory. I pray the Lord will raise up one of those pockets here in my little town. Yes, God, we want You and please do not remove Your hand from us! In His Goodness….

TIFFANY ROCHE

Menlo Park, California

HIT BY SPIRITUAL LIGHTNING TWICE

While standing in line to testify of being healed from low blood sugar, I was also going to ask for prayer for neuropathy damage. There in line, the Holy Spirit told me not to ask for that, but rather to ask for the anointing that He wanted me able to take out my own trash (referring to infirmities). I did exactly what the Holy Spirit said. Prophet/evangelist Todd reached out and grabbed me in a bear hug and lifted me (I'm 230 pounds) up off my feet into the air. When he did that, a lightning bolt of Holy power hit me as never before since God called me in 1976.

When Todd stood me back down he blessed me with his mantle, plus double, and told me that he only did that when God told him. And again God's power hit me the second time. I danced with that lightning bolt of God's Holy power, and I never dance. The Holy Spirit's wind hit me, throwing me backward past all of Brother Todd's catchers. Five days later, the Holy Spirit still keeps coming in on me at various times during the day with no respect for where I am or who I'm talking to. Praise God! Everywhere I go people are looking at me as though I have two heads. It's okay; I smile because I know why.

RONALD PHILLIPS

Winterhaven

2007-07-03

15-YEAR-OLD GIRL HAS SUPERNATURAL ENCOUNTER WITH ANGELS

Right after I recommitted my life back to Christ, the Lord instructed me to give up my old friends, and my old life, and I did. About a week after I had done that, the Lord blessed me with new friends, not people, but angels! About a week after I renounced my old life and friends, I was praying at about 10 P.M., and then someone said my name. I turned around and a huge angel from my ceiling to the floor spoke to me and I got scared; but he said, "Don't be afraid, Alyssa, I bring you great news." He spoke with me for hours about what the Lord was going to do in my life.

Then, I went to sleep and I saw in a dream our whole house being taken over by angels, and even the Lord came into our house, walked around our beds, and blessed us and secured the whole place. Then the next night, a whole room full of angels came in and spoke with me and said, "We are so happy to have you back, ALYSSA!" Then a beautiful angel, named Mary, came and said, "We are here to believe in you." They stayed for a week and then left, but they told me after they left, "Even if we leave this room we will still be friends forever." This has changed my whole life! I'm hoping to come down to The Super Natural [*sic*] Training Center soon!

> ALYSSA, 15 YEARS OLD
> Clackamas, Oregon
> 2007-04-05

NEW FFM PARTNER HAS ANGELIC VISITATION

I just became a partner with Fresh Fire Ministries two days ago. Over the past year [2006] I have been experiencing angelic encounters, especially after I took the "School of the Supernatural Realms of Heaven."...Two days ago (August 22, 2006) I was soaking in my room and immediately I found myself in front of a door. I was kneeling down on my face in front of the door because the presence was so strong. The door opened and an angel walked out of the room. The angel was carrying a large book. I couldn't read what the book said, but it was big.

The angel then proceeded down (what appeared to be) a long hallway of doors (then it ended). Today (August 24, 2006) I was praying and the Lord instructed me to lay down and soak in His presence. As I was laying there soaking (to Todd's "Marinating" CD), the Lord spoke to me and said that I was entering into a position of soaking over a period of time and that He is going to send angels to me. I continued soaking and within minutes the same angel that I saw two days ago was standing before me, with the same book again....

JASON HOTHCKISS
FFM Harvester Covenant Partner
Holmdel, New Jersey

HOME VISITATION

Two months ago [February 2005] my husband and I experienced the most amazing presence of the Lord in our home. We were having dinner in the kitchen and the presence of God came so strong we couldn't even finish eating. My daughter fell on the floor in travail, I starting laughing uncontrollably, and we all began praying and crying. It was amazing. My husband and I went to bed later and the bed was shaking. My husband actually saw a cloud for three days.

He works out of home and could not work for four days. He cried and spoke in tongues the whole time.

We are amazed at the grace and mercy the Lord has had on us. It is nothing we have done. Ever since the tent meetings last summer, God has restored and healed our marriage and done wonderful things for us. After Todd prayed for my husband at the luncheon last summer, there have been great answers to prayer and great restoration and miracles in our family.

Hallelujah! I was at the Sunday night service and when I heard Todd say that God is going to visit homes with a great presence, I felt like shouting, *He has already done this for us!* In fact Richard and I said the same thing when this happened to us, that God is going to do amazing things in people's homes. We love Fresh Fire.

FRANCES
Langley, British Columbia
2005-04-27

TALKING WITH THE CLOUD OF WITNESSES

I was at Todd Bentley's conference in Dudley, U.K., in February 2005, and as I waited on God (during the soaking session), I suddenly saw this angel sitting in front of me. I was taken to a round room that was similar to an amphitheatre. I had the sense that this was a serious place, almost like a courtroom. I saw who I believed to be the apostle Paul, Kenneth Hagin, Kathryn Kuhlman, and others. They were all engaged in conversation. I thought, *Hey, this is great! I'll get to hear some great stuff here!* However, to my alarm, they all stopped talking, looked at me, and asked me to come down to where they were. I felt unworthy and humbled to be in such a place. I went down and the apostle Paul asked me to ask them a question.

I didn't know what to ask but a thought came and I said, "Tell me about binding and loosing."

The apostle Paul laughed and said, "You're at Todd's conference, aren't you?"

"Yes," I replied.

"Well, what Todd's told you about binding and loosing is right. He got it from here. He comes here a lot." They started to talk about Todd in very fond and favorable tones.

Then Kathryn Kuhlman took my hands and said to me, "Honey, you asked the Lord for my anointing when you were ten years old, didn't you?"

"Yes," I said. Immediately I had a picture of myself at age ten in New Zealand. I saw the room and exactly where I was standing. The memory was very vivid.

"Don't worry that it's many years since that time. Many, many, many people need this," she said. Then the group of people gathered around to pray for me. As they did, the vision ended.

This encounter left me a bit in awe. At the time, I wondered if I was suddenly going to be healing the sick like Kathryn Kuhlman. Instead, I received an increased awareness of the Holy Spirit and sensitivity to grieving Him. At times in prayer, I have felt the presence of the Lord so strong that I can do nothing but cry. I realize that this was a part of Kathryn's anointing—her strong sensitivity to the Holy Spirit. I believe I have to press in further to receive the fullness of that anointing, and it seems the Holy Spirit is guiding me to do that, giving me more of a desire to seek the Lord.

ROBYN TAN

London, England

February 2005

CONFERENCE VISION/ENCOUNTER

I received the clearest vision I have ever had on Friday, September 21, 2005, at the "Prophetic Seers" conference in Dudley. During the evening meeting as we were worshiping, I felt as though I was being lifted up. I looked down and saw in the spirit that I was standing on a snowcapped mountain. God told me straight away that the snow represented His purity (see Isa. 1:18). I lifted the snow and saw that there were loads of bright, colorful flowers, which represented the Church— children of God. Each one was not damaged by the snow that rested on it, but shone with the color which I believe represented the gifts and grace given to each one.

God said, "I have kept My church hidden up until this time, because I was saving the best until last." I then saw the snow begin to melt and form a stream that ran down the mountain into the cities below (the world). I watched the stream as it took the purity of God into the world and the flowers shone from the mountain, illuminating the mountain of God's presence. I looked down and saw a clump of unmelted snow at my feet. I felt as though God told me to pick it up and inhale it.

I took a deep breath; my eyes were now open but the vision was still so real. I was still there. As I breathed out, I felt overwhelmed by the vision and began to cry a lot. God was definitely releasing me of an anger and frustration I have had about the church (and myself as well) not really fulfilling our calling and being a true representation of the love of Jesus to the world. I couldn't tell anyone the vision for about an hour, because it was so real and overwhelming.

I walked away from the place where I received the vision and calmed myself down. Later I went back there and started to see it again, as though it had saturated the place where I had been standing. God later gave me the Scripture Romans 8:19 (AMP), "For [even the whole] creation (all nature) waits expectantly and longs earnestly for God's sons to be made known [waits for the revealing, the disclosing of their sonship]." God's amazing. There was such a sense of intimacy with God at the whole conference. Thanks for all the hard work your team put in to help us press in to God even deeper.

DAVID GLOVER

Leicestershire

SUPERNATURAL ENCOUNTERS AFTER PROPHETIC DECREE

In August of 2004, my wife and I drove down from Edmonton to Penticton, where I had lived as a child, for a one-week holiday. I had read Wes and Stacey's book, *Welcoming a Visitation of the Holy Spirit*. So we decided to drive down to Kelowna on Sunday, the day after we arrived, to visit their church. That particular service had a guest speaker named Todd Bentley. I was a little disappointed because I had just assumed Wes would be speaking that day.

Anyway, Todd comes on the platform, and I'm thinking to myself, *What is this? He's dressed like a thug, and talking so fast that I can't comprehend a word he's saying… And loud!* All I knew was that it was something prophetic or prophetic decrees or something. At that time I didn't even understand what that was, much less care. Honestly, I didn't think it was ever going to end. It did. My wife looks at me and says, "Well, what do you think?" This is about the time in my Christian walk where I was just learning to keep a bridle on my tongue. So I just said, "No comment. Where's the exit?"

My wife Marlene, by the way, thought we should buy Todd's CD: "Soaking in the Secret Place." We had a little "discussion" over that, and she won as usual. We headed back to our motel in Penticton. I should say here that although I had read the aforementioned book, and even though it does contain some prophetic things, this wasn't something I understood at that time. What drew me was the idea of a Holy Spirit who would actually manifest His presence to me personally. Even, in me, and upon me. Somebody that I would or could FEEL.

That same Sunday night I had a dream, in our motel room. Normally at home, it was my practice to get up early before work and go downstairs to pray for an hour or two. I have a special room downstairs where I can close the door and be alone with God before the world starts to stir. Even though I was very diligent about this, my prayers were very regimented. I would even watch the time and assign a certain amount of time to each particular topic. However, I dreamed I was back at home and it was early morning. I was in my prayer room as usual. But instead of my usual sitting position, I was on the carpet flat on my back. There was an extremely heavy invisible Presence pushing me down against the floor and not letting me get up. As I was struggling and fighting to get up I heard a loud voice say, "You can resist Me, or you can give in. It's your choice!" At that moment I knew if I wanted to get up, I would be able to do so. But I said, "No, I'll stay." I knew it was the Holy Spirit. I just let Him smother me in His glory. It was overwhelming. I woke up with glory all over me.

The following Sunday we arrived home from our trip, and Monday morning I went downstairs as usual and closed the door behind me. I was so depressed with my circumstances at that moment. Even with my prayer life. For the first time in a very long time, I didn't sit down to pray. I told God I was tired of praying and getting nowhere. I told Him I was just going to lie down on the couch and do nothing. I had enough. Now, you must understand that I have no idea what soaking is at this time. I have a CD player in that room already, and that's also where Todd's soaking CD wound up after the trip. So I thought that I might as well listen to it while I lay down.

I set my cell phone alarm for when I had to get up and lay down on the couch with the intention of getting a little extra sleep, really. Next thing I remember, I heard a sound behind me. I knew exactly where I was and what time it was. I was wondering why I couldn't hear the CD playing, because it should be. But the sound. It was coming from behind me, from the other side of the room, and I thought to myself, *The furnace is sure kicking in loudly. There must be something wrong.* Then it got louder and closer. I was just about to get up and, wham! It was on me. It's hard to describe. Imagine a freight train or a hurricane bearing right down on you with all of the wind and all the vibrations. And then at the same time, pure liquid glory splashing right through you, like tidal waves. When I started to open my eyes, it would diminish and when I closed my eyes it would start right back up again.

I was literally buzzing all day. Needless to say, I could hardly wait to get back downstairs on Tuesday morning. I put the CD on, and again I found myself in the wind tunnel. But man, what a wind! Next thing I know, Jesus is standing beside me, but He's so big that His upper body is clear through the roof. I couldn't make out the details of His face, but I knew it was Jesus.

Then the fear of the Lord hit me, and I couldn't get small enough. And then little tornadoes were in the room. They were all lit up and had shining, glittering, gold-colored flecks swirling within them. And the rest of the week was pretty much the same. Since then, the frequency is down, but it is still happening. I've resumed praying as well, but with a lot more joy. Not that long ago, I nodded off a little, while praying and once again there was that rumbling in the distance. I thought to myself, *I know what's happening next. Get ready for the wind!*

Just as I thought that, the wind suddenly stopped short of me, hovered there for a few seconds, and then, wham! I got hit with such an electrical charge that I literally bounced in the air. I thought I heard God say, "You haven't got Me figured out yet!"

I grew up feeling very alone and rejected. No hugging, kissing, or touching. All my life I felt untouchable, unlovable, dirty and ugly. I was miraculously delivered from severe alcoholism and other things, six years ago when someone handed me a book called *The Bondage Breaker*, by Neil Anderson. I was instantly delivered of addictions overnight. Since that day I have lived a godly life. But I could just never feel God the way I wanted to. That is why I finally decided to let you guys know how you changed my life.

I'm very sure that there are a lot of people just like me who desire intimacy with God, but it just seems so impossible. May I suggest, stop trying so hard to make Him love you. Just lie down with your desire and wait. He will come!

REN HARMS

Edmonton, Alberta

VISITING GOD'S HOME

In November 2003, I attended a conference in Kansas City. Todd Bentley spoke in the evenings and Patricia King hosted a *Glory School* in the daytime. I went with little enthusiasm because I was in the throes of a very long spiritual dry spell, and I was not wholly sold on the recent teachings I'd heard from Patricia King and Todd Bentley about the availability of the spiritual realm. I'd had one or two profound spiritual experiences in the past, but they were rare, and now I was being told that the spiritual realm was where believers are supposed to live—a realm that is easily available to every one of us who desires it.

On the last day, the first of several visions began. I stood with Jesus in mid-heaven and looked below us to see the great expanse of the earth. We were so far above it that I could easily see its curvature.

"What do you see?" He asked. I looked below at the vast, blue sparkling waters of the ocean, the green and brown of the continents, and the gauzy haze of floating white clouds high above. My heart burst with love for my terrestrial home.

"It's just beautiful, Lord. It's safety. It's security. It's where I live!" I told Him enthusiastically.

"Don't let this (earthly planet) cap your experience with Me," He said. Answering as a small child, I was pleased to comply, "OK!"

The scene suddenly changed below us, and now we were standing above the throne room. I was shocked to see that there was no one sitting on the throne!

"Lord," I exclaimed in alarm, "Why aren't You sitting on the throne?" Speaking slowly and enunciating clearly as if speaking to a very small child, He explained, "I reign from there, but it is not where I live."

More amazed than before, I asked, "You don't?" and speaking very slowly and clearly He smiled and said, "No. I live in another universe."

Stunned, I exclaimed, "You DO?"

"Yes," He said, "Would you like to come and see?" I couldn't believe my ears! He had just invited me to "another universe," to His very own home!

"Yes!" I exclaimed.

He pointed up into the black sky above us and said, "Follow the first star until morning." His finger pointed to a bright object in the heavens that looked somewhat like a planet. Immediately I rocketed toward it. As I drew closer, I could see that it was very lovely and luminescent, and resembled a fresh water pearl, more pear-shaped than round. Then, in an instant, I had arrived.

I found myself in a room that I knew was His living room. Although it was a regular size, it was the most glorious room I had ever seen. Narrow rays of golden light emanated from myriads of points around the room and shone across to their opposite side. Each ray fanned out as it traveled from its point, and every ray was lovely beyond description and seemed to dance. Because of the abundance of light, I could see nothing, not even Him, though I knew He was very near.

He invited me to sit down. I looked around but could see no furniture.

"Where, Lord?" I asked.

"Oh—just anywhere." I continued to look for a place to sit but could see nothing, not even the floor. I knew the floor was down there somewhere because I was standing on it, so I just tossed myself backward, knowing that I would find it. Instead of falling to the floor, rays of light quickly rose from below and caught me, holding me in a reclining position!

Because I couldn't see much, I closed my eyes and just enjoyed reclining beside Jesus. I reached out to Him, silently asking for His hand, which He gave me. I drew His hand to my lips, pressed an adoring kiss into His palm, then opened my eyes and was shocked and amazed. His palm was a hand of light! I gazed in wonder at it and had a powerful revelation that this was a *supernatural* hand—a hand that could do anything.

Tonja Dillard Clark

Missouri

November 2003

Vision in Chicago Releases
Salvation in Uganda

I had applied to go with Fresh Fire Ministries to Uganda, Africa, in November 2002. Shortly after, I was at a hot dog stand in Chicago when I suddenly had a vision. In it, I saw a man in a yellow shirt, sitting under one single African tree. He held something I'd never seen before.

I said, "God, what am I seeing?"

He answered, "That is an instrument in his hands. I want you to tell this man that I am Lord, I am going to heal his teeth, he will make music unto Me, and he and his whole family will be saved."

When I arrived in Jinga, Uganda, I had forgotten the vision. However, as part of a prison ministry team, we'd gone to a prison; and as I sat on the sidewalk in front of the prisoners and looked out into the concrete yard, I saw one single African tree! Sitting beneath it (just as in my vision), was the man in a yellow shirt!

"Lord, I can see You are working here, but in the vision You showed me he had an instrument in his hands. Well, God, where is the instrument?"

No sooner had I prayed than across the prison courtyard came two men carrying the very instruments that were in the vision! They were some sort of lyre or stringed instruments, seemingly made of wood and strings. The Holy Spirit was so all over me at this point that I just HAD to bring this word forth!

I stood up and called this man out: "When I was in America buying food, God gave me a vision and a message for you, sir," and I pointed to the man in the yellow shirt. All eyes turned to him, and he himself turned around to see whom I was pointing at. When he realized it was he, I told him to come up to the front. I said, "Jesus wants you to know that HE is Lord and that He is going to heal your teeth," at which point the man's whole facial expression softened and was visibly moved. I continued, "Those men over there are going to teach you how to play those instruments that they are carrying."

A huge roar and cheer came from the crowd. "You will make music unto the Lord and you and your whole family will be saved."

I asked him if he had ever given his life to Jesus and made Him Lord of his life, and he said, "No."

"Do you want to?" I asked, and he said, "YES!"

He had been a Muslim, but he gave his life to Jesus that day. While I was waiting and watching this man earlier, I kept hearing the name, "Daniel." I somehow knew that when Muslims leave the Islamic faith that they are cut off from their family and, in essence, lose their name. Out of my mouth came, "Well, God is giving you a new name today. Your name is Daniel," and I continued to prophesy as the Lord led. It was like someone turned a light switch on inside this man and he could not stop smiling, laughing, and praising God! He went over, danced, and sang with the band as they played worship music.

Think of the supernatural sovereign power of God to take a girl from Wisconsin, give her a vision (while buying a hot dog in Chicago), and send her to Africa to prophesy to a prisoner under a tree (he missed the altar call)—all to save his soul!

God said to me very clearly that afternoon, "Eileen, NOW, will you please embrace the prophetic call I have on you?" God was asking if I would step out of what I wanted and embrace what He had given me.

Finally, humbly, I said, "Yes, Lord, yes." Since then, God has brought forth many more things through His awesome power and my simple obedience.

EILEEN BERGLUND
Racine, Wisconsin
November 2002

REVELATIONS IN THE TENT OF MEETING

In April 2002, I went to the *Open Heavens Conference* in Abbotsford, British Columbia. We received very clear teaching about accessing the third Heaven. Todd and others laid hands on us for impartation and for the activation of our spiritual senses, and I had my first encounter in Heaven, seeing very clearly the things God wanted to show me.

On the way home the Lord said, "When you go home, go to the store and buy a tent. I will meet with you in the tent. I will restore to you the Feast of Tabernacles." I arrived home at 11 P.M., drove straight to Wal-Mart and bought a small tent, and then set it up in my living room.

My wife, Lynnie, sheltered me from the distractions that would normally fill my day as I began to spend many hours in the tent. Inside, I'd zip it shut, listen to instrumental music, and soak in the presence of the Lord. As a result (of soaking), I experienced and saw Heaven.

In one encounter, I was walking through a green field in Heaven on a pathway lined with round stones that had eyes that looked at me. I wondered, *What is this... stones with eyes?* Immediately the answer came, "Everything in Heaven is made of living substance. That is why the rocks can cry out and praise Me and why the trees of the field can clap their hands." As I meditated on that thought, the Lord said, "When My people spend time with Me in Heaven, they will absorb the very life of Heaven. When My Church spends time in Heaven, it will spring forth with new life. Remember Aaron's budding rod? It spent one night in the Holiest Place and the dead stick came alive." I realized that God has a plan to catch the Church up in the Spirit and to bring forth new life within her.

After I spent several weeks and many hours in the tent, my wife said, "I like it when you spend time in the tent."

"Why?" I asked.

"You come out tender," she replied.

I soon started to notice that my character was changing, and that revelations, words of knowledge, words of wisdom, prophecy, and healings were becoming more abundant in my life. I also began to see many Scriptures in a new light, and I received a deposit of new understanding that has transformed my preaching and teaching. As I look back on the last three years, I can say that they have been the best of my whole life. But the Lord says, "This is only the beginning. The best is yet to come!"

DENNIS WALKER
Las Vegas, Nevada

THE SEVEN SPIRITS OF GOD

Since I began walking with the Lord in 1989, God has blessed me with tremendous prophetic encounters and visitations. In June 1994, during an increased time of holy desperation, I went to a Benny Hinn conference and received a powerful deposit of the anointing. My life was radically impacted. The Lord began to move mightily through my ministry in ways I had not experienced before—healings, signs and wonders, and power demonstrations that impacted thousands in many regions.

Over the course of the next few years, we had several meetings that exploded into extended meetings. Thousands of lives were changed, and the Word of God and His power demonstrations impacted many regions. Our ministry saw and moved in a very powerful anointing of the Holy Spirit up to this point. That brings me to the prophetic encounter that I had when Todd came in August 2002.

In spite of all that God was pouring out, I knew deep in my spirit that there was something more! When we began planning the *School of Revival* with Todd Bentley in August 2002 in Amarillo, Texas, the Lord spoke to me that something powerful was going to take place. I began pressing in and calling out to go deeper into the things of God. Little did I know that what was about to take place was literally going to catapult me to another level in the Lord.

During one of the sessions, I was caught up in this life-changing prophetic encounter. All of a sudden, I saw a huge, mighty angel, and he shouted, "Open up your mouth." I instantly obeyed. He said, "Eat this!" and then he threw something at me. I felt it hit inside my mouth and I ate it! Then the encounter was over.

Out of all the spiritual experiences and visitations I'd had, I must admit, this was a new one. I was blown away. I immediately looked in my Bible and marked several passages that pertained to what had just happened (see Ezek. 3:1-4; Rev. 10:8-11). My team came to me and asked,

"What just happened to you?" I was still in shock but managed to stammer, "I just ate a scroll or book or something. This big angel threw it at me."

On Sunday morning, Todd preached on eating the scrolls for new commissionings of the Lord. As he was preaching, this word was literally imploding in my inner man. I had not said anything to Todd about my visitation, and here he was preaching a message on the scrolls and the books just as I had encountered earlier! This event would start a series of prophetic encounters with the Lord over the course of the next three months that impacted not only me, but my family and our ministry.

A few weeks after the school, the Holy Spirit woke me early one morning and prompted me to pray. I drove to our office and as I walked through the front door, immediately I knew that it was going to be a very, very powerful time. The atmosphere was charged with God's presence. I instantly kicked off my shoes. As I walked through the hallway, I looked up and with my natural eyes—not in a vision—as real as any person, there stood the same mighty angel that told me to eat the book.

He was huge and radiated strength, power, and authority. I tell you the truth, I was undone. I immediately made a sharp right turn into my office and began to pray. The Holy Spirit revealed some incredible things of the Lord. After about 45 minutes of divine downloads, I asked the Holy Spirit about the angel in the hall. He spoke to my heart and said, "He has names written upon his arm and legs. Go look at the names."

Now you must understand, this guy was massive in

splendor and I was actually somewhat afraid to look at him again. I slowly cracked my office door and kind of peeked to see if he was still there. Yep, he was. I mustered my courage and leaped into the hall. I saw names written on each shoulder, arm, and leg. Then he was gone. For the next few hours, I was literally undone as I thought about what had just taken place.

In October, I was invited to do a meeting called *Seven Days of Glory*. As I was preparing in the pastor's office, I asked the Lord for the counsel of Heaven for the meetings, the church, and for the region. All of sudden, I was caught up before the Lord's throne. He was just blazing with great power and glory!

It is an incredible experience to see the Lord in power. People ask me, "What was it like?" I don't have words adequate to describe the magnitude of power that was radiating from Him. It is unexplainable. My breath was literally taken away.

All of a sudden, I saw the same mighty angel who gave me the scroll and visited me in the office. This angel walked up to the Lord, and the shape of the Lord's hand became visible. I could see that He was holding an envelope. He handed it to the angel and the angel walked over and handed it to me. At this point, I was completely blown away. I took the envelope to read what was inside and I was so stunned that I dropped it! The angel picked it up and handed it back to me. I looked again at the contents of the envelope and two Scriptures were written inside, Revelation 4:5 and Isaiah 11:2. Both of them speak about the seven Spirits of God.

Since the angelic encounter in Amarillo, I have been on a powerful journey with the Lord to learn about the seven Spirits of God. I now teach and minister out of a deep revelation and deep flow of the seven Spirits of God. I want to honor Todd as a man of God and as my friend. The Lord has used Todd to dramatically impact my life and ministry.

KEITH MILLER
Stand Firm World Ministries
www.sfwm.org
Amarillo, Texas

"JESUS IS SITTING ON MY BED!"

In October 2001, Ivan Roman and I were living in an apartment next to the Fresh Fire office in Abbotsford, British Columbia. Although I wasn't saved yet, I had been working for Fresh Fire for about three months and I would pray constantly as I went throughout the house. Ivan was a very good tutor in helping me learn how to pray; however, I wasn't praying for anything in particular and I definitely wasn't expecting a visitation from Jesus! One night around 10 P.M., I went into my room and got my Bible off the end table. I sat on my bed and started reading and meditating on the presence of the Lord. What happened next was astounding!

All of a sudden, my bed started moving! At first, I thought Ivan had come into my room and sat on my bed, but when I looked down at the front right-hand corner of the bed, I saw Jesus sitting there! He turned around and looked right at me! Well, the only thing I knew about seeing Jesus was that it meant it's your time to go! So I got up and ran out of my bedroom. I shook all over and stood in the hall until Ivan saw me and asked what I was doing.

"Jesus is sitting in there on my bed! He is here to take me to Heaven and I'm not going back in there because I'm not going!" Ivan walked into my bedroom to check it out and said the presence of the Lord was strong and that it was a heavy visitation. It's something I will never forget. I know that I saw Jesus sitting on my bed.

After that, there were more visitations, and almost every day for two weeks I'd suddenly become slain in the Spirit. At times, I'd simply walk through the door of my apartment and fall under the weight of God's presence. The Holy Spirit would throw me on the floor, and I would lie there and "vibrate" sometimes for as long as 45 minutes. Ivan would have to drag me out of the apartment so we could go have dinner. We would go to a restaurant, eat lunch or dinner, and as soon as I walked through the door, I would find myself back down on my face. I will never forget those very exciting experiences.

That first visitation was the start of many amazing things that Jesus would do in my life. I really believe that this was how the Lord chose to draw me to Himself. Within a month of that first visitation, I went to Toronto, Ontario, with Fresh Fire and gave my heart to the Lord on November 14, 2001. My life has never been the same since!

DAVE BENTLEY
Abbotsford, British Columbia
January 2005

SEEING DEMONIC SPIRITS FLEE

When Todd Bentley ministered in Pensacola, Florida, at Brownsville Assembly of God, I watched the services on the Internet. Todd spoke about taking spiritual authority over the areas where he ministers, including the airwaves. At the end of the service, he began to move in the word of knowledge and the cameras scanned the attendees. I couldn't believe what I was seeing! When he would give the word of knowledge, I could see demonic spirits leaving different people. I was able to see the spirits two different ways: Some of the related spirits were gray and like overlays on the people, and the others were black. When the word of knowledge was released, I saw the demonic spirits leave people. Prior to this night, I had never had supernatural experiences like this. I have seen demonic spirits, but not in association with particular illnesses being revealed and never so many at one time. It's occurred a few times since then in other circumstances.

SHERRY FURLOW
Millbrook, Alabama

ANGELIC ENCOUNTER, HEAVENLY PORTAL, AND MIRACLES

I have been blessed to travel with Todd Bentley and Fresh Fire Ministries periodically since 2002. During these times of fellowship and ministry with Todd, there have been numerous encounters with the supernatural reality of God and the

Kingdom of Heaven. I first met Todd on October 24, 2001, in Springdale, Newfoundland. The Lord also opened my spiritual eyes and I began to both hear and see angels in those meetings. I saw an angel standing behind the worship team and I gazed on him for about 20 minutes. He was about 10 feet tall with a fierce countenance, and he wore a white robe and carried a large sword.

Later, Todd preached about the angel I'd seen (his name was Revival Harvest) and shared how it had visited him in Pastor Dave Mercer's office. On the last night of those meetings, Todd prayed for me so as to impart the healing anointing. As I was under the power, I began to see into the spirit realm. I saw Jesus descend into the church through a portal. Words cannot describe the glory and overwhelming love that invaded my spirit. Jesus then walked over to me, stood over my prostrate body, took my left hand in His, and blew into my palm. Oil began to run down my arm, and Jesus commissioned me with the Scriptures of Matthew 28:18-20 and Jeremiah 29:10b-14. I was unable to move for a long time, and it took nearly two hours before I could speak. A friend told me that my face was glowing!

After this encounter, I immediately began to walk in the supernatural reality of God. The anointing for miracles and healing immediately manifested in my life along with the word of knowledge. The Lord miraculously opened the door for me to travel to the nations and to step out into full-time ministry. Today, my wife, Kathy, and I have traveled to 23 nations to preach the Gospel. We have seen 14,000 plus salvations, over 120 deaf healed, about 100 plus blind healed, and over 100 tumors vanish. Now thanks be to God who always leads us in triumph in Christ, and through us diffuses the fragrance of His knowledge in every place. To God be the Glory!

KEVIN BASCONI
Grandview, Missouri

GRANDMA GOES TO MALAWI

In 2002, I attended the *Glory School* in Kansas with Patricia King and Todd Bentley. When Todd began to speak of an upcoming trip to Malawi, Africa, the Holy Spirit fell on me, and it was as if the words were coming straight from Him through the mouth of Todd. My spirit began to be gripped with a desire to go on that trip with Fresh Fire, but there was a struggle going on within me: *Are you crazy? You're a 66-year-old grandma, and you're not able to come up with thousands of dollars.* Years earlier, I had been an evangelist going to the streets during Mardi Gras in New Orleans and other places doing street evangelism, but that had waned with years of comfort.

Todd called people to line up for impartation, and when he came to me, he roared over me and I hit the deck. The Holy Spirit said it was the roar of the Lion of Judah. I felt a download from Heaven of holy boldness, and I felt nine feet tall in the spirit. When I stood up, I was a different woman. I knew I received impartation. I immediately began to witness wherever

I went during that conference. I felt I had fire shut up in my bones as the prophets said, and I knew that the spirit to witness was restored.

That night after returning to my hotel room with my friend, I began to have a visitation. The Lord took me into an open vision where I was sitting on a stage behind Shonnah Bentley in Africa at a crusade where Todd was preaching. I saw thousands of Africans responding to the Gospel, miracles, and healing. Most profoundly, I saw Jesus walking through the crowd, and many were being healed as He walked among them. I then knew beyond a shadow of a doubt that I was to go with Todd to Malawi. I think it only really hit me the night the vision came to pass as I was in Africa sitting on that very podium, in the exact place I had seen myself watching Todd preach. Then I saw Jesus walking through the crowd just as in my vision.

Today, I feel about 16, and that old boldness I once had is not only restored but also more intense. I also know that the anointing to have dreams and visions was imparted because I've had an increase of them since I sat under Todd's ministry. I'm looking for more opportunities to go to the nations and lead people to the Lord. I told Him I wanted to go out in a blaze of glory. I am so excited about Todd and young people like him who are going mach speed to get things done in the Kingdom. I just laugh and ask these young ones if I can grab onto their coattails. It's going to be a fiery ride!

PATRICIA MASON
Spring Hill, Kansas

GOD'S GLORY VISITS THE MALL

During Fresh Fire's *Canada Ablaze* in Toronto in spring 2004, God's Kingdom came in the mall! At the end of the day, we were all to meet at the mall by Dundas Square before heading back. There were groups of people from *Ablaze* in the mall and it was an all-out glory fest in there! People were being led to the Lord and the love of Christ was being shared all over the place!

There were some people from our group who targeted the escalators. Two were on the main floor (looking over at the down escalator) throwing Holy Ghost fireballs on people, and another *Ablaze* guy rode the escalator doing it too. I watched as people were hit with fire! They'd jump or just gaze up to see what was affecting them. The Kingdom of God was being released and people were definitely being touched. Some saw angels riding the escalator with the *Ablaze* kid! It was cool! We were having a hard time even functioning at that point because the glory was so thick, and at times we couldn't even walk and had to hang onto things.

Our leader came toward us to scold us a little because as the power increased we drew a lot of attention. As he approached, a portal opened up in the middle of the mall, and a perfectly round shaft of light came down from the ceiling and fell on the floor before the group of us! This caused him to pull back from the glory and shield his face as he was hit by the glory of God! Then he began shaking and manifesting in the glory along with everyone in our group. It was incredible.

The very atmosphere in the mall had been changed

because the Kingdom of God had been released over those three days through every *Ablaze* person! Now I know that the Kingdom of Heaven is being released from within us, just as Todd had preached in one meeting. I saw it, experienced it, and felt it.

Before *Toronto Ablaze*, I was a Spirit-filled believer who was so frustrated because I felt that there had to be more. After that week, I knew there was!

KIM GLOVER

Mattawan, Michigan

ANGELS, MANTLES, AND THE GLORY OF GOD

Through my friendship and association with Todd, I have learned much about the supernatural world and the operation of angels. Not only was I activated in the spirit for supernatural encounters, but he also helped me understand previous encounters I had with the angelic and their significance in my ministry, call, and function. Shortly before God launched me into the healing revival ministry, I had a profound encounter with both God's glory and the angelic. I was traveling with Todd for a month in Europe, in August 2003, and we were in one of our last meetings in Estonia. It had marked the one-year period of my "internship" with Todd, through whom I had learned how to operate in the word of knowledge and flow in the prophetic healing anointing. I knew in my heart it was like Elisha following and serving Elijah. I was waiting for a double-portion mantle.

During the meeting, I walked over to Todd on the platform. As we stood about two feet from each other, a strong angelic presence manifested on the platform between us. We both instantly knew it was the Angel of the Lord. As I passed my hand through the space of air between us, it became electrified with the presence of God. It was the presence of an angel being sent to help minister to the heirs of salvation. In that moment, I lifted my hands into a tangible glory cloud over our heads. I cried out to Todd, "Lift your hands. The glory cloud is over us!" As we did, miracles began happening all around the room as deaf ears, blind eyes, tumors, and many other sicknesses were instantly healed.

I then walked over and stood on the side of the platform as Todd released the anointing over the people. That moment became the crowning moment of my first year with Todd. Suddenly I felt a mantle being placed over my head and shoulders. It felt like a heavy blanket. As I shared with Todd what I was experiencing he proclaimed, "It's the mantle for mass crusades!" That night, through a supernatural encounter with the Angel of the Lord and the glory of God, I received a mantle for mass crusade evangelism. From there I have gone on to minister in mass crusades throughout India and Europe, seeing thousands saved, healed, and delivered, and we are currently making plans for Africa and South America.

MATT SORGER
Selden, New York

HOLY SPIRIT BOMB GOES OFF

I want to thank Fresh Fire Ministries for changing my life physically, emotionally, and spiritually through *Toronto Ablaze*. It was as if a Holy Spirit bomb went off in my home when I returned. My children immediately started seeing visions, and my nine-year-old daughter began to be taken to heavenly places where she dances with angels and talks with the Lord. My husband's heart was so hard when I got back that even the children prophesying over him the visions they saw didn't soften it. However, when he saw me shaking in the deep of sleep, the Lord broke off the religious spirit and let him see it was all real. I ache to be in the fullness of Him again, watching the Kingdom come and playing in the refreshing of His Spirit. Thank you for bringing the reality of His fullness.

JULIE MCHUGH
Plainwell, Michigan

IMPARTATION, PROPHETIC ACTIVATION, AND ANGELIC VISITATION

I went to see Todd Bentley at Pastor Severio's church in the Spanish Harlem in the Bronx because I was hungry for more of God and I wanted to experience supernatural things. Todd went around imparting the anointing (in his very special way) to everyone at the church. It was so fast that I wondered, *How effective could that be?* However, that night in the hotel, I clearly heard the voice of God in my sleep. He said that my daughter, Sydney, was set apart and her future was with Him. I woke up and I knew that this was an experience different from any other dream. I realized that I received a new anointing that night when Todd had prayed for impartation for me. It was the first of many other prophetic messages.

A few weeks later, I was abruptly awakened at around 12:30 A.M. I opened my eyes and I saw a portal on the ceiling of my room. The opening looked like moving ripples of light and water mixed together. The room was completely illuminated because it was full of angels in motion that were beaming with light. It looked like they were coming right at me, and I got scared and screamed, "JESUS!"

I looked around my room to make sure I wasn't dreaming. Their heads and bodies were like the sun. I covered my head, cried, and worshiped (the Lord) as I felt paralyzed. I shook all night and was in shock.

This past week, during the second week of fasting, I was awakened again at around 3 A.M. I saw a huge angel standing next to me. I made sure I looked at him really well. This angel was bright, full of light, and his garment was white but simple. I had fallen asleep sad and discouraged but was praying and giving God my burden. This angel brought me comfort and was a reminder that God was protecting me while I slept. Two days later, I was awakened abruptly, and I saw an angel between my husband and me. Again, I felt protection and comfort from God. We are in a battle, but God reigns and we'll be victorious!

MONICA SCALA

Toms River, New Jersey

TWELVE-YEAR-OLD RECEIVES PROPHETIC ANOINTING

I went to the Fresh Fire Ministries conference with my mother in Irving, Texas, in 2004. I didn't want to go and I was not walking right with God. At the conference, the second night during worship, the Holy Spirit miraculously touched me. No one prayed for me or laid hands on me, and the next thing I knew I had repented and was on the floor laughing and crying. Later, I found out that a friend from church had been praying for me intensely those three days I was at the conference. Since then, I've been right in my walk with God and I've tried to help my friends at Junior High by prophesying to them when the Holy Spirit tells me to do so.

I believe the Lord gave me the gift of prophecy at the conference, even though I didn't know it at the time. One night at Junior High, we were in worship, and I heard Him tell me to pray for Brittney who was standing in front of me. I was very scared and annoyed that the Holy Spirit would want me to go pray for her in front of everyone. But He kept nagging and nagging. It was as if He wouldn't shut up until I got it done. So finally, I went over to pray for her. I heard the Holy Spirit tell me to lay hands on her, and naturally, I asked Him what I should say. He said, "Lay hands on her and you'll find out." He tends to say that every time I ask those types of questions.

So I laid my hands on her and immediately I felt doubt, rejection, hopelessness, and sadness, and I knew that I was feeling what her spirit felt like. After I told her something, she started crying and I could feel that the Holy Spirit was giving her something and changing her. I praise the Lord for what He has done in my life.

RACHEL CURYLO

Dallas, Texas

VISITATION OF THE ANGEL OF COUNSEL AND MIGHT

In November 2003, at the Fresh Fire and Master Potter Ministries' joint *Glory Week Conference* with Todd Bentley, Bobby Conner, Paul Keith Davis, and me, the angel of counsel and might visited. That same angel visited Todd and two of his interns; both were at two different locations, but it was during the same period.

At this time, I experienced a profound angelic visitation about the sword of the Lord, end-time martyrdom, and the key to apostolic authority. Here's what happened. Bobby Conner came into my session when I was ministering, so I greeted him and grabbed his hands with a good morning handshake. The moment I touched his hands I felt a portal of glory open above me. A huge angel, 30 feet tall and towering above me, suddenly was knocking me around the front of the room. I could see the glint of a brilliant sword in His hands and a golden sash. The heavens started to open as angelic activity moved powerfully throughout the room. A realm of revelation and angelic activity permeated the atmosphere as I ministered prophetically to the people.

Simultaneously, this mighty angel visited Todd in his hotel

room and offered him the sword. It had a ruby stone in its handle and the blade of the sword was inscribed with Hebrews 4:12. Todd knew that this was the revelatory anointing of discerning hearts and thoughts. Then the angel told Todd that it was for Paul Keith who was ministering Saturday night. That afternoon Todd moved powerfully in words of knowledge under an open Heaven.

That evening Paul Keith was handing me the microphone to end the meeting. As he did, he said, "Oh, there's an angel on the side of the stage. Would you like to go up there?" Immediately I replied, "Yes" and came up on the stage. Suddenly, the power of God hit me and I was violently flung to the floor. Swiftly, without warning, a huge living sword was literally plunged into my chest. Pinned to the ground, I looked up and saw a huge warring angel, towering approximately 30 feet tall, standing in front of me. By revelation, I instantly knew this was the angel from the morning session, the angel of counsel and might, who was piercing me with the same sword of Hebrews 4:12.

As this realm of Heaven engulfed me with liquid fire and glory, I could not move. Finally, when I was able to get up, my hands shot out in front of me and I was holding this awesome living sword of light. The sword was drawn before me as lightning shot from the blade into the eternal realm.

Standing behind me, this angel of the Lord was holding my hands. I was this little child, engulfed in His arms, as we held this magnificent, shimmering sword together. The sword was the living Word full of authority, and as I held it, the fear of the Lord and the holiness of the Eternal One radiated throughout my being. This encounter continued for several hours.

I believe that the angelic encounters Todd and I experienced, the releasing of this sword to Paul Keith, the keen and key prophetic interpretation from Bobby Conner, and my own visitation of encountering the living sword of God reveals a prophetic picture for the Body of Christ as a whole. Like piecing together a puzzle, we all operated in a cluster anointing to put together all the clues in the Spirit of what God was saying.

I believe that we (like Joshua in Zechariah 3:8) are a living sign of an impartation God is releasing in His hour. It's not just for Todd or me; it's for everyone! The Lord is releasing a Hebrews 4:12 living Word of God sword to all who are willing to pay the price for it. If, like Joshua, we exchange our filthy garments for the rich robe and clean turban God is offering (see Zech. 3:4), the Angel of the Lord (see Ezek. 44) will place the Zadok sword in our hands.

God is changing our weapons of warfare! We cannot model them by elements of the past because the Lord is not only changing the guards, but also re-mantling the Body of Christ in new garments. As we learn the difference between the profane and holy, and use this season of grace to fall on the rock, lest the rock fall on us, we will wear new garments in the Spirit.

Jill Austin
Los Angeles, California

378

SUPERNATURAL JUSTICE

On March 3, 2004, I saw an angel standing over me. He said, "Write down these words for they are faithful and true. 'I have come to strengthen you for the days ahead. I give you this scroll, now eat it. Soon. Twenty-eight days.'" Twenty-eight days later Todd came to Dudley, England, to teach a healing school. On the Sunday of the conference, he shared on the honey scrolls. I ate the honey scroll that the Lord gave to me that morning, and since then I have known an increase in the revelatory realm. In 2004, I had five visits from angels who have come to me in inner visions, and this continued in 2005.

One particular encounter came out of Todd's teaching on heavenly courts and divine judgments. At the same time as the healing school, my husband and I were involved in a court battle with a kitchen company that had knocked a hole in our kitchen wall while fitting a new kitchen. They had failed to finish the work and refused to give us our deposit back. While in prayer seeking divine judgment, I saw a door open at the bottom of a turret.

The Lord called me up, and at the top was a man in the form of a servant dressed in a simple white robe with a rope sash. He gave me a scroll and said that it was the tactic. On it was a picture of the top branches of a tree. All the branches began to be lopped off until all that was left was the main trunk. Then I heard a voice say, "Even now the ax is laid to the root of the tree." Then I saw the trunk severed, and the root removed and thrown into the fire. I used this revelation with the Scriptures Matthew 3:10 and Isaiah 1 to pray for divine justice, that the Lord would chop down all the lies and deceit of this company and restore our money.

In July, we went to court and recovered all our money with compensation! While we were at court, my parents looked after our children and witnessed the local authority remove a tree opposite our house exactly as it was shown to me in the vision! They were so intrigued that they took numerous photos showing the whole process from the lopping off of the branches to the removal of the root. What was going on in the heavens was taking effect not only in the courtroom but also across the road in front of our house!

DEBORAH ORGILL
West Midlands, England

CHILD VISITS HEAVEN IN A DREAM

In the third week of January, I was soaking in the presence of God while listening to Todd's *Marinating* CD. My daughter, Jessica, who is seven years old, asked me if she could sleep on the floor with me. We fell asleep while the CD continued to play all night. In the morning, I asked her if she had any dreams. She said she dreamt that the whole family went to Heaven: "We went through this beautiful gate made of pearls, and there was this very clear water and we drank and played and ate some beautiful delicious fruits." She said it was so beautiful. She was very casual about it but still remembers her dream to this day.

NONNIE ROBERSON

Temple, Texas

THE REALITY OF THE SUPERNATURAL WORLD IN OUR HOUSE

Last August, 2004, Todd put on one of his Healing Schools in Amarillo, Texas. I knew that, despite the 15-hour drive, I had to be there. The school proved to be a life-changing event. I know I received major impartation from Todd and his team. I experienced levels of God's glory that I hadn't seen before. I had gold manifest on my hands for the first time, saw angels, and even saw glory clouds throughout the week.

The event that I believe affected Misty and I the most was when Dave Bentley, Todd's father, prayed for me to have a visitation of the angels involved in the ministry of William Branham. It was significant that the school was in Amarillo, because William Branham had lived there and I believe he was also buried in this city. Todd, Dave, and others from Fresh Fire had the chance to visit these sites and therefore had the opportunity to receive a fresh impartation.

Not fully knowing all that I received from that week, I hurried home to pray and give this impartation to my wife. The very night that I got home, the visitations began. As I began to pray for Misty to receive this impartation, she started to manifest gold dust on her face and arms. The anointing of the Holy Spirit was very strong in the room and the (spiritual) wine started to flow. It became obvious that we were not alone in the house.

The next month [September] we were with Todd again at Mahesh Chavda's church in South Carolina. Todd said something during this time that really spoke to our hunger, and out of eagerness to grow, we spent the Day of Atonement in fasting and prayer. It was not long after this event [October] that our house became a habitation of God's glory...Misty and I had started praying when, almost immediately, the anointing came. The atmosphere in our living room changed so suddenly that we were surprised when the presence of God and a strong anointing settled in. The thick stillness of God's splendor filled our house in a hazy glory cloud. This startled us, and the only thing we knew to do was begin to worship. At one point, an angel of revelation came, and Misty, under the anointing, sat down, went into a vision, and began to prophesy.

That marked the beginning of many encounters with God's glory and strong visitations of His ministering spirits. Since then, we've also had the awesome privilege of seeing angel feathers fall in most rooms in our house, as well as numerous glory clouds. Misty and I had heard about these things from ministers, books, and of course the Bible. However, we didn't realize that it was available to us. Just being common people, we thought these encounters were reserved only for ministers. Of course, all of these encounters have changed our lives forever.

Todd has really taught us to always give away what we have been given; nearly every time we pray for someone, we pray the prayer of impartation and visitation. I have gotten testimonies from people whom we have prayed for who began to have visitations and see angels with open eyes.

LADD AND MISTY DENISON
Thompson's Station, Tennessee

VISION OF GRACE AND MERCY

Visions were for great men of God in international ministry who had fasted for 40 days. Visions were not for a single mom with two girls who worked in the home-care service and who was a sinner. Well, that's what I thought before Todd Bentley's conference at Revival Fires in Dudley, England, in October 2004. I was just a normal Christian struggling to read my Bible and find time to pray like so many others. However, this was about to change. During worship, I suddenly found myself caught up in heavenly realms, and over the next five days, I had vision after vision!

[In one meeting] I was suddenly caught up in a living moving vision. I found myself standing in what looked like a warehouse. There was no end to the room. I asked what this place was, and immediately I sensed that this was a room in Heaven. The Holy Spirit said, "This is the room of Grace and Mercy." The Holy Spirit showed me the blankets of grace and mercy and that there were more than enough to go around all the people in the entire world for all of history. The Holy

Spirit showed me I could take blankets of grace and mercy to everyone who wanted one; however, He also said, "Not everyone in the world throughout all of history has wanted a blanket of My grace and mercy."

I began to walk through these vast corridors of racks of blankets, and I came across a golden table and a golden chair with red velvet cushioning on it. The Holy Spirit said, "The chair's name is Mercy." The table was called Grace, and I was surprised to see that it was untidy. I could see papers on it and they were in a state of disarray. I wondered why the table of Grace was so untidy. The Holy Spirit said, "Because grace and mercy have been neglected by the church. It has fallen into a state of disarray; however, I am calling My Church to tidy up the table." I could sense part of this involved bringing the message of grace and mercy to the Church. I now have an understanding of grace and mercy that I never had before.

JULIA KEMMISH
Somerset, England

DREAMS RELEASE GREAT BUSINESS FAVOR

I've had two prophetic dreams that have impacted my life tremendously. In the first dream, Todd was standing on the street and he told me to seek God at 6 o'clock in the morning. He said, "Seek God at six sharp; not four or five." Then he said, "God will do a miracle in your life!" For the first couple of days, I was obedient, but then I became lazy and began to miss doing this each day. I missed the third and fourth day; then on the fifth day, I received another dream.

In this dream, while I was having my meal with the rest of my family, a telephone call came. So I decided to get up and answer the call. Before I picked up the phone, I thought I should check to see who was calling me. On my call display, I saw the word *HOLY*. I was so scared. When I picked up the phone and put it to my ear, I heard a voice speak to me: "MAHENDRA SINGH, this is ABBA calling." I was shocked and couldn't move in my dream. Since that day, I have been seeking the Lord at 6 o'clock in the morning, no matter how tired I am or how busy my schedule is. Since I have been obedient, God has been doing miracles in my life, business, and ministry!

In my second dream, I opened a door and went into a room. I saw Todd sitting inside the room and it was full of glory. He was so anointed and the light of God was shining so brightly there. As I approached him, Todd hit me three times on my head, and it felt like I was being hit by a "two-by-four." After this dream, more miracles started to happen! God started to give me favor with people, and when I would go and speak to them about the love of Christ, they would listen to me. I would walk into a business and I'd be given a contract for my cleaning company! The owner would say, "We were just thinking of calling a company to come and do our cleaning and here you are!"

On April 12, 2005, when I was passing by a certain business in Maple Ridge, I wondered about the possibility of getting a contract with them. Five minutes later, I received a phone call from this same business, and the owner said, "We need someone to come and give us a quote for the janitorial work." So I went there later in the afternoon, and after presenting the quotation, the owner gave me the job. Glory to Jesus! Things that I just think about and start to desire in my heart start to happen in my life! The favor of God has come upon me.

Since that day when Todd hit me on my head in my dream, I believe the wisdom of God has been imparted to me, because whenever I minister to people they listen to what I have to say. It's as if they are glued to every word that comes out of my mouth. It's the favor and the blessing of the Lord. Doors that were shut for many years have started to open, in both business and ministry. To Him be all the glory and all the honor.

MAHENDRA SINGH
Abbotsford, British Columbia

DESPERATE TO ENCOUNTER GOD

After listening to the Fresh Fire tape series on the manifest presence and the secret place, I was inspired to contend for the supernatural. I began to have increased supernatural encounters that drastically changed my life, such as sweet smelling aromas, visitations, and the anointing of the Holy Ghost's fire and power. I also began to experience greater degrees of the glory with supernatural surprises and manifestations of the Spirit when I least expected it. The revival phenomena I experienced were unknown to me, so when it happened, it turned my world upside down. The following is one of many that changed my life from being an ordinary believer to a radical witness who is always in a state of expectation for another encounter.

One morning at 2:00 A.M. I woke up from a dead sleep and experienced, without question, the tangible, visible, holy, fearful, and overwhelming presence of God. It appeared as if a face with a personality was hovering over my face just inches away. The presence appeared to be like a cloud of smoke with white light emanating energy, power, authority, judgment, and other attributes of God. This Spirit of the fear of the Lord hovering over me had a presence that felt like a person who could see right through me and had so much power that I wanted to hide under my sheets. I finally just passed out under the weight of this tangible Holy presence. I could not speak the next day.

This experience caused me to be empowered with fearlessness and a reckless abandonment to be His witness to the lost as I had never been before. The power to be a witness came upon me, and my life was never the same again. The places I have gone to reach the lost and dying with the life-saving Gospel of Jesus Christ only could have happened with this encounter with God. Our church would do 24-hour soul winning, with the goal to win 500 souls in one night to the Lord. I remember times of going over 20 souls per hour! The fruit of this experience carries on until this day, with greater service in the ministry of helps and evangelism.

I thank God and give Him all the glory for what He has done with Fresh Fire and all the souls who are being impacted and saved for all eternity.

MICHAEL SWAINE
Cambria, California

FAST FORWARD INTO THE SUPERNATURAL REALM

I attended your recent school of the supernatural in Toronto. Since the school, I have been taken to a new level spiritually. It's as if God has hit the fast forward button. Every time I go to pray, it seems almost immediately I am taken into visions and prophetic experiences! Angels, the throne room, living creatures, different rooms up in Heaven, Jesus Himself coming and sitting with me and us having long conversations…you name it. It's quite overwhelming. Prayer is now a completely different experience for me. It's like the presence of God is just waiting for me to step in, and bang, off we go! In fact, it's so overwhelming at times that some days I have to take a break from prayer because I'm getting so much revelation that I have to take some time to reflect on what I have already received. Now I just lie down on the floor, and by the time I say "dear Jesus" I'm in. It's like electricity going through my body. Jesus walks into the room, angels show up and lay hands on me, or I look around and see I'm in the Garden of Eden or a room up in Heaven. This has completely changed my spiritual life. Praise God!

FRANKLYN SPENCE
St. Lazare, Quebec

Chapter Fourteen

FRESH FIRE REPORTS OF SUPERNATURAL SIGNS

In the ministry of Fresh Fire, we have watched with awe as God has demonstrated His supernatural Kingdom to the multitudes with signs and wonders. The result? Hundreds of thousands of people's lives transformed by Christ's saving, delivering, and healing power.

Following are several reports and accounts of God's awesome supernatural manifestations during, and as a result of, our conferences, meetings, and crusades around the world. God has truly drenched our ministry with His favor as evidenced here and in our growing number of news updates. We have used excerpts from various accounts and edited or paraphrased versions of them. This is just a small sampling, and other accounts of God's supernatural works are available on our Website: www.freshfire.ca. Below are some of those reports—it's time for us to testify of our God's goodness, love, and power!

SUPERNATURAL DISPLAY IN GROCERY STORE PARKING LOT

After shopping at a grocery store and prophesying accurately over the cashier, two of our interns began to put their groceries away into their vehicle when they sensed the Holy Spirit wanted them to minister to a woman in the parking lot. They began to tell her about the reality of the supernatural realm, about how they have seen gems from heaven, gold dust, diamond dust, and many other manifestations of the kingdom. Right then and there she started to get covered by it herself! Within a minute her whole body had oil, diamond dust, gold dust, sapphire dust, and silver dust coming on her, and within two minutes she was a sign and a wonder! She said she would be coming to their church the following Sunday!

FFM REPORT

JULY 2007

THE SPIRIT AND POWER OF ELIJAH IS ALIVE TODAY

Recently when a close associate of Fresh Fire was one of the preachers at Holy Ghost tent revival meetings in Alberta, he had a dream from the Lord. In the dream he heard the Spirit of Wisdom speaking and declaring that God was going to release the double portion of Elijah and purity across the land of Alberta. [Alberta is one of Canada's ten provinces, situated between British Columbia and Saskatchewan.]

The following day, while preaching, the Lord told him to make a decree about the release of the double portion of Elijah and purity. Then, under the inspiration of the Holy Ghost, he called down fire on the "prophets of Baal." [It's interesting that the prophets of Baal, among other evil practices, would sacrifice their sons with fire as a burnt offering to this idol.]

The result of this proclamation got everyone's attention big time because in the natural, within a couple of hours of the meeting, a local hotel used by pimps, drug dealers and prostitutes as a sex brothel was burned to the ground. The fire department could not figure out the cause of the fire!

FFM REPORT

Spring 2007

CHARIOTS OF FIRE SIGNAL SUPERNATURAL SIGN

Another amazing demonstration of God's power happened through this same associate at a recent conference in Cedar Rapids, Iowa. After the Holy Ghost told him to preach about overcoming the fear of the supernatural, He said to tell them that He wanted to release a greater dimension of open heavens, and if the people would repent for their urge to be in control and for their fear of the supernatural, then He would open the heavens.

So, out of his mouth came these inspired words: "As a sign to you that this is the word of the Lord there will be many people in the city and region who will begin to experience 'Book of Acts type of experiences' with God. Many will have supernatural encounters with Jesus Christ and they will even have Elijah-type experiences."

That night, about 15 minutes after the meeting, a man (who was not even in the meeting) was driving with three friends on the outskirts of Cedar Rapids. At 11:45 P.M., in the natural, they saw two chariots of fire appear alongside of their car. They fell into a trance and "woke up" 30 miles down the road! The man had been having struggles in the past with the supernatural!

Since the Lord confirmed His word immediately with this supernatural sign, FFM's associate discerned it was a sign from God that a spiritual drought in that region was over and the heavens were now open for the people of God to experience the supernatural!

FFM REPORT

AUSTRALIAN WOMAN REVITALIZED

A woman visiting and attending our tent meetings in Stony Plains and Lloydminster, Alberta, recently reported (August 3, 2007) that on the seventh day Todd prayed for her and she fell out under the power. She said, "It felt like someone hit me in the guts and I was dizzy for a moment." She reported that when she got up she knew she'd been completely healed of pneumonia and a low immune system, which had caused her to have a fever for over a year. In her testimony she also said that previously and in a dream, Todd had "visited" her home in Australia. He knocked on her door and invited her to come outside and eat pizza and then she went outside and "chatted" with Todd and his ministry team. It was after that experience that she decided to attend the meetings, and that's when she received the healing. She reports that she has a completely new lease on life!

FFM REPORT

WOMAN "HIT" POWERFULLY WHILE WATCHING TELEVISION BROADCAST

Susan J. Perry from Edgewater, Florida, reports that on August 9, 2007, while watching Todd speak on GOD TV about healings and God encounters, experienced a powerful encounter and healing:

We had never heard of him or this ministry before but we happened onto the channel by divine appointment. My husband and I often join in during television ministries by raising our hands in agreement and praying along with whomever we are watching, but last night was the BOMB!...I have had a problem with weight loss, feeling sluggish, and just not myself—knowing this just isn't me nor my portion! But I have trusted in the Lord for my very existence each and every day, in hopes that my body would change in the precious name of Jesus.

Well, as Todd Bentley called out to the television audience to lift their hands and receive, we obeyed. And I never felt such power open my mouth and travel through my body! It was as if a freight train was running through a tunnel of air, going into my mouth and traveling within my body. It was a slam of power! I felt it primarily in my throat and esophagus; perhaps my thyroid too. I don't know what the Holy Spirit did, but it was all powerful and I willingly received it! Then I began to get a round mark, like a bug bite or something on the outside of my throat, on the skin. God said, "Let this be a mark of what I did!" Glory to God!

SHARING THE FIRE

A woman wrote that she, her husband, and two sons traveled from Washington State to San Jose for our revival meetings in the summer of 2006. Here's her account:

Jeremy [her husband] received an impartation to see in the spirit, and then he moaned, "Oh Lord," all night long on the hotel bed. It wasn't food poisoning, but visions, dreams, and angelic encounters. I was already experiencing these before; but the increase of accuracy, words of knowledge, and visions for people, while we are ministering has been AWESOME. The words are so right on, that people just break down and cry, or fall over under the power.

We were so touched by the "model" that your ministry demonstrates: the proper spiritual father and son relationship being displayed, and the integrity of being "real" in the spirit. We started a ministry last year and struggle with the words to tell people, since many of the places we go are "on the small grid," but they are so hungry. It was great to be with your ministry and tell people, "We do that!" It exploded the things that God is telling us to do and be, when we watched you and your team. You are a great model. Just your living testimony of who you are is a huge encouragement!

Our ministry team is coming together so fast and so strong, that people are literally jumping on board with us to be a part of what God is doing. I love the impartation stuff so much. I think we'll take a group up to BC [British Columbia], so that the whole team God is putting together here can get all of the spiritual gifts and increase in ministry. We really feel we are a three-fold-cord team.

Craig especially touched us, by sharing his visions as a revivalist. I have had some of the exact same visions sometimes, but I didn't know what to do with them. God is calling us to create a "nest" here in the Northwest. He's been drawing an amazing number of people to this small town of beauty and spiritual history to start an amazing fire of revival for the Northwest, and you help us so much with the impartations we receive through your ministry.

Also, the intern that kind of sounds like a turkey in the Spirit, we love her. I think she is doing the battle cry of a tribe between the Middle East and India, and that she is hearing the battle cry of Heaven for those nations and all nations. We love to be a part of the Spirit pouring out on your team. My son, who is seven, called the fire tunnel line a "human wash," and was really touched. He is seeing angels, and so are all six of the children under the age of eight years old on our ministry team.

We ministered at a church this past Sunday and had a fire tunnel, and prophesied on many coming out on the other end. God is rallying the senior intercessors! That's part of my job for this last day's revival generation. Thank you for imparting the increase. You rock.

Jenn Beebe

MOSSYROCK

JESUS REVEALS HIMSELF TO UGANDAN NATION
by Kevin Basconi, FFM

This is a report of one of our crusades in Uganda (2003) where God literally opened up heavens above the crusade grounds on the final night. Later in the report, you will read about the incredible fruit of this supernatural manifestation.

Over 20,000 Gather and Over 4,000 Saved

Thursday—Tonight Todd began the crusade by calling out several words of knowledge. He told the crowd of over 20,000 that God was going to confirm the Gospel by releasing miracles before he preached and that a mighty healing wave was going to sweep through the stadium.

He then began to pray over the entire crowd, releasing a healing word. Todd proclaimed that Jesus was walking through the crowd! Immediately miracles broke out and the crippled began to walk.

In all, seven crippled people walked onto the platform to testify that the power of God had hit their bodies and they were now able to walk! During the wave of healing that continued for over one hour, dozens were healed or received impartation. Here are some highlights:

A woman who had been shot three times in the leg by rebels was able to walk.

A five-year-old deaf mute child was healed and able to speak.

Three people were healed of blindness in the right eye.

Three women with paralyzed right arms were healed and able to move their arms freely, one for the first time in 16 years.

Nine tribal chiefs responded to a word for an impartation of healing.

Numerous other healings took place throughout the stadium—hundreds came forward to give testimonies of healing. After Todd's message he gave an invitation to accept Jesus and 302 people responded. These heart transformations, of course, were the greatest miracles!

Outreach to Orphans—Jesus Heals All!

Friday—This morning a team from the mission base traveled over one hour into the bush country outside the city of Kampala to the Bodarie Orphanage. The team presented a brief message of the power of the cross and the blood of Jesus. After giving a word of knowledge for deaf ears, six children (every deaf child present) were healed of deafness—two of the children were deaf from birth. One child also spoke for the first time in his life.

In all, the team prayed for 286 children, and they all reported healing from stomach problems, headaches, and fevers. Jesus healed every sick person in the orphanage! The team then imparted the healing anointing to the children so they could pray for others' healing!

Miracles and Revival in Kampala

Todd opened the evening crusade by sharing that the Lord had given him a vision of the Father releasing an anointing to break witchcraft and generational curses. Proclaiming that revival was coming to Uganda, he called for those who practiced witchcraft and divination to come forward. A challenge was issued to see who was the greatest: Jesus or the devil. Todd told the crowd that the Lord had given him authority to pray and break the power of generational curses and the spirit of python, which was the dominant spirit over the region.

As he began to pray and take authority over these demonic powers, dozens of people violently manifested demons, and those people were carried from the crowd of 24,000 to the front of the platform. At one point there were over 120 people, almost in a huge pile, manifesting demons. Todd told the crowd that as these people were delivered, miracles would happen in the stadium grounds.

Here are just some of the miracles that we are aware of (as hundreds came forward to give testimonies of healing). Again, the Lord healed seven paralytics, bringing the total for the last two nights to 15, with one healed by the team in the crowd.

One man's blind left eye opened and was able to see for the first time in ten years; another blind man was healed after 30 years. One boy with withered hands for seven years was able to move them again. Dozens with tumors were instantly healed—they testified that the tumors simply vanished! There were literally hundreds of healings and miracles. The healing wave lasted for one and a half hours.

Todd then briefly shared with the crowd that Jesus was the

only way to Heaven. He pointed out that God had demonstrated the Kingdom of Heaven for them. He said that he had not come to Kampala with words only, but with a demonstration of the power of God. The fact that the blind were seeing, the lame were walking, the deaf were hearing, and the devils were being cast out was proof that Jesus was God and the only way to be saved. When he invited the crowd to the altar for salvation, 523 new converts came forward.

Team Enters Slums to Preach Gospel

This day the Fresh Fire Missions team traveled to Mengo Kisenyi, one of the worst slums on the face of the earth. People here suffer from deep poverty, abuse, and the ills of prostitution. In this area, many women born into prostitution entertain up to 30 customers a day. They usually earn less than one American dollar for a day's work. When the team arrived, they began the quarter-mile walk through the stench of 3-inch-deep mud and sewage to find the Christianity Focus Center.

During the night, a small twister had wreaked havoc on the crusade grounds that are just a few hundred yards from the area where the prostitutes ply their trade. Local pastors worked feverishly to reconstruct the Fresh Fire platform, extensively damaged during this freak storm. Many of the local pastors pitched in to help with the repairs and to prepare the grounds for the crusade Friday night.

Pastor David Kiganda started the church here less than three years ago. The land that the Focus Center sits on was at one time a pauper's grave site—local thieves would sleep there during the day, before venturing out into the city of Kampala to rob and steal. The pastor bought the land (located right in the middle of the brothels) and bulldozed it.

Now the pastor ministers the Gospel to these desperate women. When the team arrived, we found Todd and the leaders of the team already preaching to a group of 18 prostitutes. Todd, with his feet caked in mud, wept and his voice cracked as he shared his testimony here in one of the darkest places on earth. Pastor David later told me that Todd and the team were the first white missionaries to set foot into the dangerous Mengo Kisenyi slums.

Later, Todd said, "I have never been touched like this in my entire ministry; these women are totally helpless and desperate." With tears of compassion welling up in his eyes, he said, "We have got to do something to help them! I don't care how we do it, but we have got to help this pastor get these women out of this place!"

After Todd finished his testimony, 16 prostitutes came forward to accept Jesus as their Savior. Todd had tears running down his cheeks as he hugged each convert, and prayed with them individually. Many of the women are infected with HIV. The women on the FFM team then ministered to these women in small groups.

Pastor David shared with Todd his vision to send converted prostitutes to a center 100 kilometers away from Kampala. There these women would be discipled, rehabilitated, and trained to find a normal job. After feeding them a good meal, Pastor David began the discipling process with these spiritually reborn women.

Outreach to the "Beer Hut"

Several of the team took advantage of the opportunity to do street ministry in the slum area and traveled by foot through the muck to the village Malwina. Here men and women sit in small huts and drink a local beer made of a grain called millet. The teams walked through the narrow muddy walkways dodging chickens, turkeys, and children to minister the love of Jesus.

One by one the teams preached the Gospel in the huts. After about an hour, they reported 103 salvations and many healings. One woman was healed of a blind right eye after responding to one of the team's word of knowledge. A small group of people came to Jesus after witnessing the miracle.

Praying for the Dead

One team was given permission to return to the Namirembre Hospital. The leader and several members believed God to raise the dead. They returned to the 4th floor to check on the patients that were prayed for in the TB ward two days earlier. There they saw an orderly pushing a dead person through the hall. When they asked for permission to pray for the dead person, the team was able to enter a "holding room" where they prayed for four dead men and women. Although they did not see God release this miracle, they pressed in and felt assured that it would happen soon. When the team entered the TB ward, they found that only 15 of the 37 were still there; many had received healing and returned to their homes.

Saturday Night Crusade—Crowd Swells to 55,000

Todd told the crowd of 55,000 that he was not going to preach to start the crusade. Rather, God was going demonstrate that Jesus was Lord by healing ten deaf. Many deaf people came rushing to the platform for healing prayer. The team prayed over them, and soon ten deaf people were completely healed; many spoke for the first time.

Todd then preached a brief message on the cross and the 39 stripes Jesus took for our healing. He told the swelling crowd that the deaf hearing was a sign from God that the Gospel he preached was real. After sharing his testimony of salvation from drug addiction, satanism, and a sinful lifestyle, 267 came forward to accept Jesus as Savior.

Todd then released a healing wave over the new converts and the crusade grounds. Immediately dozens began to manifest demons and were brought to the front of the platform. Many were healed and delivered. Some of the documented miracles include:

- A child, whose right testicle was the size of a fist, was instantly healed. The father testified that he saw the tumor shrink right before his eyes—he immediately accepted Jesus as Savior!
- An eight-year-old child's blind eyes were immediately healed.

- One infant was able to move and sit up for the first time ever!

- One man, blind in his right eye for eight years, was healed.

- Many reported that their cataracts dissolved under the power of God.

- Three people with broken legs began to walk normally with no pain.

Open Heavens Releases Miracles

During the worship God released an incredible display of His power! It was the Scriptures of Joel 2 and Acts 2 coming to life before multitudes of people! The heavens opened and the glory of God fell! There was an incredible sign in the sky: brilliant colors and heavenly light shimmered across the crusade grounds! Hundreds of people began to worship, falling on their faces before God! Literally dozens of people began to violently manifest demons as the glory and power of Jesus swept through the crowds! The portal in the sky lasted for 22 minutes and eventually was transformed into the face of Jesus, then into the Lion of Judah!

Todd preached a short message to about 55,000, bringing the total attendance for the Uganda Crusade to over 140,000. He preached on the Holy Spirit from Matthew 3:11, Acts 1:5, and Acts 2. Todd told the country of Uganda that they need the power of God and the Holy Ghost. There were millions hearing the Gospel on the radio nightly. When Todd asked people to indicate who had been healed while listening to the radio, hundreds of hands went up! Only God knows how many have been saved over the radio. Dozens also came forward to testify of healing while listening to the radio. These included:

- A woman with an issue of blood for seven years.

- A healing of malaria from 100 kilometers away.

- One man who received a financial miracle.

- A woman with arthritis in her entire body.

- One blind man who was also healed.

Next, Todd called for the deaf, and an entire deaf school came on to the platform! There were 13 in all; many of them were mute as well. As Todd and the team prayed for them, 12 of the 13 were healed and seven mutes began to speak for the first time!

During the altar call, 884 ran to the platform to receive Jesus! Todd then prayed for the new converts and people in the crowd to be filled with the Holy Spirit and fire, The power of God swept into the grounds—tens of thousands were filled with the Holy Spirit and began speaking in tongues!

All glory to God for His mighty acts and life-transforming power!

THE RELEASE OF SILVER AND GOLD

On the Day of Atonement, the Lord began to speak to Charlie Robinson (an FFM associate minister) about the finances

He was about to release to His people, starting this year. Knowing that the root of the Hebrew word for gold and for glory is the same, Charlie has prayed for years for the release of the gold (the finances) for the Body of Christ. The Lord revealed to him that He wanted to bless the Church with great wealth to fund the great harvest to come. Hand in hand with this outpouring of wealth and harvest would come the glory of God. On September 24, 2004, the day before the Day of Atonement, Charlie felt the Lord prompting him to pray aggressively for the gold that He was about to release in the earth.

The Lord spoke to him that the church would walk through the Second Chronicles chapter 5 pattern in restoring God's glory to His Church—the glory which would usher in a great harvest of souls. In this chapter, after the preparation of the temple was complete, Solomon brought the silver and gold into the treasury, and then the glory of the Lord filled the house of God. The Church today is about to follow those same steps: preparation, silver and gold, and then, finally, God's glory (with harvest).

Note: A powerful "first-fruits" prophetic fulfillment of this word from Charlie about silver and gold came only a few weeks after he gave the previous Destiny 2005 word. On a ministry trip in California, the "Golden State," people in meetings threw gold and silver into the offerings. In one particular meeting, ushers counted 24 rare gold coins, and 40 rare silver ones. In another meeting, the offerings contained small bars of gold and silver. Immediately after one of those meetings, the Lord confirmed that this was a first fruit of the financial release that He was bringing to fulfillment. (After this meeting) Charlie turned on a television and the first thing that flashed on the screen was a photo of a 1881 Morgan Silver Dollar, identical to one of the coins just received in the offering

FFM Report, 2005

Unusual Visitations!
by Brian Hill of Living Stones Fellowship

Iowa, U.S.A. (2001)—Our meetings with Todd Bentley culminated Sunday night. By now most of the people had attended at least two meetings and the level of intimacy had deepened within the group. Todd spoke of how Jesus breathed on His disciples and said, "Receive the Holy Spirit." Todd said the act of breathing dispensed the Holy Spirit, but the command to receive was for the disciples to be open and accepting of Him.

He then talked about the River of Life and asked, "Does anyone want to drink with me?" He told everyone to imagine holding a barrel and to dip it into the River. He led the congregation in prayer to receive the Holy Spirit and then drink from their barrels. They did so three times. The fire of God came and the fire of the Lord was released. The congregation burst forth in praise as they called upon the Lord to release Revival Fire upon the land. Anointed joy burst forth as the Lord released His blessings on the meeting and people fell under their chairs in hysterical laughter.

Then a sober quietness descended upon the congregation. The Holiness of God settled in the room. Todd said that the Spirit of judgment was present to purge the flesh with burning. Many people were on their faces, crying out to the Lord.

Another wave of joy swept through the room followed by another period of quietness. Todd could barely stand on the platform because of God's power and he staggered drunkenly between the musical instruments. A few people from the congregation went up to physically support him and as they did so, everyone there, including Todd, fell under the power because the presence of God was so thick.

After some time, Todd managed to stand, but his feet were rooted in one place and he was unable to move and said that his feet were on fire. He shook uncontrollably as God gave him numerous words of knowledge for healing. He had Ivan (part of the Fresh Fire team) move among the respondents, as he was unable to move out from behind the podium. This lasted for about 45 minutes and then as quickly as it all started, it stopped.

"Wow! Whoa! Bam!" was all Todd could say for a few minutes. "It was like my body was in a trance, but my mind was still here in the room. Man—that was weird! Wow!" Todd explained (that when) the natural realm was stripped away one could experience the supernatural as tangibly as the natural realm (even with the five senses of taste, touch, sight, smell, and hearing).

As Todd continued this teaching, the lights in the room seemed to flicker. It did not seem to be anything significant at first, but then it continued at irregular intervals. Todd became particularly fascinated by this phenomenon. He said that sometimes, when the Holy Spirit comes into a meeting, the power surges and lightnings occur. This is the lightning of the Lord! Todd said that he'd only experienced this phenomenon a few times and that it was significant. Several attendees actually reported that they saw streaks of light shoot across the room.

The overhead lights were turned off, except for a single red spotlight that (unintentionally) illuminated the large "Power Connection" banner on the platform's back wall. People began to lose focus in their prayers as they searched the room hoping to see where the next strike would occur. Todd urged everyone to not search out the manifestations but to continue to focus on Jesus. As soon as they refocused and pressed in again, the manifestations returned.

I was sitting in the sound booth at the back of the room. The red spot and the soundboard flickered and flared several times during this long period of quiet reverence. In the few years I have been coming to Living Stones Fellowship, I do not recall seeing the lights ever do this. A heavy tangible presence, like a warm blanket enveloped the meeting room, and everyone lay still.

Sounds were muffled, and we suddenly felt a cool breeze. In the summertime, this would be normal with the building's air-conditioning system, but it was December, and so usually the air coming through would be warm from the furnace and not the cool, refreshing air we felt. As people lay quietly, a banquet of fragrances filled the air and people reported that they could smell cookies, spices, flowers, and fields of grain. Several reported other smells that confirmed to me that there was no natural explanation, such as bathroom air fresheners or deodorizers.

As the fragrances filled and permeated the air, some people saw into the realms of the spirit. Don Stevens, a recently saved young man, told me that he saw what he described as the Garden of Eden. He said he was standing at the edge of a forest, looking into a meadow filled with huge flowers. He saw a small hut off to the side and there was a group of children frolicking in the field. He recalled seeing this before he smelled the fragrant air. He said the scents were familiar but also brand new at the same time, as if different facets of the fragrant odors were being revealed to him. Don's account is of significance, because he was into his vision before the others announced seeing similar images. In other words, his experience was not influenced by the testimonies of others. "That I may proclaim with the voice of thanksgiving and declare all your wonders" (Ps. 26:7 NASB).

Steve Libby is one of the regulars at our revival meetings. He always has a wonderful testimony of the Lord. The entire night, Steve had been heavily "under the influence" of the Spirit. He stayed slumped in his chair and did not move or speak to anyone. As everything came to a close, he came out of his trance and announced he'd been in God's library and he told us that the winds were God's promises. The "lightning" continued throughout the entire event.

MIGHTY MEN CONFERENCE
by Andy Barnes, Pastor, Living Joy Christian Centre

October 22, 1999—Todd's message on Friday was very challenging to the men as he shared on the "kingly oil and anointing" and the "priestly oil and anointing." Almost every man was stretched out before the altar in a state of repentance and desire for the authority of the kingly oil, which comes after walking in the priestly anointing. Ministry was great; each person received personal ministry, and Todd had a prophetic word for several.

On Saturday morning, Todd shared on recognizing and releasing the prophetic and how we experience the presence of God. At the end of this session there was a time of practical application as men were paired off and believed God for a word of edification, exhortation, and comfort for each other. Many people prophesied for the first time and were greatly encouraged.

Todd also ministered Sunday morning and evening and Monday and Tuesday evening in meetings that were open to the public. He shared powerfully along the same theme of relationship and intimacy with God. The prophetic word was very encouraging, and Todd also ministered in the word of knowledge, with several people receiving prayer and healing for specific health problems that were identified. Once again powerful praise and worship was a part of all the meetings, and there was great freedom, rejoicing, and praise to God, as well as awesome times of sensing the intimate,

410

wonderful presence and glory of God during times of reverence and worship.

Monday night during ministry, two of the worship team members heard wonderful high harmony voices join them in their singing. There were no others present, and it was felt that these were angels singing with them...awesome!

During ministry times God displayed His love and power in a variety of ways. Some of the miracles included a girl healed of a crooked spine—it became perfectly straight, shoulder problems instantly healed, and people freed of depression, fear, and anger. While Todd was here in April, a man got saved whose wife was already a Christian. They have been going to her church, and he has remained free of any desire for alcohol and has been growing in his relationship with God. This time, their three sons were saved and they rejoiced in tears over the fact that the entire family was now saved.

A lady came to Tuesday's meeting intending to have Todd pray for her mother. On Thanksgiving Day her mother had an asthma attack, and while being rushed to the hospital, had a heart attack in the ambulance. At the hospital, doctors discovered a hole in one of the heart valves, and also that she had diabetes. She remained in a coma for eight days, during which time they gave her insulin and waited for her to recover enough to do heart surgery.

The next day she (the daughter) phoned the hospital to see how her mother was and was told that she had been released to go home. On contacting her mother, she found that there was no longer any trace of diabetes and the heart problem had improved so dramatically that it would be more dangerous to operate than to let it remain, and she was strong enough to walk about four blocks. Praise God, both the mother and the daughter gave God glory for this miracle.

During the time since Todd's last visit in April, there has been a drawing into a deeper relationship, intensity in prayer and intercession, and a release of different gifts for expression of worship to the Lord, for example, painting during worship and praise, and poetry and dance.

The meetings were powerful with the presence and power of God displayed. There was a strong call and anointing for intercession, with groanings of the Spirit, which was released on Tuesday evening. These things will have a lasting effect on the church and community.

Newspaper Report of Dental Miracles

In the May 1, 1999, issue of *BC Christian News* (formerly *Christian Info News*), [i] reporter Peter T. Chattaway wrote about the then recent reports of people throughout British Columbia receiving gold fillings and similar miracles. Among those whom he interviewed were people who had attended Todd Bentley's revival service at Mission Foursquare Church where reportedly seven people had received dental miracles. In researching this phenomena, he interviewed Todd who'd reported that the Mission church miracles were the first manifestation of that type of miracle in his meetings, but that they had manifested in consequent meetings as well. "In addition to the gold-teeth," wrote Chattaway, "churchgoers also report gold dust and oil appearing on their hands...." According to his report, Paula Spurr, a musician and former deejay said that "her hands began to 'sparkle' during a "God Rock" service led by Bentley at Burnaby Christian Fellowship March 26 [1999]....[23]

ANGEL IN ALBANY
by Todd Bentley

*The excerpt below comes from a report of the angel that appeared during the healing revival in Oregon which lasted for months and drew thousands of people from all over America and beyond. Hundreds were saved, healed, and delivered. This portion was taken from **Journey Into the Miraculous**.*[24]

In February (2001) I saw an angel, 20 feet tall, which stretched to the ceiling of the Albany auditorium. At the time, I didn't realize that this was the same angel I'd seen in Grants Pass. The Spirit gave me a sign that this angelic visitation was real. A woman in the audience, Muffy Joe Howell (the daughter of Dale Howell, the pastor from Grants Pass), could also see the angel and when I asked her, she would describe the same vision I was seeing. She whispered, "Todd, there's a huge angel in the pulpit." Muffy had been crippled with an infirmity in her hips from birth. However, suddenly she screamed out, "The angel just touched me," and she was healed. Now I really knew God was up to something.

The audible voice of the Holy Spirit, which accompanied the angelic encounter, instructed me not to speak to the angel. (In subsequent encounters I also heard the audible inner voice of the Holy Spirit.) The angel had a key, just like a mayor holds the key to a city. Its commission was to turn this key over to pastors by imparting wisdom, authority, revelation, and anointing so they could take healing back to their churches. The angel stayed in the pulpit and released a healing anointing while I prayed for over 30 pastors that night.

I knew by the Spirit that the angel's name was Healing Revival. He was like the angel in John 5 that stirred the pool of Bethesda. This angel was a prophetic sign that God is going to fulfill the vision of the coming healing revival I had received about a year before. I believe God sent the angel to Albany to establish healing revival and regional breakthrough. This angel is one of the many that I saw in a stadium in Heaven waiting to be released to fulfill end-time purposes.

Conclusion

As you've just read, men, women, and children today are experiencing the supernatural realm as it invades their natural world. The voice of God and revelations from Heaven are for every believer. I believe that while you've been reading through this book God has begun to open your eyes, more than ever, to see how natural it is for us as Christians to expect to live in the supernatural realms of Heaven. We can expect to regularly experience signs, wonders, miracles, and healings!

I encourage you to pray the prayers in the previous chapters often, with a passion to lay hold of everything God has for you. Then you will grow in intimacy, purpose, and power as you, like the others you've read about in these pages, enter into the reality of the supernatural world!

Endnotes

1. John Paul Jackson, "Naturally Supernatural," www
.streamsministries.com, 1999. Used with permission.

2. Jackson, "Naturally Supernatural."

3. William Branham Website and Forum, "Boy Raised From the
Dead," available from http://www.williambranham.com/raised_
from_the_dead.htm (accessed August 27, 2005).

4. James Strong, *Strong's Exhaustive Concordance of the Bible*
(Iowa Falls, IA: Abingdon Press, 1986), Greek Dictionary, 31.

5. Strong, Greek Dictionary, 32.

6. Rick Joyner, *The Final Quest* (Charlotte, NC: Morningstar
Publications, Second Edition, 1996), 89-90.

7. Joyner, *Final Quest*, 89-90.

8. Joyner, *Final Quest*, 89-90.

9. General William Booth, "Is This Your Life?"; available from
http://www.myfaith.com/William-Booths-Vision.htm.

10. Booth, "Is This Your Life?"

11. Strong, Greek Dictionary, 72.

12. Strong, Hebrew Dictionary, 147.

13. Strong, Greek Dictionary, 6.

14. Strong, Greek Dictionary, 5.

15. Kenneth Hagin, "Reverend Kenneth Hagin"; excerpt from the book *I Believe in Visions*, available from http://www.near-death.com/forum/nde/000/90.html (accessed September 1, 2005).

16. William Booth, "A Vision of the Lost"; available from http://www.sendrevival.com/pioneers/General_William_Booth/vision_of_the_lost_wb. htm (accessed September 1, 2005).

17. Booth, "A Vision of the Lost."

18. Howard Culbertson, "Missions Slogans and Quotes From Missionaries"; available from http://home.snu.edu/~hculbert/slogans.htm (accessed September 1, 2005).

19. R.F. Youngblood, *Nelson's New Illustrated Bible Dictionary*, revised edition (Nashville, TN: T. Nelson), in LaserD (CD-ROM).

20. Gary L. Thomas, "Historical Profile, Brother Lawrence"; The Center for Evangelical Spirituality, 2005; available from http://www.garythomas.com/resources/classics/lawrence.html (accessed September 5, 2005).

21. R. Dean Davis, *The Heavenly Court Judgment of Revelation 4–5* (Maryland: University Press of America, 1992), 163.

22. Strong, #4487, Greek Dictionary, 85.

23. *BC Christian News* 19, no. 5 (May 1999). Formerly *Christian Info News*, archived at http://www.canadianchristianity.com/cgi-bin/bc.cgi?bc/bccn/0599/teeth.

24. Todd Bentley, *Journey Into the Miraculous* (Ladysmith, BC: Sound of Fire Productions, 2003), 142-143.

Author Contact Information

MAILING ADDRESS:

c/o Sound of Fire Productions
PO Box 1163
Ladysmith, BC
Canada V9G 1A8

SHIPPING ADDRESS:

Sound of Fire Productions
40 1150 Walkem Rd.
Ladysmith, BC
Canada V9G 1A8

ADDITIONAL CONTACT INFORMATION:

Telephone: 1-250-245-7003 or FFM 1-604-853-9041
Personal assistant e-mail: trudybrennan@freshfire.ca
Todd Bentley cell: 1-604-217-1793
Agent/Contact: Darcia Bentley 1-250-245-7003
darciabentley@shaw.ca
mailto:soundoffire@shaw.ca
soundoffire@shaw.ca

TODD BENTLEY RESOURCES
FROM
Sound of Fire

MARINATING ... *Pickling in God's Presence*
SOAKING CD ~ by Todd Bentley

This CD is sure to take you into the glory and presence of God. You will hear Todd speaking powerful soaking prayers over inspiring instrumental sounds and sweet female vocals. This CD is for those who want to be saturated with the presence of the Holy Spirit and whose hearts long for deep intimacy with Jesus. During recording, Todd experienced visions and visitations of heaven. Todd and others present in the recording studio felt the tangible presence and anointing of the Lord in a new and exciting way. This anointing is transferable and is definitely captured on this very special recording.

SOAKING IN THE SECRET PLACE
SOAKING CD ~ by Todd Bentley

If you have ever heard Todd's teaching on the Secret Place (Soaking), or as he puts it, pickling in the presence, then this prayer CD will help you come into the Father's House and sit at the feet of Jesus. Join Todd on a journey into the Presence of God with prayers from the bible and prayers that come from a deep passion and longing for Him. This is a meditative, contemplative CD that combines piano style music and numerous sounds such as: rain, flute, trumpet, shofar, and more, for a deep prayer experience.

*Both of the CD's above are also available in **instrumental versions** which do not contain any prayers or vocals on them, only the music.*

FRESH FIRE MINISTRIES

Fresh Fire Ministries is an international ministry called to global harvest. Todd Bentley and the FFM team take God's saving, healing, and delivering power to the nations of the world, sparking revival fires and equipping the body of Christ in power evangelism and healing ministry. FFM conducts healing crusades throughout Africa, India, South America, Mexico, Europe and beyond. Hundreds of thousands have been saved, delivered and miraculously healed. Each year, Fresh Fire also hosts several conferences, teaching schools, and anointing services, accommodating the training and equipping of thousands.

Fresh Fire is also active in humanitarian and mercy ministry, communicating the gospel of Jesus Christ, not only in word and power, but also in compassionate action. This practical ministry includes the building of orphanages and homes, feeding outreaches, providing medical supplies and treatment, and clothing distribution.

Our vision is to see people revived in a new passion for Jesus, burning with the fire of evangelism to reach the lost. We achieve this goal through conferences and training schools, the Jesus Road School Intern Program, the Supernatural Training Center seven-month equipping program, and short term missions trips to the nations.

For more information about:
Todd Bentley and Fresh Fire,
FFM missions trips, ministry partnership, and all of our
resource products, please visit our website.

Fresh Fire Ministries
P.O. Box 2525 Abbotsford, BC, Canada V2T 6R3
Phone: (604) 853-9041 Fax: (604) 853-5077 Email: info@freshfire.ca
www.freshfire.ca